DECOLONIZING UNIVERSALISM

Studies in Feminist Philosophy is designed to showcase cutting-edge monographs and collections that display the full range of feminist approaches to philosophy, that push feminist thought in important new directions, and that display the outstanding quality of feminist philosophical thought.

STUDIES IN FEMINIST PHILOSOPHY

Published in the Series:

DECOLONIZING UNIVERSALISM

A Transnational Feminist Ethic

Serene J. Khader

OXFORD
UNIVERSITY PRESS

OXFORD
UNIVERSITY PRESS

Oxford University Press is a department of the University of Oxford. It furthers
the University's objective of excellence in research, scholarship, and education
by publishing worldwide. Oxford is a registered trade mark of Oxford University
Press in the UK and certain other countries.

Published in the United States of America by Oxford University Press
198 Madison Avenue, New York, NY 10016, United States of America.

Library of Congress Cataloging-in-Publication Data
Names: Khader, Serene J., author.
Title: Decolonizing universalism : a transnational feminist ethic / Serene J. Khader.
Description: New York, NY, United States of America : Oxford University Press, [2019] |
Series: Studies in feminist philosophy | Includes bibliographical references and index.
Identifiers: LCCN 2018009726 (print) | LCCN 2018026193 (ebook) |
ISBN 9780190664213 (updf) | ISBN 9780190664220 (epub) |
ISBN 9780190664237 (online content) | ISBN 9780190664206 (pbk : alk. paper) |
ISBN 9780190664190 (cloth : alk. paper)
Subjects: LCSH: Feminist ethics. | Decolonization. | Postcolonialism. | Universalism. | Globalization.
Classification: LCC BJ1395 (ebook) | LCC BJ1395 .K43 2018 (print) | DDC 170.82—dc23
LC record available at https://lccn.loc.gov/2018009726

CONTENTS

ACKNOWLEDGMENTS

I have always thought of philosophy as a conversation, and my work in this book benefited from the contributions of many conversational partners. I am especially grateful to Linda Martín Alcoff, Daniel Susser, Monique Deveaux, Alison Jaggar, Diana Tietjens Meyers, Charles Mills, and Allison Weir, who commented on significant portions of the book. I also thank Alia Al-Saji, Amy Baehr, Ann Garry, Justin Bernstein, Elizabeth Brake, Saba Fatima, Kiran Grewal, Nancy Hirschmann, Martina Koegler, Tracy Llanera, Keya Maitra, Lisa Mirachi, Catriona Mackenzie, Rachel Ann McKinney, Uma Narayan, Nkiru Nzegwu, Anne Phillips, Elena Ruiz, Lisa Schwartzman, Eric Schliesser, Wendy Salkin, Lisa Tessman, Krushil Watene, Kyle Whyte, Heather Widdows, and Scott Wisor for conversations and written comments that significantly impacted my thinking about this project.

A couple of institutions have also supported the work in this book. A fellowship from the Ethyle R. Wolfe Institute at Brooklyn College provided valuable teaching release time in 2016 and 2017. The Institute for Advanced Study at the University of Birmingham hosted a workshop in 2015 on a draft manuscript, at which I received many helpful comments. The Centre for Moral, Social, and Political Theory (CMSPT) at the Australian National University provided space for me to complete the final chapters.

Parts of this book have appeared as journal articles, and I wish to acknowledge *Hypatia, Feminist Philosophy Quarterly*, and *Politics and Gender* for permission to print revised versions of "Development Ethics, Gender Complementarianism, and Intrahousehold Inequality," "Transnational Feminisms, Nonideal Theory, and Other Women's Power," and "Do Muslim Women Need Freedom," respectively.

I thank my editor at Oxford University Press, Lucy Randall, for her enthusiasm for this project and her expert guidance. Hannah Doyle, also of Oxford University Press, provided valuable editorial assistance. My research assistant, Alyssa Colby, offered much-needed help in preparing the manuscript.

The moral, emotional, and intellectual support of my friends, my parents, and my siblings has been invaluable during my writing process. I am deeply fortunate to be surrounded every day by people whose passion for knowledge and justice inspires me.

And finally, thanks to my partner, Matt Lindauer, for his singular combination of empathy and intelligence—and for a love that has made me, and the arguments in this book, much, much braver.

DECOLONIZING UNIVERSALISM

INTRODUCTION

IMPERIALISM IN THE NAME OF FEMINISM

As I write, it has been twenty-three years since the Office of the High Commissioner of Human Rights announced a need to end "harmful traditional practices" that affect women and girls (OHCHR Fact Sheet 23), sixteen years since Laura Bush (2001) used the presidential radio address to pronounce "the brutal oppression of women . . . a central goal of the terrorists," eight years since Nicholas Kristof's and Cheryl WuDunn's *Half the Sky* described poor women as an "untapped resource," four years since a book urging women at the highest economic echelons to "lean in" to corporate success began to top bestsellers lists, and three years since Malala Yousafai won the Nobel Peace Prize. Has the time come, as Valentine Moghadam (2010) ironically asks, to declare that we are all feminists now?

Anti-imperialist feminist concerns suggest the answer is not so simple. Although the above developments do seem to reflect a growing consensus about the value of women's health and education, as well as widespread enthusiasm for women's entrepreneurship, Western interest in "other" women seems highly selective—and, in some cases, only tenuously connected to feminism. George W. Bush notoriously supported the contemporaneous war on US women's access to abortion and contraception. He rarely used his platform to criticize harmful traditional practices that affect U.S. women. A Pakistani girl who criticized drone strikes received a distinctly icier reception in the United States than Yousafzai (Fatima 2014). *Half the Sky* depicts men in the global South as barbaric and focuses on the instrumental value of women in the global South (see Narayan 2010). Despite international zeal for increasing women's earning power, a growing body of evidence shows that women's gendered labor burdens are increasing, while their household bargaining power is decreasing (Chant 2006, 2008; Wilson 2015). The international community seems to have no vision for a world in which most unpaid labor is not done by women, and disproportionately shifted onto the global South at that (Jaggar 2013; see World Bank 2012).

The causes related to women in the global South that capture Western fascination are often those whose discussion participates in justifying—or at least does not challenge—imperialist domination. In spite of this, the need for feminist activism, particularly cross-border feminist activism, remains urgent and undeniable. The facts of militarism, cultural domination, and transnational economic exploitation mean that Western women are complicit in "other" women's oppression. New forms of gender injustice, such as the overrepresentation of women among the poor, global increases in women's unpaid labor burdens, the constitution of women as an ideal transnational manufacturing force, and the subjugation of women by politicized and conservative religions are caused partly by transnational processes of neoliberalism and militarism. The cause of ending sexist oppression is also urgent in its own right; women around the globe find their life prospects systematically curtailed in ways that those of the men in their communities are not.[1] Anti-imperialist feminists in our time can neither retreat into the local nor refuse to make moral and political judgments.

The way forward can only be to articulate a normative position that criticizes gender injustice without prescribing imperialism. We need greater clarity about which values feminists should embrace when engaged in transnational praxis, and we need to be able to explain why these values do not license projects of Western and Northern domination often undertaken in their name. Such a normative position has been difficult to forge because of the frequency with which universalism and normativity are assumed to be aligned with support for Western values and interests. Westerners often assume that what is universally valuable for women *just is* (an idealized form of) the Western way of life. In many theoretical discussions, this peculiar narrow and ethnocentric variant of universalism is what is meant by "universalism." The assumption that Western ethnocentric universalism is the only universalism has the consequence, to borrow a phrase from Isis Giraldo (2016, 165), of "foreclos[ing] the possibility of defining female emancipation in terms other than Western hegemonic understandings" (165). It is thus unsurprising that the challenge of decolonial, postcolonial, and transnational feminisms has seemed to many, on both the Western and anti-imperialist sides of the debate, to be a relativist or anti-normative one. In my view, the universalism/relativism framing of debates about decolonial feminisms has blocked attention to the important normative claims that suffuse anti-imperialist feminist theories.

This book develops a feminist normative position that rejects this anti-imperialism/normativity dilemma. I argue that an understanding of feminism as opposition to sexist oppression, coupled with an understanding of transnational feminist praxis as aiming at justice enhancement in a world characterized by historical and ongoing imperialism, can form the basis of an anti-imperialist and universalist feminism. Anti-imperialist feminisms, in my view, contain substantive normative claims. Instead of sidelining them by defending Western values and interests as though they embody the only plausible universalist positions, feminists should ask whether the specific values that have been accused of being vehicles for imperialism should or must be part of the normative position we call "feminism."

The book begins from the idea that that anti-imperialist feminisms offer good reasons to question certain values that Westerners have taken to be central to feminism. Some of these are individualism, autonomy (and its associations with secular worldviews), and gender-role eliminativism. I show that feminists engaged in transnational praxis can, and in some cases should, reject controversial variants of these values. Because opposition to sexist oppression is imaginable without them, and because they get in the way of feminist politics in an unjust world characterized by historical and ongoing imperialism, questioning or abandoning them is less threatening to feminism's status as a normative doctrine than some Western feminists have feared.

The Argument of the Book

The overarching argument of the book can be thought of as follows: feminism requires universalist opposition to sexist oppression, but feminism does not require universal adoption of Western—or, more specifically, what I will call "Enlightenment liberal"—values and strategies. The mistaken view that it does, a view I call "missionary feminism," results from misunderstandings of the role normative concepts should play under nonideal conditions and conditions of moral diversity—and, sometimes, from noninnocent idealizations of Western culture as aligned with moral progress. The reasons transnational feminist praxis does not require the universalizing Enlightenment liberalism to which I appeal throughout the book are the following:

1. We do not need a thick, justice-monist ideal of the gender-just society to oppose gender injustice.

2. Feminism is mostly a view about the appropriate power relations that should obtain among groups in a society, not a view about which goods make an individual life go well (and so feminism is compatible with a number of different social and cultural forms).
3. The effectiveness of strategies for change varies based on the material conditions and moral vernacular(s) of a given context.[2]
4. Many Western values, even ones that have helped erode sexist oppression in the West, can contribute to sexist oppression in other contexts and bear no conceptual relationship to its absence.

Points 1 to 3 reject the notion that feminist praxis requires a single cultural blueprint to have normative bite. I propose that the normative core of feminism is opposition to sexist oppression, and that conceiving it this way avoids the idea that feminism requires remaking the world according to a single culturally thick vision. Opposition to sexist oppression underdetermines which strategies for change should be chosen in any particular situation. Because it mostly makes a point about how goods and power should be allocated, rather than a point about which goods and powers are important in every context, and because it focuses on what is wrong instead of what is ideal, the notion of feminism as opposition to sexist oppression refuses to offer a single recipe for how to achieve the right gender relations.

Point 4 about the effects of adopting Western values is particularly important to my argument in this book. Much of what I reveal in these pages is that the widespread view that adopting Western values causes feminist change often has more to do with ideological associations than conceptual or empirically substantiated ones. Enlightenment liberalism is a view according to which moral progress occurs through the abandonment of traditional values and unchosen relationships, as well as through the universalization of economic independence. It is a caricatured and crude view to be sure, and one that I'm sure few feminist theorists would explicitly avow, but it is difficult to understand a number of unjustified Western feminist assumptions without an unstated view like it lurking in the background. Enlightenment liberalism seems in particular to animate the assumptions behind many popular media depictions and advocacy discourses, including, for example, the assumption that unregulated capitalism will benefit women and the assumption that traditional adherence is deeply at odds with feminism. Even Western feminist theorists who eschew such assumptions in the abstract fall into them when they are evaluating specific cases related to "other" women and making prescriptions for them.

Enlightenment liberalism's teleological narrative about the West as the apex of human progress supplies an explanation of why feminism is meant to require the adoption of Western cultural forms; according to the Enlightenment liberal retelling of history, moral progress means the erosion of community and tradition that the West has ostensibly already achieved. Western willingness to erode communal bonds (rather than, say, Western willingness to engage in imperialism) explains the ostensible economic, military, and ostensibly moral superiority. The Enlightenment liberal association of Western values with moral progress also helps explain why Western feminists easily lose sight of feminism's true normative core: opposition to sexist oppression. Oppression is a set of social conditions that systematically disadvantages members of one social group relative to another (see Frye 1983; Young 1990). Yet it is all too often uncritically assumed that feminism is just improving women's well-being within an oppressive system, or that feminist change will occur if women have the ability to reject the trappings of their religions or cultures or to earn incomes.

The only way out of unreflective assumptions that Western values are the feminist answer is to raise explicit questions, and consider arguments and empirical evidence, about which values can motivate reductions in sexist oppression under conditions of global injustice. I tackle the specific values I do in this book largely because they have been the most controversial—accused of being Trojan horses for imperialist activity. Putatively feminist values can become vehicles for imperialism in two distinct ways. First, they can serve justificatory roles. They can make direct rule, militarism, economic exploitation, political domination, white supremacy, and marginalization of minoritized cultural groupings seem like good things—even things that would advance their victims' gender interests. Second, values can play a constitutive role in imperialism. That is, they may be parochial values that when imposed on cultural "others," become part of a regime of cultural domination.[3] The values of individualism, autonomy (sometimes discussed as secularism), and gender eliminativism have all been accused of playing both justificatory and constitutive roles in imperialism.

In addition to its thesis about how the values accused of being vehicles for imperialism are less central to transnational feminist praxis than it may initially seem, this book can also be read as developing a methodological thesis about the decolonial, postcolonial, and transnational feminist literatures. My methodological thesis is that reading the anti-imperialist feminist literatures as statements about action under *nonideal* (that is, unjust) conditions can disarm the allegation that they are relativist. What Western feminists read as "other" women endorsing sexism is often their taking seriously the demands of making change in a world where injustices intersect, and where justice cannot be brought about in a single stroke (see also Nnaemeka 2004).[4] Because social change almost always involves long-term negotiation with existing structures of power and systems of meaning, and because such social change often imposes costs on the vulnerable, recommendations about how to achieve it will rarely be articulated as visions of ultimate gender justice. Instead, they attempt, to use Maria Lugones's (2003) words, to "refigure the possibilities of the oppressed from within the complexities of the social" (116). Anti-imperialist feminists often articulate their strategies in opposition to Western interventions that aim to institute a new, supposedly independently desirable status for women but that fail to understand what is morally at stake in a given context. Critiques of Western feminist interventions often take aim, not just at cultural or local misunderstandings, but also at failures to understand the ways in which individual women's interests are harmed by oppressive structures besides sexism—such as the imperialism, unrestricted capitalism, and white supremacy in which Western feminists are implicated, but also by heterosexism, ableism, cissexism, and other axes of oppression. It is much simpler theoretical business to know that certain forms of oppression are unacceptable than to know what to do under conditions in which multiple oppressions are likely to be affected by any single strategy, and in which appeals to precedent and existing power relations are unavoidable parts of political praxis. Whereas philosophers have tended to trade in determining what is and is not acceptable relative to an ideal baseline, anti-imperialist feminists have emphasized questions about what to do given the complexities of political praxis under nonideal conditions.

Once we recognize the nonideal character of much anti-imperialist feminist theory, we can see that what are often reductively assumed to be assertions of the value of unqualified respect for culture are actually attempts to introduce moral and political considerations that are genuinely relevant under nonideal conditions. Consider the common argument that the burqa enhances women's agency by providing portable seclusion (see Papanek 1982; Abu-Lughod 2013). It has been read by many Western feminists as suggesting that walking around "shrouded from head to toe" is "on the whole a desirable way to live" (see Okin 1999). But the latter only follows if we ignore the historical character of judgments about what improves women's status over time; a burqa is likely genuinely better than complete seclusion. Similarly, consider the objection of many indigenous women to political strategies that pit them against the men of their groups (see Moreton-Robinson 2000; Curchin 2011).

Those who see such women's silence or refusal as caused by embrace of sexist traditions miss, among other things, the rationality of the suspicion of settler women in a context where indigenous people have been harmed by policies intended to "help" them, how criticisms of indigenous cultures are likely to be interpreted by settlers in ways that justify further harm, and the possibility of internal reform. This book is guided by the idea that useful insights about how to craft our moral and political concepts lie within anti-imperialist feminist theories, but also that to understand these insights, we need to see those anti-imperialist feminist projects for what they are, and to understand that the philosopher's project to a certain extent *should* be to help guide political action in a world characterized by ongoing imperialist and gender injustice.

The Chapters: From Relativism and Universalism to Specific Values

I have said that I aim in this book to develop a way out of the anti-imperialism/ normativity dilemma. This dilemma suggests that we have a choice between abandoning feminism on the grounds that it is an imperialist imposition or biting the bullet and accepting that, if feminism is an extension of Western chauvinism, so be it. My solution is a "nonideal universalism" that thinks of transnational feminisms as a justice-enhancing praxis (see Sen 2009) that aims at reducing or eliminating sexist oppression. It is a solution to the dilemma for two reasons. First, nonideal universalism rejects the notion that there is a single feminism-compatible cultural form, thereby also undermining the idea that an idealized Western culture is the feminist solution. Second, and relatedly, a focus on justice enhancement rather than justice achievement opens up space for criticism of imperialist interventions, especially those taken in the name of Western values or interests that worsen, or do less than they could to improve, women's situation. In chapters 2 to 5, I show how nonideal universalism yields the conclusion that feminism does not require the endorsement of certain objectionable forms of the values of individualism, autonomy, and gender eliminativism.

First, however, I make theoretical space for the idea that universalism could be part of an anti-imperialist feminist solution at all. I show in chapter 1 that the "missionary feminism," an objectionable Western feminist position I see as crystallized in Lila Abu-Lughod's "Do Muslim Women Need Saving?" is not required by moral universalism. Missionary feminism is instead characterized by a brand of universalism that is ethnocentric, justice monist (beholden to the idea that there is one possible set of gender-just cultural forms) and that is beholden to epistemic habits of idealization and moralism (the reduction of political actions to moral statements) that inure Western culture and Western intervention to criticism. I develop my nonideal universalist position, which states that feminism is opposition to sexist oppression and that transnational feminist praxis is a justice-enhancing exercise whose practical implementation requires actively attempting to offset imperialist idealizations. I also discuss an example of transnational feminist activism in the Freedom without Fear Platform in the United Kingdom that aligns with nonideal universalism. Readers who do not need to be convinced that normative universalism can be distinguished from support for imperialism can focus in this chapter on the theoretical habits I do claim participate in justifying imperialism—or they may wish to skip the chapter altogether.

In chapter 2, I turn to the value of individualism and attempt to disentangle the forms of it that play justificatory and constitutive roles in imperialism from those that feminists must endorse. I argue that independence individualism, the imperialism-complicit form of individualism, is conceptually unnecessary for feminism and actually unhelpful for opposing sexist oppression under gender-unjust and imperialist conditions. Drawing on examples from anti-imperialist feminist literatures, I identify four types of harms to women that appear to their proponents to be required for feminist change. These harms, including neoliberal governmentality harms, feminization of responsibility harms, cultural harms, and kinship harms, actually seem to those who enact them to constitute benefits. This sense that women must benefit from what are actually harms to them stems from a tendency confuse personhood individualism, which is important for feminism with independence individualism, which is not. The latter, the view that people should be economically self-sufficient and that only chosen relationships are valuable, gains its appeal more from an idealization of Western culture than from the conceptual entailments of feminism. Further, independence individualism impedes transnational feminist praxis by referring to a parochial Western moral vernacular, worsening women's gendered labor burdens relative to men's and obscuring the transition costs of proposed feminist change. Two of my aims in this chapter on individualism are to show what is wrong with feminisms that fail to apprehend the value of women's inherited attachments and embedded communal forms of life and to precisify feminist criticisms of neoliberalism.

I take on the value of autonomy as freedom from tradition (also sometimes discussed in feminist literatures as the secular) in chapter 3. Feminists who place a high value on freedom from tradition are easily co-opted into clash-of-civilizations rhetoric and the enmity toward "other" cultures it justifies. Recent work on feminist complicity in Islamophobic policies bears witness to this concern; proponents of policies ranging from the US invasion of Iraq to bans on forms of Islamic dress in Europe portray Islam as the source of women's oppression. Additionally, the idea that human lives go badly when individuals accept reasons for acting that are externally dictated, or when they refuse to subject all elements of their traditions to critical scrutiny, is often accused of being a parochial Western value. I argue that feminism does not require value for what I call "Enlightenment freedom," the ability to reject or question traditional dictates *because they are traditional dictates*. If we understand feminism as opposition to sexist oppression, we can see that whether practices and beliefs contribute to oppression or not is a function of their content and effects—not their perceived origins. As a result, feminisms based in traditionalist worldviews are possible, even ones based in worldviews that take some religious or traditional dictates to be beyond question. The chapter can also be read as a response to the work of Saba Mahmood in which I argue that, though feminists cannot embrace the content of conservative Islamist views that deem women inferior, they can embrace other views that share Mahmood's ethnographic subjects' pedagogical and metaphysical view that some traditional dictates are beyond question.

Chapters 4 and 5 focus on the value of gender-role eliminativism. Western feminists have often argued against sexist oppression by referring to fundamental similarities between or among genders. Western gender regimes have often played both justificatory and constitutive roles in imperialism. The institution of Western gender roles has, in many non-Western contexts, increased sexist oppression, as well as increased women's vulnerability to imperialist domination. In chapter 4, I argue that though feminists need not embrace gender-role eliminativism, some gender-emphasizing worldviews cannot constitute feminist *ideals*. These are headship-complementarian worldviews that build asymmetrical vulnerability into gender roles, and according to which women should specialize in household labor and defer to men's authority. I consider defenses of headship-complementarian worldviews that take them to be feminist because they valorize women's well-being. Through a discussion of intrahousehold inequality supportive norms and practices, and a reminder that sexist oppression requires caring about the design of society and not merely about individual women's well-being, I show that feminists cannot conceptualize headship-complementarian gender roles as part of a gender-just end state. However, I acknowledge that nonideal universalist commitments suggest that headship-complementarian strategies can be worthy of support under certain conditions. These conditions include ones in which women's basic well-being is extremely low, and there are few non-headship-complementarian strategies that are likely to be successful in increasing it, or ones in which women will reject improvements in their condition that are not defended in headship-complementarian terms.

Whereas I focus in chapter 4 on gender-emphasizing worldviews that feminists cannot embrace, I focus in chapter 5 on cases in which gender-role eliminativism overreaches. I argue that the tools of nonideal universalism can help Western feminists avoid the mistake of assuming that gender-emphasizing metaphysical views always represent acceptance of sexism. Western feminists need to see that gender-emphasizing strategies can be attempts to improve women's condition under nonideal conditions or to rehabilitate and reimagine precolonial gender roles in ways in which gender difference does not translate into asymmetries of power. I focus my argument on postcolonial feminist objections to the idea that women should be incorporated into a gender-neutral public sphere. I identify three missionary feminist confusions that transform engagement with defenses of "other" women's feminized power into opportunities to assert the ideality of Western culture and the nonideality of "other" cultures. I then show how the underdetermination of the ideal of opposition to sexist oppression and the idea of transnational feminist praxis as a justice-enhancing project concerned with resistance instead of ideal gender relations can reduce the likelihood of such missionary feminist confusions.

A Worry: What about Feminist Solidarity?

The conception of feminism I offer will seem to some to not be normative enough. After all, I define feminism negatively, as opposition to sexist oppression. I argue that feminists do not need a single ideal of the gender-just society, that it is acceptable for the indices of advantage and disadvantage and the moral languages in which feminist strategies are articulated to vary somewhat from context to context, that empirical contextual considerations matter in determining which strategies should be chosen under nonideal conditions, and that Western feminist interventions can turn out to be more imperialist than feminist and to sometimes do more harm than good. It may thus seem that I want to excise positive visions from feminism and, if not make feminist solidarity impossible, limit it to being only temporary and painstaking.[5]

I have three lines of response to this worry. Before I describe them I want to emphasize that many Western feminists, especially Western feminists involved in advocacy and policymaking roles, could do with taking a more painstaking approach to solidarity. As I will point out, Western feminists often assume that what it would mean for "other" women to become feminist is that they will adopt Enlightenment liberal values. Such assumptions are, in addition to being parochial, sometimes out of touch with the empirical realities of what would actually improve "other" women's lives. For example (as I argue in chapter 2) the assumption, endorsed by many feminist philosophers, in addition to development advocates,[6] that income generation will liberate women is out of touch with the fact that women need more household negotiating power and supports for household and dependency work. The result of such ill-thought-out interventions can be genuine harm.

But to begin answering the question of whether my approach undermines solidarity, I clarify that I am not arguing against all uses of positive ideals in feminist praxis. Positive ideals of gender justice have been vital for actual feminist organizing. They motivate people and help them cultivate capacities to imagine gender relations otherwise. Nothing in my account precludes local and culturally specific ideals. In the broader transnational context, I am against two things: ideals that are treated as transcontextual recipes for what to do and ideals whose content seems decided more by Western and Northern self-representations and interests than by genuine empirical engagement, intercultural dialogue, and attention to what "other" women actually need. To begin with the latter, my worry is that Western feminists are letting ideological representations of the superiority of the West, including the Enlightenment teleological narrative I describe in chapter 1, appear as truths about what all women need—without empirical evidence and without deliberation with the women whose lives they are attempting to shape. I am open even to universalist transnational feminist positive ideals that are the result of intercultural negotiation and empirical engagement, but I am unconvinced many such ideals have been allowed to emerge in the contemporary transnational political landscape.

I am also against treating positive ideals as recipes in transnational contexts. By this I mean that feminists need to see that an ideal of gender justice does not determine what should be done to achieve it in any particular context (I discuss this at length, especially in chapters 1 and 5). So even if transnational feminists did come to agree on an ideal of gender justice, I would want them and, in particular, Western feminists to remember that knowing what the desired end state is different from knowing how to get there, as well as to recognize that the latter is likely to be context specific. Knowledge about which political strategies would work is likely to require first-personal information from the people affected and attention to the fact that women have interests besides gender interests—including human interests, such as basic health, and other group-based interests, such as interests in not being victims of imperialist domination. The openness to positive ideals I am describing here may seem in tension with the opposition to justice monism I articulate in chapter 1. However, I there only oppose a *thick* vision, and my aim is mostly to hold open space for alternative visions of gender justice in a world where Western visions easily dominate other ones without a warrant.

My second response to the question of whether my view undermines solidarity is to point out that my view is more normative than it may initially seem. In chapter 1, I argue that transnational feminists should take the goods that are the objects of human rights to count as a nonexhaustive and minimal list of universal indicators of advantage and disadvantage. Moreover, my claim that indices of advantage and disadvantage can vary should not be read as a claim that it is impossible to make true judgments about what the indicators of advantage and disadvantage are in a given context. My view is that Westerners should not assume that the familiar indices or familiar instantiations are the correct ones. The upshot is not that solidarity is impossible tout court; it is that meaningful solidarity is impossible until the indices of advantage and disadvantage in a given context, evidence of their gender differential distribution, and what is at stake in practical strategies for changing them are known.

Third, I point out that my approach does not merely emphasize epistemic difficulties and context specificity; it also emphasizes historical and ongoing imperialism. I bring this up because the primary argument of the book is not that contexts and normative systems are too diverse for Western feminists to trust their normative judgments; it is that Western feminists are too embedded in imperialist power relations and the false representations that buttress them to see the lives of "other" women clearly. The fact of imperialism means that there are some solidaristic actions that Western feminists can take that draw on relatively noncontroversial value judgments. One, which Alison Jaggar (2005) has argued for, involves advocating for the stopping of harm to "other" women through Northern and Western policies. Another, which has been discussed by Uma Narayan (1997), is for Westerners to reject or minimize strategies that portray "other" women's oppression as caused by their cultures or lack of modernity. What is wrong with Western feminist judgments, this book suggests, is often not that they are wrong about the badness of unfamiliar practices; it is that they advocate for changing them in ways that worsen the lives of those they advocate for and do so because of the missionary feminist precommitments I describe in the first chapter.

Methodology and the Challenges of Normative Theorizing across Disciplines

My aim in this book is ambitious—to answer questions about what the core values of transnational feminist praxis should and should not be. These questions are not easily answered from inside a discipline. Philosophy offers indispensible tools for normative theorizing, but the theoretical questions that arise out of transnational feminist praxis do not map neatly onto known philosophical debates. The decolonial, postcolonial, and transnational feminist literatures are themselves interdisciplinary but tend to be developed from qualitative social science. In my view, their engagement with social movements, and their empirical and political orientations more broadly, enhances their ability to identify questions that are genuinely morally and politically urgent. At the same time, however, the normative questions anti-imperialist feminist literatures raise are often restricted to analysis of particular phenomena or left at the level of critique. To answer the questions I want to answer about how values do and should figure in transnational feminist praxis, I have had to develop the book along argumentative contours that do not neatly follow debates in philosophy or interdisciplinary feminist theory. Philosophical readers are thus likely to find that I sometimes dwell in examples and place conceptual and logical distinctions more in the background of chapters than they would like, as well as to find it unusual that I treat the political implications of adopting moral and political concepts as germane to their acceptability. Feminist theoretical readers may find my emphasis on distinguishing between the objectionable and necessary forms of values and precisifying the role of certain values at odds with their desire to criticize entire social imaginaries. They may be surprised by my insistence on preserving normativity. Both audiences will likely find familiar insights in the chapters, but I hope that normative precision can cut through some dilemmas in feminist theory and that attention to real-world gender injustices can draw attention to some issues that have been largely neglected in political philosophy.

What I have tried to do is address questions about values as they arise in transnational feminist praxis. My hope has been that tools from philosophy, especially analytical precision and its repertoire for describing moral and political concepts, can help illuminate what is at stake and help us get clearer about what the objects of anti-imperialist feminist critique are—and whether, and to what extent, they are in tension with feminism. Anti-imperialist feminist projects have been largely critical and often concerned with calling for greater attention to contextual variation and particularity. This emphasis is justified in a world where Northern and Western intervention in women's lives often causes harm, and where the harm sometimes comes through the assumption that women everywhere want or need the same things. I attempt here, however, to ask what can be learned from these criticisms at the level of normative theory. Which values, when subjected to both analytical scrutiny and attention to their real-world effects, will turn out to be emancipatory? Does criticizing Western values mean criticizing normativity as such, as some decolonial and postcolonial feminists allege? When is sensitivity to context important, and are the forms of it that feminist politics needs incompatible with any form of universalism? These are the questions I hope the tools of philosophy can help feminist theorists answer.

Writing a work of political philosophy that foregrounds the concerns of the anti-imperialist feminist literatures challenges the methodology of Anglo-American political philosophy in three ways that are worth making explicit. First, these literatures discuss values as they impact political life, which does not always match up to how they are articulated in academic philosophical texts. This has made it all too easy for philosophers to claim that anti-imperialist feminists address value positions that nobody actually holds, but I think the reality is more complicated. Addressing values as they impact public life is surely worth doing in its own right. But philosophers can help themselves to both normative and non-normative commitments that are not explicitly articulated in their texts. Readers will undoubtedly find many cases where I criticize feminist philosophers for holding positions they do not explicitly endorse. My reason for doing this is usually that their judgments about particular cases are informed by more than their explicit theoretical positions; they are informed by unstated background assumptions, often ones that are at best empirically suspect and at worst only made plausible by imperialist epistemic contexts. Practical prescriptions that are informed by uncritical assumptions about the causes of "other" women's oppression and the superiority of Western cultural forms are, in my view, quite commonplace in philosophy. To avoid drawing discussion away from the issues at hand and toward scholarship on individual Western feminist philosophers, I have tended to put examples of philosophers making objectionable judgments about cases in the endnotes rather than the body of the text.

As Cheshire Calhoun (1988, 452) argues, theoretical traditions can draw their appeal from assumptions that "are not logically entailed by any particular theory and might be denied by individual theorists were those beliefs articulated." For example, I argue in chapter 3 that philosophers who take seriously the fact that we all inherit values and practices from our cultures continue to help themselves to unstated assumptions that tradition is the source of patriarchal oppression. Though few philosophers explicitly argue that traditions are sexist because they are traditions, more than one offers freedom to question traditions as a *feminist* (and not merely a comprehensive liberal) solution. Moreover, the value positions that animate public life, even when they are not identical with the ones operative in political philosophy, can bear associations to philosophical ideas that are themselves worth exploring. For example, as I argue in that same chapter, the idea that moral progress comes from the rejection of tradition resonates heavily with certain ideas in the history of liberalism, including Mill's claims that traditionalism stifles human nature and Kant's views in "What Is Enlightenment?" I try in the body of the book to be clear about when I am criticizing public justificatory discourses and when I am criticizing explicit philosophical positions, but I ask readers to keep in mind both that public discourse often draws on philosophical ideas and that philosophers often draw on background assumptions in making judgments about cases that they would likely disavow were those assumptions made explicit.

Second, the decolonial, postcolonial, and transnational feminist literatures do not treat the prescriptive content of moral and political philosophies and their logical implications as the only elements of them worth discussing. These literatures suppose that studying the ways values operate in the world can give us insight into whether those values are good values. As feminist philosophers have long argued,[7] refusing to consider the social functioning of moral and political concepts can prevent us from seeing the extent to which such concepts gain their popularity and apparent coherence from their ideological functions. An important benefit of considering the ways concepts function to promote injustice is that it draws our theoretical attention to logical inconsistencies, unforeseen implications, ways of seeing underlying our normative prescriptions, and moral and political alternatives that it is easy to miss from the armchair—and from the socially dominant and empirically limited positions from which most philosophers begin their inquiries. Such limitations are especially likely to cause problems when theorists from the West and North attempt to discuss "other" women and women from the global South.[8] It is difficult to imagine theorizing about them responsibly without attention to the ways values operate in real-world discourses that affect their lives.

Third, contemporary Anglo-American political philosophy is dominated by debates within liberalism, and much anti-imperialist feminist literature is critical of liberalism. The view that liberalism is the only defensible normative viewpoint makes it difficult to imagine the possibility that one may criticize liberalism, or elements of it, without being a relativist. I have already mentioned that liberals often respond to criticism of any form of liberalism by arguing against relativism. This is a question-begging response, and the only way for feminists to develop a more adequate one is to engage with "other" traditions and practices and the arguments for women's emancipation they furnish. This is not the same thing as looking for the presence of liberal values in other traditions,[9] though I do not deny either that moral overlap exists across cultures or that some of it concerns liberal values, broadly construed. Feminist projects grounded in liberal values have occurred all over the world, and this is an important fact, but it certainly does not establish that liberalism is the only moral vocabulary hospitable to feminism. Nor do I mean to undermine the idea that certain values associated with liberalism, such as freedom of speech, are universally valuable. I mean more simply that the philosophical tendencies to begin from arguments within liberalism and treat liberal viewpoints as self-evidently offering the solution to oppression are insufficient responses to the difficulties of transnational and cross-cultural political engagement.

Terminological Clarifications and Scope

A few remarks about terminology and scope may be helpful. Feminist readers may see three elements of my analysis as divergent from trends in contemporary feminist scholarship. First, the book's focus on analyzing and correcting Western feminist values and ways of seeing may seem out of step with recent arguments for "Southern theory" (see Connell 2014, 2015) and border theorizing (see Mignolo and Tlostanova 2006; see also Anzaldua 1987). It may seem that by focusing on critiques of Western values, I have repeated colonial epistemic practices, causing what Uma Narayan (1997) calls the mirror dynamic in which academics treat encounters with "other" cultures only as opportunities to reflect on themselves. Global justice clearly requires greater epistemic justice, in my view. Southern theory is a crucial part of this enterprise. Indeed, the Western feminist assumption that Western social and cultural forms are the (only) potentially gender-just ones—the assumption this book attempts to dislodge—is clearly fueled by a failure to think about human life and the world from any position outside the cultural and economic center. Yet I believe a continued critique of Western feminism is part of the project of dislodging this assumption and creating intellectual and political space for "other" women's political and theoretical interventions. So long as Westerners continue to believe that their values are the only ones that can promote feminist change, and so long as global conditions afford them disproportionate power, Westerners are likely to continue engaging in imperialism in the name of feminism. Furthermore, imperialism is not merely perpetuated by a *lack* of (or lack of exposure to) Southern theory. As I argue throughout this book, Western feminist epistemic habits exert a blocking force; they filter what feminists can do with new information about "others."

Second, it may seem outmoded to define feminism as opposition to sexist oppression. I discuss this concern in chapter 1, but it is worth saying from the outset that I take embracing this definition of feminism in the transnational context to be in the spirit of intersectionality rather than an alternative to it. Oppressions such as imperialism, racism, heterosexism, classism, ableism, and cissexism undoubtedly intersect with sexism, and it is often difficult to differentiate the effects of sexism from effects of other oppressions in actual women's lives. At the same time, it is useful—partly *because of* the fact of intersectionality and partly because oppression is a group-afflicting phenomenon—to be able to distinguish what would improve individual women's lives from what would reduce sexist oppression. In some cases, many of which are imperialism-related, available alternatives present a choice between advancing gender interests and other identity-related interests. It is undoubtedly true, as intersectional feminists argue, that the lives of women who are victims of imperialism and sexism would be improved by the end of both systems. But it is also true that acts and strategies that promote sexism can be in the short-term interests of women who are multiply oppressed, because individual women can benefit from meeting the standards of oppressive regimes and because reducing imperialism may, in the time frames that activism occurs in, be more likely to improve their lives than reducing sexism.

I do not think it is helpful for navigating a world where sexism and imperialism both exist to imagine away potential conflicts between the goals identified by each. Intersectional feminist theories are correct to dictate that feminists should proactively seek strategies that reduce women having to choose between their gender and racial or anti-imperialist interests, wherever possible. Intersectional theories are also correct that in some cases the effects of gender oppression and other forms of oppression are indistinguishable in human lives. But from the perspective of evaluating strategies under conditions of multiple oppressions, it can be useful to see when women are negotiating trade-offs among interests related to different identities, as well as what is being traded away for what. Rather than defining away the possibility of forced tradeoffs between gender and other identity-related interests, I prefer the idea Australian indigenous feminist, Aileen Moreton-Robinson, articulates about the implications of intersecting oppressions. As she puts it, "Feminism must accept that it is not the political home for women all of the time" (Moreton-Robinson 2002, 68).

Third, it may seem surprising that I spend little time discussing what many have taken to be the core prescription of transnational feminist praxis, recognition of "other" women's agency. It is certainly true, as I argue in chapter 5, that Western feminists often ignore "other" women's systems of value and reasons for choosing what they do, and that this ignorance and objectification are pernicious. However, as I have argued at length elsewhere (see Khader 2011, 2014), I do not think feminist questions are resolved by concern with agency (or "relational autonomy," a term that has become increasingly popular in feminist philosophy and political theory[10]). It is possible to be fully agentic and to also perpetuate one's own (or others') oppression. Feminism requires opposition to oppression, not just the ability to make meaning and act in ways one cares about in the world. Feminists should be interested in promoting not merely agency, but women's emancipation or gender justice as well, and doing this inevitably means making judgments about the content of agency or what agency brings about in the world. This does not imply that such judgments should be made lightly or without contextual sensitivity, but it does imply that respect for agency is an insufficient feminist normative commitment. An anti-imperialist transnational feminist praxis must certainly demand taking women's analyses of their own situations and their reasons for acting as they do within them seriously, but there is no guarantee that political strategies and social movements that are agentic are necessarily *feminist* (see Madhok 2013). And in this book, I am interested in asking, not whether women are reflective or which values they actually hold, but rather what values *should* motivate transnational feminist praxis.

Finally, I pause to clarify some of the terms I use frequently in this book. First, despite the fact that the West is not internally homogenous and that geopolitical relations in the contemporary world do not map clearly onto a Western/non-Western binary, I mostly use the term "Western" to refer to commitments associated with Euro-American positions of cultural, economic, and military dominance. I hope it goes without saying that the points of view I call

"Western feminist" in this book are neither held by all Westerners, nor held exclusively by them. Complicating matters is that some of the forms of imperialism I am interested in are more directly related to neoliberalism than to Western culture. Neoliberalism is typically discussed in North-South terms, where "North" refers to the affluent. Because the justificatory discourses surrounding poverty and women's oppression so often attribute affluence and gender justice to cultural superiority—and gender injustice (more on this in chapter 3) and deprivation to cultural failure—the idea of the North and the idea of the West are overlapping. I thus often use the term "West" to include both the ideas of West and North. Indeed, as Giraldo (2016, 168) argues, drawing on Walter Mignolo's idea of re-Westernization, countries with rising affluence that may not have been culturally Western at earlier points in history sometimes begin to cast themselves as Western now. I do, however, use the terms "North" and "South" to discuss cases where the form of domination is primarily economic.

I use the term "other" women, borrowed from Uma Narayan (2002), instead of the term "third-world women" to capture both the decline in the use of the term "third world" after the Cold War and the fact that women who are perceived as culturally "other" now live throughout the West and are often marginalized through internal imperialist dynamics.[11] I do not mean in using this term to suggest that "other" women bear some common characteristic besides their relation to the West. Instead, much of the point of my analysis here is that Western interactions with "other" women are more closely based on ascriptions of what Chandra Talpade Mohanty (1988) calls "the third-world difference" than on the types of context-specific and historical understandings that are relevant to political action.

Finally, I use the term "anti-imperialist feminist" to capture the postcolonial, transnational, and decolonial feminist positions. These literatures share an interest in the effects of imperialism on gender relations and Western difficulties apprehending them. However, the differences in these literatures are significant, and I use the terms "postcolonial," "decolonial," and "transnational" individually when referring to claims characteristic of only one of the literatures. Postcolonial and decolonial theory both criticize the ways in which Western universalist claims are often false and built on assumptions about the inferiority of "others." Both also emphasize the ways popular Western analytical and moral notions are products of ongoing colonial processes that continue to participate in justifying colonialism. Postcolonial theory originated mostly in discussions of the Middle East and South Asia. Decolonial theory, the strain I engage with least in this book, is more grounded in contemporary Latin American thought, traces colonialism back to the late fifteenth century, and offers extended discussions of the genesis of the concepts of the human and being. Transnational feminist theory is a twenty-first-century innovation that attempts to identify possibilities for cross-border activism created by globalization, with an emphasis on the ways in which neoliberalism in particular generates new oppressions and new feminist opportunities. I group the feminist variants of these three schools of thought together as anti-imperialist because of their shared normative commitments to opposing imperialism and sexism. In the following pages, I clarify these normative commitments in the hopes of imagining a feminism that does not perpetuate imperialist domination but is capable of responding to gender injustice on a global scale.

1 TOWARD A DECOLONIAL FEMINIST UNIVERSALISM

Feminist critics of imperialism are often thought to be relativists.[1] Because many Western feminisms[2] set themselves up as "universal, morally correct," and "exhaust[ive] of how we imagine emancipatory possibilities and projects" (Khoja-Moolji 2017, 378), critiques seem, to use Shenila S. Khoja-Moolji's words, "regressive, backward, premodern and against the principles of human rights" (377).[3] Explicit disavowals of relativism have now become standard in decolonial, postcolonial, and transnational feminist writings—presumably to pre-empt such accusations.[4] But denying a commitment is not the same thing as not having it, and Western feminists have exploited this ambiguity to great effect. The anti-imperialist feminist tendency to use the terms "universalist" and "normative" pejoratively has inadvertently fueled the Western feminist worry.[5]

The universalism/relativism framing, I claim, makes it impossible for the normative claims in anti-imperialist feminisms to register as such. The notion that universalism itself causes imperialism (or, as some Western feminists would have it, causes what *appears* to be imperialism) produces a dilemma forecloses the possibility of anti-imperialist feminisms. According to this anti-imperialism/ normativity dilemma, we can have a feminism that saves "other" women to Western culture or no feminism at all. But the dilemma only obtains if the only possible form of universalist moral argument is one that endorses Western values and conceives Western actors as a sort of moral vanguard.

I contend, however, that what makes feminisms complicit in imperialism is not primarily universalism, and that because of this, we can imagine what I call a "nonideal universalism" that is simultaneously feminist and anti-imperialist. The key to imagining such a position is to demonstrate that the commitments that cause

Western feminisms to become complicit in imperialism are not central to feminism's status as a normative doctrine. These objectionable commitments constitute a perspective I refer to as "missionary feminism"—a schematized perspective I think few feminists explicitly endorse, but whose commitments lie in the background of many feminist theorists' and activists' advocates about actual interventions. Missionary feminism, I argue, stems more from ethnocentrism, justice monism, and idealizing and moralizing ways of seeing that associate Western culture with morality (and thus prevent Western culture and Western intervention from becoming objects of normative scrutiny) than from universalist commitment to the value of gender justice. Ethnocentric justice monism is the view that it is only possible to actualize gender justice within one set of (Western) cultural forms. Idealizing and moralizing ways of seeing describe the world according to a false social ontology wherein the West's putative moral superiority derives from endogenous cultural factors and suggest that political actions are to be evaluated as expressions of moral judgments rather than negotiations of interests and power.

After distinguishing the imperialism-promoting commitments from the universalist ones feminists need, I sketch an alternative feminist normative framework that is responsive to the needs of transnational feminist praxis in a world characterized by historical and ongoing imperialism. According to it, feminism is opposition to sexist oppression, and transnational feminist politics requires visibilizing the effects of global structures on contemporary practices and acknowledging the practical character of many transnational feminist political judgments. I begin with an example of a real-world feminist political strategy that is complicit in imperialism and end with one that is more redemptive.

Two terminological points will be helpful in mapping out this argumentative terrain. First, I call the position that women's subjugation is acceptable because people believe it is, or because it is widespread in certain contexts, "moral relativism" because this matches the usage in the existing feminist debates. Admittedly, the substance of these allegations is better conceptually understood as sexist apologism than relativism, since the accusation against anti-imperialist feminists is often that they only value cultures,[6] not that they deny that anything has universal value. Second, unless otherwise specified, I use the term "universalism" to refer only to moral or normative universalism. Moral universalism is the notion that some things are better and worse for human beings across all contemporary contexts. By defending universalism, I do not mean to claim that all (or even familiar) universalist feminist views are correct or feminist. Instead, I mean to say that it takes much more than the universalist *form* of moral argument to drive imperialism, and that we can develop an anti-imperialist transnational feminist praxis by training our focus on these other elements.

Missionary Feminism and the Problem of Saving "To"

According to Uma Narayan (1997), many Western feminisms assume the "missionary position" by assuming that "only Westerners are capable of naming and challenging patriarchal atrocities against third-world women" (57). Since the easiest way to argue that Westerners are uniquely positioned to make feminist change is to claim that their form of life is the best one for everyone, it is unsurprising that missionary feminists are typically universalists. To get a more complete picture of the content of missionary feminism, its relationship to universalism, and anti-imperialist reasons for opposing it, I examine and abstract from the case-specific criticisms Lila Abu-Lughod makes in her influential essay "Do Muslim Women Need Saving?" In a particularly pithy and evocative phrase, Abu-Lughod (2002) argues that missionary feminisms save *to*: "When you save someone, you imply that you are saving her from something, you are also saving her *to* something" (789), she writes. Saving involves a sense of superiority by Westerners and a lack of reflection about "the violences entailed in . . . transformation[s]" (789). Missionary feminism, rather than being reducible to a view about the possibility of cross-cultural moral judgment, includes views about who can make change and about the form of life "other" cultures should ultimately be changed *to*.

Since Abu-Lughod's essay, like most anti-imperialist feminist work, responds to a particular event and context, reconstructing the general commitments of missionary feminism requires some theorizing. I take missionary feminism to comprise six overlapping commitments, which I will describe here. Abu-Lughod's original essay discusses the mobilization of feminist rhetoric in favor of the US invasion of Afghanistan (and, later, of Iraq). Because it has been fifteen years since Abu-Lughod's essay appeared, I will also draw from Sujatha Fernandes's (2017) work on the Afghan Women Writers' Project (AWWP) for examples of missionary feminism at work in Afghanistan.[7] To be clear, missionary feminism is a somewhat stylized position, designed to make sense of the patterns of Western feminist moral attention. It needs neither to be endorsed in its entirety, nor embraced explicitly, to be motivating Western feminist theory and politics.

The West as the Single Gender-Just Endpoint

According to Abu-Lughod, missionary feminists already know the details of what Afghan women will look like after "salvation." This improved society will be free of the cultural forms that mark Muslims in the Western imaginary; women will, for example, be free of veils of any kind. Western cultural forms *just are* the gender-just way of life. The AWWP audiences, who are Westerners listening to stories crafted by Afghan women about their experiences of war and reconstruction, take this assumption so far as to treat patriarchal elements of Western culture as liberatory. They discuss how lucky they are to live in a country where they can shop and wear makeup (Fernandes 2017, 658), and are fascinated by tales of Afghan women who long to go to the prom (655) or wear white dresses, rather than burqas, at their weddings (656). Of course, some of what the missionary feminists take to be desirable is genuinely worth having, such as access to education. But instead of asking directly about what would increase gender justice in other contexts, missionary feminists always already know that their own form of life constitutes it. The possibility of "other" forms of life being refigured to support gender justice and the possibility that Western culture is gender unjust do not register.

In other words, missionary feminists believe that there is one possible gender-just cultural form, and Western culture embodies it. They recognize no conceptual space between the idea that the situation of Afghan women is gender unjust and the idea that everyone should adopt Western culture; what "other" women need to be saved *to* is (an idealized) Western culture.

A Single Moral Vernacular

One part of the view that Western culture is the gender-just endpoint is worth discussing in its own right, because it receives so much attention in anti-imperialist feminisms. Abu-Lughod (2002) claims that missionary feminists cannot imagine that Afghan women might be "called to personhood, so to speak, in a different language" (788)—one in which they wish to retain forms of life with strong family ties or orient their lives toward religion. Abu-Lughod's implication is that missionary feminists believe that only one set of moral self-understandings is compatible with feminism. The typical candidate is the self-understanding offered by what I called Enlightenment liberalism in the introduction, a crude liberalism that opposes custom and values individual self-sufficiency.[8] Instead of asking questions, or opening up space for others to ask questions, about how moral vernaculars other than

Enlightenment liberalism contain emancipatory possibilities, missionary feminists suppose that other moral languages are bankrupt.

The Enlightenment Teleological Narrative

Abu-Lughod and Fernandes note that missionary feminists describe Muslim women as stuck in the past and Western culture and Western intervention as "other" women's future. Abu-Lughod (2002) reminds us that direct rule of Algeria was supported by the view that France, for the first time, was giving Algerian girls the ability to have "a share of this world" (785). A contemporary AWWP reader listens to an Afghan woman's description of freedom as the ability to veil from whomever she chooses and replies that covering the body is what Western women used to do in the 1920s (Fernandes 2017, 656–657). Embedded in this rhetoric is the sense that there is a single destiny for all societies, and that "others" currently inhabit the past of the West. This way of thinking has the effect of transforming cultural changes that would otherwise need justifying into part of inevitable historical progress.

This association of the West with the future of humanity can be traced to a common narrative about modernity that resonates with thought of many Enlightenment philosophers[9] and has been extensively theorized in decolonial and postcolonial thought.[10] According to it, the world is divided into "primitive" and "modern" societies, and all societies are naturally progressing toward modernity—some more quickly than others. Gender justice is a byproduct of modernity, which the West achieved more quickly because of its internal features. The narrative capitalizes on ambiguities in the terms "modern" and its companion term "civilized." Both terms seem to many to simply connote points in time; to live in the twenty-first century just is, at first blush, to be "modern." At the same time, however, both terms are normatively laden; being modern is a positive thing, associated with scientific and moral progress and, in particular, acting out of principle rather than custom. Yet one need only scratch the surface to see that the word "modern" (and thus morally advanced) is not applied equally to everyone living in the twentieth or twenty-first centuries. This distinction between *modern* and *primitive* functions as a de facto color line, separating the West from "others" (Razack 2008). The packing of Westernness, justice, and futurity into the single idea of modernity permits the view that the adoption of Western culture is inevitable and required for gender justice—and the view that the steps on the path to gender justice will be the same in every context.

Western Intervention as Women's Salvation

Missionary feminists see Western intervention as the preferred feminist solution partly because they ignore, and conduct their politics absent, contact with organizations led by "other" women. Abu-Lughod (2002) remarks that during the colonial period, direct rule was believed to be the only way of ending practices such as child marriage and the "tradition" of sati in India (785).[11] Fernandes shows how, contemporarily, Afghan women face Western incentives to frame their narratives in ways that support the notion that Western involvement is the solution to their problems. In one example, a woman who is reading her poem about the horrors of war precedes it with a discussion of how positive the effects of US intervention have been for Afghan women, feeling obligated to claim that exposing Afghan men to America is an important path to cultural change (Fernandes 2017, 662). The view that Western intervention is the feminist solution is a natural outgrowth of the Enlightenment teleology, which tells missionary feminists that "other" women are destined to adopt Western culture and that the backwardness of "others" is caused by endogenous factors. Who better to bring moral progress to others than representatives of the culture that embodies the height of human progress?

Invisibility of Costs of Intervention

Abu-Lughod (2002) argues that both the harms of war and the contributions of war to women's subordination are simply ignored in missionary feminist calculations about intervention. More broadly, feminisms that save *to* ignore the "violences entailed in . . . transformation" (789). The occlusion of the effects of war on Afghan women is evident in the forgetting of US responsibility for the ascent of the Taliban during the Cold War. More contemporarily, Fernandes argues that audiences of the AWWP ignore the extent to which war imposes gendered costs on women. AWWP participants write about war increasing poverty and vulnerability to rape (Fernandes 2017, 654–655)—both of which create incentives for early marriage. Yet the effects of war on early and forced marriage are simply ignored by the Western women who use these stories as opportunities to pontificate about their own good fortune in being able to choose marriage partners. To generalize these points, missionary feminists ignore the harms of Western intervention in the lives of "other" women.

Misplaced Priorities

Abu-Lughod observes that missionary feminist supporters of the 2001 invasion of Afghanistan seem more preoccupied with veiling (ranging from burqas to hijabs; recall George W. Bush's neologism "women of cover") than issues like starvation and women's health. She treats the invasion of Afghanistan as continuous with early twentieth-century colonial feminisms, which were preoccupied with unveiling Egyptian women but cared little about educating them—and were in fact supported by some who were vocal opponents of women's suffrage in England (Abu-Lughod 2002, 784). She also criticizes missionary feminists for failing to prioritize changing global structural contributors to "other" women's oppression. She asks not only why those who are worried about Afghan women's situation often fail to acknowledge the role of the US government in installing the Taliban,[12] but also why they are not focusing their political energy on fighting the structures that produce global poverty and inequality (789).

The charge Abu-Lughod is making is about misplaced political priorities, not just hypocrisy. Westerners intervene in the lives of "others" in ways that do not track what is genuinely morally urgent. A feminist politics that cares more about markers of cultural difference than starvation, violence, and lack of education and their gendered effects—and one that is unwilling to engage in politics that would reduce these harms by challenging global structures—is vulnerable to criticism for ignoring what is genuinely morally important.

Resort to the Cultural

Abu-Lughod criticizes missionary feminists for taking oppressive practices in Afghanistan to be caused by culture or religion—instead of by the history of the Cold War or the earlier European division of the Middle East. One example from the AWWP is particularly illustrative: a woman tells of having been engaged to her cousin since she was an infant and having fallen in love with him through speaking to him on the phone. Because of the need for patronage from a warlord to survive the war, her family forced her to marry a warlord instead in exchange for employment opportunities for the men in her tribe (Fernandes 2017, 654). Rather seeing the ways in which war can worsen women's vulnerability to this "cultural" practice, Western audiences lump the arranged and forced marriage together as belonging to an Afghan culture in which women lack choices.

The Western notion that unchanging "other" cultures, rather than global politics or internal power struggles, produce sexist practices has a long history (see Narayan 1997; Mohanty 1988). Abu-Lughod names this explanatory strategy "the resort to the cultural."

Is "Missionary" Another Word for "Universalist"?

Universalist commitments are straightforwardly linked to two of the missionary feminist views: the notion of the West as the gender-just endpoint and the idea of a single moral vernacular. But it is possible to reject these elements without rejecting universalism, and this is important for retaining feminism's status as a normative doctrine and grounding anti-imperialist feminist praxis.

Universalism: Part of the Problem Worth Retaining?

Since missionary feminism needs universalism to get off the ground, rejecting universalism may seem like the anti-imperialist fix. A logical point can help us see why rejecting missionary feminism does not require rejecting universalism: one needs to be a universalist to be a missionary feminist, but not the other way around. Nonetheless, the fact that we *can* retain universalism and be anti-imperialists does not mean that we should. Some important considerations militate in favor of decolonial, postcolonial, and transnational feminists embracing some type of universalism, however. One consideration is familiar; it is unclear how feminism can be a meaningful normative doctrine without universalist commitments.[13] Any plausible feminism will include the view that some things that happen to people because of their gender are genuinely wrong, and cross-contextually so. Lest the idea of cross-cultural validity seem unnecessary, it is worth remembering that it is difficult in the contemporary world to avoid encountering and judging the practices of "others." A parochial morality is not enough in a world characterized, not just by frequent cross-cultural interaction, but also by cross-border exercises of power—including the worsening of "other" women's oppression by imperialist forces. Universalist moralities have justified imperialism, but feminists cannot afford to forget that relativism, too, as Kiran Grewal (2012) puts it, "is often used to reinforce positions of privilege and power" (579). Allegations of Westernization that have been used to delegitimize feminists outside the West (see Narayan 1997), and allegations of whiteness that have been used to delegitimize women of color within the West (see Moraga, Anzaldua, and

Cade Bambara 1983), often depart from the idea that opposition to sexist oppression is a parochial value.

Another reason for feminists to retain universalist, or at least highly general, forms of normative theorizing is the increasing need for cross-border feminist politics brought about by geopolitical changes. Chandra Talpade Mohanty argues in recent work that new cross-border formations of power, such as an increasingly neoliberal global order, demand transnational organizing. Though Mohanty (2013) initially became known for emphasizing "historical and cultural specificity in understanding [third world women's] complex agency as situated subjects," she now cautions against seeing such forms of analysis as requiring the abandonment of "all forms of generalization" (967; see also Mohanty 2003). In fact, Mohanty argues, the view that cross-border analysis is totalizing plays directly into the hands of the forces of neoliberalism and white supremacy. The weakening of states, increasing militarism (including the militarization of domestic security forces), the transnational rise of patriarchal politicized religion, and global capitalism are creating new forms of gender injustice (Mohanty 2003, 231). Mohanty argues that cross-border similarities in the operations of multinational corporations and the economic policies they prefer states to adopt have resulted in the emergence of new forms of low-wage, gendered, and racialized manufacturing labor. Opposing such global systemic injustices requires seeing cross-contextual similarities and being able to draw consistent moral judgments about them.

Finally, it is unclear that rejecting universalism can yield coherent anti-imperialist positions. The logical tension between relativism and anti-imperialism is similar in structure to the tension between relativism and feminism, but it is deeper, since imperialism, by definition, is a border-crossing phenomenon. Imperialism typically involves cultural differences between the dominator and the dominated, and we want criticisms of imperialism to be able to show more than that imperialism *appears* wrong from the perspective of the dominated. Relativism also interferes with opposition to imperialism in another, related way: it precludes normative views originating from the colonized from having universal force—that is, from having moral purchase on Westerners. As Linda Zerilli (2009) describes the worry (though in the context of a different problem), if local ideas cannot become universal "There [can] be no place within local traditions from which to begin the political process of articulating a new universalism, because aside from . . . the (truly universal universals in non-Western Cultures), traditions are closed" (302; see also Connell 2015).[14] Of course, not all values need universal force to do their work. But if the harms of imperialism or gender injustice turn out to be traceable in some way to

Western (or other) values, cross-contextual rejection of those values will have to be possible.

Ethnocentrism and Justice Monism

If anti-imperialist feminists must be universalists, the path to avoiding the anti-imperialism/normativity dilemma has to be to reject some other elements of missionary feminism. In my view, the objectionable theoretical habits underlying the missionary feminist errors I described above are ethnocentrism, what I call "justice monism," and idealizing and moralizing nonnormative assumptions. Once we recognize these theoretical habits for what they are, it will become clear both that it is possible to have a universalist normative perspective without them and that missionary feminism cannot successfully be opposed by rejecting universalist forms of moral argument. Because missionary feminism combines a strange species of universalism with particular ways of construing nonnormative facts, opposing missionary feminism means changing both the structure of existing universalist moral ideals and ideological ways of seeing. Ethnocentrism, the first theoretical habit constitutive of missionary feminism, is judging "others" according to the moral standards of one's own culture. Ethnocentric judgments always run the risk of being morally arbitrary, because ethnocentrists refuse to raise questions about whether what is culturally familiar is genuinely morally important. Ethnocentrists typically make judgments about cases by assuming that what is familiar tracks what is genuinely morally important. The missionary feminist who believes that the true feminist gender protocol is one in which women wear makeup and white wedding dresses rather practice any form of veiling assumes that Western gender norms are the morally correct ones.

The idea that some cultural forms are *the* gender just ones bespeaks, not just ethnocentrism, but a theoretical commitment I name "justice monism." Justice monism is the view that only one type of social or cultural form can house gender justice. It is analogous to what Amartya Sen calls "transcendental institutionalism," the idea that there is one possible sort of just social arrangements.[15] Justice monism is the heart of the idea of saving *to*; if morally acceptable gender arrangements might take culturally multiple forms, the notion that some particular, culturally specific set of gender arrangements should replace existing ones requires much justification. If, on the other hand, one begins from the notion that gender justice has a single cultural form, and one is already an ethnocentrist, saving *to* just is what feminism requires. Neither the concept of universalism nor the demands of transnational praxis require the notion of a single gender-just cultural form. Justice monism is a specific, thick interpretation of universalism, not a logical entailment of it.

Idealization and the Idealized Global Social Ontology

Yet Abu-Lughod's article is clear that missionary feminism is more than a view about what would constitute gender justice. Saving *to* is saving, and saving rhetorically suggests that some people are in a special position to reveal moral truths to others. Instead of being based in a view about the normative content of feminism, the idea that some people are uniquely situated to bring about moral progress draws on a certain way of construing the *nonnormative* facts about the world. Indeed, one of the major contributions of decolonial, postcolonial, and transnational feminist theories has been to excavate the nonnormative (or not directly normative) ways of seeing that make imperialism seem legitimate, and even necessary. Missionary feminists take the West to be an agent of morality, and they preserve the deep psychological and ideological association between the West and morality by filtering away information that might reflect poorly on the West or its values. The strength of the ideological association between the West and morality ensures that criticisms of the West seem to be criticisms of values as such. The nonnormative ways of seeing that filter information to preserve this association are idealization and what I will call "moralism."

The theoretical practice known as idealization is at the root of the Enlightenment teleological narrative and the resort to the cultural. Onora O'Neill (1987) argues that idealization occurs when, in the process of abstraction required by theorizing, we represent objects in ways that distort them. The distortion usually occurs by falsely attributing (putatively) positive features to the object or by downplaying negative ones. As feminist philosophers have consistently argued, practices of abstracting about objects in order to theorize about them risk—under unjust background conditions, at least—not random forms of distortion but rather emphasizing attributes that are associated with the dominant or that justify domination.[16] As Charles Mills (2005) has summarized this idea: idealization can be ideological. Mills argues that a common object of idealization in moral and political theories is the ontology of society. Moral theories, though they claim to trade only in explicitly normative claims about what we should not do, cannot avoid being shaped by assumptions about what the objects to which prescriptions apply are like (168). Because Mills criticizes liberal theories of domestic justice, he focuses on the social ontology of separate, self-interested individual persons, whose fates are determined by their choices. The idealized social ontology relevant to missionary feminism is transnational, and its object is the global political and economic structure.

According to missionary feminist idealizations, the world is divided into two types of societies. Although one type, the civilized, modern type to which the West ostensibly belongs, is more advanced than the other, their origins are unified. The backward type of society is defined by hierarchy, adherence to custom, violence, and poverty, and the modern type is defined by affluence and adherence to moral principles, including respect for individual rights and the rule of law. The differentiation was brought about by endogenous factors, or natural evolutionary processes. This division of types of societies and the view that the Western form of life is the future for all is embodied in the Enlightenment teleological narrative that I claimed above was central to missionary feminism. The notion that endogenous factors are the cause of the backwardness of some and the "progress" of the West is the missionary feminist resort to the cultural.

Recognizing these elements of missionary feminism as forms of idealization clarifies just how the association between Westernness and moral authority is produced. The Enlightenment teleological narrative makes certain normative claims plausible while seeming only to present a relatively general account of geopolitics and world history. This is because, like all generalizing narratives (pernicious or not), the Enlightenment teleological narrative selects facts that count in favor of the generalization and facts that don't. Facts about the negative impacts of the West on "other" women are downplayed or omitted. Missionary feminist idealizations deny, as Mohanty (1992) famously puts it, that "a place on the map is a place in history." Rather than being randomly selected, the facts that are suppressed by the Enlightenment teleological narrative are those that would acknowledge historical Western responsibility for unjust situations "other" women are currently in. The suppressed facts concern the realities of settler and metropole colonialism, as well as of neoliberalism and militarism.[17]

This idealized global social ontology also helps explain why methodologically individualist interventions seem to missionary feminists like the right feminist political strategy.[18] If widespread Western responsibility for "other" women's oppression is impossible, then intervening in individual cases—rather than changing global structures—is what Westerners should do. Abu-Lughod (2002) notes that missionary feminists refuse to ask how Westerners might contribute to "making the world a more just place" (790), one in which their nations' policies are less harmful. If Westerners are the bearers of civilization or the discoverers of moral principles, and if the backwardness of "others" is endogenously caused, Western intervention in individual cases is likely to seem like the way to end women's subjugation. The Enlightenment teleological narrative, in other words, updates, and makes slightly less explicit, the notion of the "white man's burden."

To risk stating the obvious, the idealization of the global order also idealizes another object, Western culture, in ways that support ethnocentric justice-monist universalism. The ideas that Western culture is the site of gender justice and that Western culture is *uniquely* capable of harboring it seem, because of the idealization of history and global structures, to be empirically and historically supported. Missionary feminists take civilization, and concomitantly gender justice, to be defining features of Western culture and take the absence of these things to be defining features of "other" cultures. Their ability to see Western culture as *the* feminist solution has much to do with a strong association between it and moral rightness, one that is tenable because of the selective apprehension of facts about history and global structures.

Moralism

Refusal to see the costs of Western intervention, as well as an inability to take seriously the kinds of questions involved in real-world priority setting, stems from a distinct perceptual habit I will call "moralism." "Moralism," as I am using it here, involves treating political activities as though they merely express general moral judgments. Being a moralist is not the same thing as making moral judgments; the latter is something feminists cannot avoid. It is instead a way of refusing to consider the practical ramifications and context-specific meanings of political actions. Of course, political actions *can* express general moral judgments, but they also always have material and discursive effects and are often motivated by interests. Moralists treat transnational political action as a sort of theater for sweeping claims about right and wrong rather than a terrain in which practical considerations are at play and power is exercised.

Missionary feminist moralism is asymmetrical about whose actions can have moral rightness attach to them. That is, it reduces all political actions to abstract moral judgments but allows only Western ones to have the correct moral *content* and count as unmotivated by interests. Where the political actions of "others" are reduced to incorrect judgments about right and wrong, the idealization of the West as protector of civilization leads to an understanding of Western political acts as expressions of lofty goals. For the missionary feminist, whether invading Afghanistan would have caused death and poverty or increased women's vulnerability to forced marriage is less important than the notion that someone was standing against the Taliban. Evaluating Western interventions only as expressions of good moral judgments also helps explain the tendency of missionary feminists to prior-itize markers of cultural difference over what is genuinely morally urgent. If the question is how to defend "civilized people throughout the world" (Abu-Lughod 2002, 784), rather than how to actually improve women's lives or reduce oppression, questions about the specific context and the merits and demerits of specific strategies become irrelevant.[19] The point here is deeper than that missionary feminism is pro-Western intervention; it is that mis-sionary feminist ways of seeing rule out questions about strategy choice and costs of intervention in advance.

Asymmetrical moralism, in addition to influencing choices about fem-inist strategy, keeps missionary feminist idealizations intact. If Westerners never intervene for reasons that are immoral or self-interested, then there is no reason to treat Western values as potentially harmful. If the downsides of Western interventions are imperceptible (or, though I will not treat this view at length here, appear to be only contingently linked to Western culture), they cannot be traced to Western values. Abu-Lughod makes this point with an anecdote from Saba Mahmood. Mahmood, a scholar of Islamist movements in Egypt, is consistently asked to discuss the harms Islamism is wreaking in the world; "but there never seems to be a parallel demand for those who study secular humanism and its projects, despite the terrible violences that have been associated with it over the last couple of centuries, from world wars to colonialism, from genocides to slavery" (Abu-Lughod 2002, 788).[20] Asymmetrical moralism cuts off many possibilities for asking when and whether Western values promote harm. This is particularly problematic in a world in which Western inter-vention has actually caused much harm, and in which extensive literatures and movements originating in "other" women, associate Western values with justifications of that harm.

What Universalism/Relativism Framings Miss: Western Transcendence

Missionary feminism, according to my reconstruction, combines a certain brand of universalism with certain habits of construing nonnormative facts that inure Western culture and Western intervention to scrutiny. My reconstruc-tion can help us see what construals of anti-imperialist feminisms as relativist get wrong. I have already argued that anti-imperialist feminist projects tend to have universalist presuppositions. Perhaps more importantly, calling the critics relativists misses the part of their aim that involves bringing *Western* values and interventions under the umbrella of what can be morally and politically criticized. Idealization and moralism are ways of seeing that protect Western culture and intervention from criticism, and revealing their role in missionary feminist judgments can help us see why missionary feminists do not bother asking whether support for universal values means support for Western ones. The ability of Western thought and values to escape criticism because they cannot be conceived by Westerners as potentially parochial is what decolonial thinkers call the "absent locus" of enunciation. As Walter Mignolo argues, co-lonial thought claims to speak about and from the perspective of humanity as such when it actually speaks from the perspective of the colonizer (Mignolo 2002; see also Giraldo 2016). The idea is not merely that Western views and activities are claimed to be universal or morally good; it is that the West disappears as a target of criticism because it so frequently attempts to align its own views with morality and humanity (and reason, but that is out of the scope of this chapter).

What anti-imperialist feminists want is for this question-begging approach to normative questions to stop; genuine normative inquiry about transna-tional projects requires asking whether some Western values and practices are parochial or harmful. To assert that we need values when the allegation is that certain *Western* ones are harmful, as Western feminists and philosophers so often do, is to ignore the substance of the allegation.[21] Imperialist idealizations and asymmetrical moralism exclude from consideration material that is abso-lutely relevant to debates about the universal desirability of Western values—that is, material about the actual effects of Western intervention. Of course, this information on its own would not resolve debates about which values to retain and which to criticize or jettison. Nor would it answer questions about which contexts parochial values might be acceptable in. But these facts do not justify simply omitting from normative debates information about the justificatory and constitutive roles Western values play in impe-rialism. After all, we can learn about the consequences of adopting certain values, their logical entailments, and alternative value systems by looking at the real-world effects of Western interventions in the lives of "others." The challenge for anti-imperialist feminist praxis is to stop letting associations driven by imperialist ways of seeing stand in for the hard work of normative judgment. For anti-imperialist feminist projects to proceed, Western values and interventions must cease to be treated as transcendent, in Abu-Lughod's

(2002) words, as issued from "outside the world looking down on the world, looking out over this sea of poor benighted people, living under the shadow—or veil—of oppressive cultures" (789). Western values and actions need to be brought back to earth.

Toward a Nonideal Universalism

Now that we have seen that critiques of missionary feminism are better understood as critiques of ethnocentric justice monism and of idealizing and moralizing associations between Westernness and gender justice, we can ask whether it is possible to imagine a feminist universalism differently. Some methodological cues for formulating an anti-imperialist universalism can be found in nonideal theory in political philosophy. Nonideal theorists, in the sense that I use the term here (following Elizabeth Anderson, Charles Mills, and, to some extent, Amartya Sen), claim that a desideratum for moral and political concepts is that they should help us diagnose and respond to existing injustices.[22] Anderson and Mills argue that one defect of ideal theories—that is, those that imagine a just world instead of offering directives about how to improve our unjust one—is their tendency to direct our evaluative gazes toward the wrong normative phenomena. Mills, as I have already noted, argues that the idea that the just society is one inhabited by equally positioned individuals, rather than by members of groups who have been subject to historical injustice, trains our evaluative focus on phenomena other than racism.[23]

If we think that what normative concepts encourage us to see and do is germane to developing them, as nonideal theorists do, the role anti-imperialist feminisms can play in developing new normative concepts become clearer. A better universalism will have to pay attention to the nonnormative assumptions held by those likely to adopt it and the effects normative concepts will produce if adopted under existing social conditions. Philosophers have tended to limit the scope of normative theorizing to prescriptions for behavior. Yet as Margaret Urban Walker (2007) argues, the expectation that responses to injustice come from "*within* a normative moral theory" misses the fact that our normative judgments about cases are driven largely by "the interpretations and associations" that have become "socially salient" to us (187). If we take blocking missionary feminist practices to be a goal in engineering a normative approach, we can begin to craft a universalism that is more responsive to imperialism concerns.

Opposition to Sexist Oppression against Ethnocentrism and Justice Monism

So far, I have cleared space for anti-imperialist universalisms. But not all universalisms are feminist. If feminism conceptually entails the values and ways of seeing constitutive of missionary feminism, the anti-imperialism/ normativity dilemma will reappear. However, I think that one intuitive and widely held normative conception of feminism is neither ethnocentric nor justice monist. It is the conception, articulated in the early work of bell hooks, of feminism as opposition to sexist oppression (hooks 2000b). Oppression, according to Marilyn Frye (1983) is a social phenomenon wherein disadvantage systematically accrues to members of certain social groups relative to members of others. Systematicity and group-based disadvantage are necessary conditions for oppression. That a person confronts episodic disadvantages, such as being last in line at the supermarket on some occasions, is not enough to make her oppressed. Similarly, a society in which disadvantages are systemic but not attached to group membership, though it may be bad or unjust, is not oppressive. Sexist, or gender, oppression is systemic disadvantage that accrues to a person by virtue of membership, or perceived membership, in a gender[24]—or as a result of a system of gender.

I will say little in direct defense of this conception of feminism, except that I think most feminists will find themselves in it, and that it is consistent with the findings of the literature on transnational feminist movements. Valentine Moghadam (2000) argues in her empirical discussion of transnational feminist networks that they converge on the notion that "family, the polity, and cultural institutions" disadvantage women and that social change should aim at improving women's social status (60). Amrita Basu (2016, xiv) argues that Myra Max Ferree's understanding of feminism as the willingness to challenge gender subordination is a useful heuristic for identifying movements that are feminist. Differences in the actual priorities and concrete strategies of different movements can be understood as different specifications of how to reduce sexist oppression in different empirical situations. For example, contexts characterized by war and political repression have led certain women's movements to focus on violence against women and LGBTQ people, whereas contexts with existing democracies have sometimes (but not always) offered feminist movements more latitude to criticize economic inequality (Basu 2016, 24). The understanding of feminism as opposition to sexist oppression undoubtedly permits the conclusion that some women's movements are not feminist. However, this use of normative criteria is ineluctable—and feminist movements all over the world distinguish themselves from movements that are merely led by women (Basu 2016, xiii),[25] especially movements led by women that actively endorse sexist oppression. In fact, some women's movements in the global South have wanted to reintroduce the language of oppression precisely to distinguish themselves from women's groups that are gender-conservative or co-opted. For example, Isis Giraldo (2016, 167) describes the Latin American feminist Julia Paredes as arguing for *despatriarcalización*, because in her context, "gender" has become an apolitical term.

The conception of feminism as opposition to sexist oppression, unlike the ethnocentric monist one underlying missionary feminism, underdetermines how gender justice should be brought about in particular cases. Whereas the missionary feminist thinks there is a single recipe for feminist change that should be followed everywhere—one that happens to involve instituting Western cultural forms—the view that feminism is opposition to gender-based oppression does not on its own prescribe particular cultural forms as the solution. The fact that it does not supply context-specific prescriptions does not imply that it is not a normative vision; systematic gender-based disadvantage, wherever it is found, is bad. But the idea that feminism is opposition to sexist oppression is compatible with different judgments about the presence and causes of oppression in different cases, as well as with the employment of different practical strategies and different moral vernaculars in different cases.

Two features of the idea of feminism as opposition to sexist oppression cause it to underdetermine what should happen in transnational feminist praxis in any particular context. First, it gives a picture of what is wrong rather than a picture of what is right. It thus rejects justice monism by not stating what the endpoint of gender justice looks like and leaving opening the possibility that multiple culturally specific ways of living gender, could embody gender justice. Feminists continue to actively debate whether a gender-just society would eliminate gender roles altogether, proliferate them, or assign new forms of power to existing ones; the notion that feminism is opposition to sexist oppression suggests that feminists, at least in our contemporary world, do not need a single answer to these questions. Feminism's status as a normative doctrine does not depend on a vision of the single gender-just endpoint. Those who believe that the alternative to universally adopting Western (or any) cultural forms is the feminist answer to relativism suppose a view must be justice monist to be normative. But there is little reason to suppose they must be, and, as I have also argued elsewhere (Khader 2011), transnational feminist praxis might gain much from a normative vision that focuses on what is wrong without a culturally particular vision of what is right.

Second, the notion that feminism is opposition to gender-based oppression does not specify what the indicators of advantage and disadvantage are in any given context.[26] This feature is particularly helpful in combatting ethnocentrism, and its manifestation in the notion of a single moral vernacular. There are in fact two types of unspecificity about what constitutes disadvantage, and I will argue that one is worth embracing only moderately. The type we should embrace only moderately is unspecificity about which goods are constitutive of advantage and disadvantage. Indicators of advantage can, and certainly do, vary from context to context. The reason for variation is emphatically not that oppression is a subjective phenomenon; whether arrangements are oppressive is not defined by whether people see them as such.[27] It is instead that societies genuinely vary in their currencies of advantage. For example, the ability to produce food is especially likely to be a source of power and advantage in agrarian societies and is less likely to be one in cash-based ones. As is often noted in feminist writings on sub-Saharan Africa, the ability to produce food is, in many situations, historically feminized and culturally associated with meaningful political roles and bargaining power (see Zeleza 2005; Pala 2005; Mikell 1997).

But because there is value in retaining the view that some goods, such as food and freedom from violence, are universal, or at least highly general, markers of disadvantage, and anti-imperialist feminists should not completely embrace nonspecificity about indicators of advantage. Feminist movements around the world seem to converge on the importance of women's access to certain goods, such as freedom from violence and the ability to determine one's reproductive life (see Basu 2016). The current pace of geopolitical and economic change offers additional reasons to refuse to make the list of goods feminists care about *completely* relative to context. First, as I have already mentioned, transnational forms of gender injustice, such as neoliberalism and militarism, are difficult to recognize without the ability to see some things as gender-injustice-undermining across contexts. To be able to, in Mohanty's words, "reemphasize connections between local and universal," (Mohanty 2003, 226) some things need to register as oppressive across contexts. Second, being free from oppression in our contemporary world probably does require access to some goods that are valuable in contexts besides one's own. It is unlikely in the contemporary world that people will never leave their particular contexts or that their contexts will not change, and it can therefore be harmful to people to make them unable to operate outside very limited cultural contexts.

Discussions of literacy, a good that has occasionally been controversial, offer an example of this point. Even if there are contexts where, in the short term, literacy is not a source of advantage or necessary to secure basic goods, it is dangerous at this point in history to assume that people can do without literacy in the long term. It is often said that children and youth who lack literacy and formal education have been "deprived of a future."

So, there is a need for a list of universal indicators of advantage and disadvantage, but combating missionary feminism means that it should not be abstracted from a specific culture and should not be taken as exhaustive. This is the form of underdetermination of indicators of advantage and disadvantage that feminists should embrace. The indicators of advantage and disadvantage should be articulated vaguely enough to be capable of being instantiated in culturally and contextually distinct ways. Since one of the goals of an alternative conception is to avoid missionary feminist ethnocentrism, any list feminists use should have been cross-culturally deliberated on and open to cross-cultural deliberation.[28] The closest available thing is the list of basic human rights. The idea that the objects of human rights have a role to play in an anti-imperialist feminism will be surprising to some, given the fact human rights are sometimes seen as a vehicle for imperialism. Though I cannot treat this worry in depth here, I emphasize that we can understand gendered human rights deficits to constitute lacks of advantage without accepting the elements of human rights that have been most objectionable to anti-imperialist feminists.

Many objections to human rights concern, not their normative content, but rather the ways of seeing of many human rights practitioners. For example, Alison Jaggar and Theresa Weynand Tobin argue that women's human rights practitioners begin from a pre-established ethnocentric analysis of why gendered human rights violations happen that makes the search for rich descriptive information before deciding what to do in specific cases seem superfluous (Tobin and Jaggar 2013, 423–424; see also Tobin 2009). Similarly, Makau Matua's (2001) argument that human rights discourse causes Westerners to think of themselves as saviors of the savage is, like critiques of missionary feminism, largely an argument about the nonnormative assumptions surrounding Western transcendence I discussed earlier. Thinking the content of the list of human rights gives a useful, but nonexhaustive list of goods whose gender-unequal distribution counts as sexist oppression can be done without accepting missionary feminist nonnormative assumptions, especially if Western feminists are encouraged to actively criticize such nonnormative assumptions, as I will recommend below.[29]

Underdetermination of the gender-just endpoint and nonspecificity about indicators of advantage and disadvantage also work against ethnocentrism in another way; they make explicit that what matters for feminist political judgments about cases is whether *oppression* is present, not whether certain cultural vernaculars or practices are. One cannot know whether sexist oppression is present in a given case without knowing the overall effects of certain social practices, which in turn cannot be understood without rich contextual information. The missionary feminist who assumes that "other" women need to be saved to an idealized Western culture either has the task backward (thinks she knows without contextual information what produces gender-based disadvantage), or has a completely misguided understanding of what the task is (thinks what matters for feminism is ultimately whether a context has adopted Western cultural forms, to return to our earlier example). What matters to her is that women wear prom dresses instead of burqas, and she either denies that both forms of dress in their contexts belong to systems that disadvantage women or is only interested in conceiving the prom dress as the desirable destiny of the woman who wears a burqa. On the conception of feminism I am advocating, missionary feminists whose judgments track the presence or absence of Western cultural forms, instead of the presence or absence of sexist oppression, may not be feminists at all.

Before I turn to discussing how a universalist feminist normative framework can resist missionary feminist construals of nonnormative facts, I consider an important objection to my conception of feminism. It may seem to exclude opposing forms of oppression besides sexism, such as racism, capitalist oppression, and imperialism—or to suggest that sexism ought to be prioritized over them. Indeed, because of such concerns, hooks (2000a) later changed her definition of feminism from the one I have just endorsed to include opposition to all intersecting oppressions. However, taking the fact of intersectionality seriously, and opposing other oppressions, does not require building opposition to other oppressions into the concept of feminism (and, in fact, many intersectional feminists do not take intersectionality to be a definition of feminism). Something does not have to be part of the definition of feminism to be morally urgent. Moreover, there is a reason specific to the project of this book for not making opposition to imperialism and racism *definitional* for feminism. Incorporating opposition to imperialism into feminism defines away the possibility of conflict between feminist and anti-imperialist goals, a conflict that is endemic to transnational feminist praxis. Sometimes, for example, anti-imperialist concerns recommend very conservative criticism of a cultural practice, while opposition to sexism requires strident criticism, or vice versa. Or, as I discuss in chapter 2, anti-imperialist concerns might recommend maximal preservation of non-Western metaphysical worldviews, whereas feminism requires criticizing the subset of these views that are oppressive to women. Because of the tragic reality of such conflict, I think refusing to make anti-imperialism definitional for feminism can be construed as a way of responding to the fact that women face multiple oppressions; it illuminates conflicts where they exist, which is key to being able to navigate and move beyond them. Understanding the potential conflicts between opposing sexist oppression and other oppressions is responsive to the reality that third-world feminists are so often silenced by internal forces who share colonial marginalization but not gender marginalization, and to the fact that missionary feminists often ask "other" women to accept imperialism to advance their gender interests.

My view is emphatically not that other oppressions should not be opposed; it is instead that feminism need not furnish all of our moral commitments. We should want to see how feminist moral commitments can be reconciled with opposition to imperialism. It is undoubtedly true that transnational feminist praxis will fail to apprehend many real-world situations if it refuses to avail itself of the intersectional insight that it is difficult, and sometimes impossible, to disentangle the effects of sexism and those of racism or imperialism in actual lives. According to Kimberle Crenshaw's (1989) famous analogy, a person who is hit by two cars at an intersection will sustain injuries that cannot easily be traced to one of the cars. The elements of Afghan women's lack of access to education that are caused by poverty and militarism and those caused by sexism are probably impossible to pull apart, and the best strategies for improving Afghan women's lives will require responding to both. Consistent with this element of intersectional feminist theory, the epistemic prescriptions described next will often recommend strategies that visibilize intersections between sexism and imperialism.

Epistemic Prescriptions against Idealization and Moralism

Because missionary feminism includes nonnormative ways of seeing, any articulation of the normative content of feminism can only go so far in displacing it. Since missionary precommitments filter information about the world in ways that associate the West with moral progress and gender justice, it is improbable that they would abandon projects of saving *to* just because they thought of feminism as opposition to sexist oppression. After all, the idea that Western culture is uniquely capable of housing gender justice and bringing moral progress to "others" may seem to them to have been arrived at through empirical observation. The only way for Western feminists to break out of the thrall of missionary feminist precommitments is to actively try to change what they see. I thus submit that an anti-imperialist feminist normative framework should include two epistemic prescriptions in addition to the idea of feminism as opposition to sexist oppression.

Call the first epistemic prescription the "imperialism-visibilizing prescription." It states that Western feminists, when attempting political engagement with "other" women, should seek information about the role global structures might have played in causing the contemporary oppression of "other" women. The relevant structures are both historical and contemporary, and they include colonialism in its settler and metropole forms, as well as militarism and neoliberalism. To be clear, recommending that feminists seek this information does not imply that imperialism is always a cause, or the main cause, of "other" women's oppression. Instead, in cases in which imperialism does play a role, the role is likely to be concealed by missionary feminists' existing epistemic habits; actively looking for noncultural causes is a way of understanding these cases more clearly. In other words, the imperialism-visibilizing prescription takes on the nonideal theoretical task of working against the idealizations that obscure imperialism, especially the idealized social ontology generated by the Enlightenment teleological narrative.

Attention to the role Northern and Western actors have played in causing "other" women's oppression can also combat the moralist tendency to take Western political actions as disinterested moral judgments whose effects are not themselves worthy of normative scrutiny. Rather than being an actor that "stands outside the world," the imperialism-visibilizing directive calls the West to come back to earth and realize its own role in creating and shaping the world it makes moral pronouncements about. Questions about remedial responsibility and a reordering of Western feminist moral priorities arise more easily when Western innocence is not the unquestioned starting point. Asking about Western causation of harm to "other" women allows reducing or eliminating harm to register as an option to be considered in the weighing of Western feminist moral priorities. When Western and Northern policies play causal roles, concerns about efficacy alone may suggest reasons to change these policies rather than intervene in local contexts. Additionally, as Alison Jaggar (2005) argues, deontological considerations, such as the idea that one bears special responsibility for repairing harm one has caused, present strong reasons for Western feminists to focus on changing transnational structures (72).

The potential costs of contemporary Western interventions are also more likely come under scrutiny if Western feminists pay explicit attention to colonial legacies and contemporary global structures. Many cases in which Westerners caused harm undoubtedly involved Westerners intending, or claiming to intend, to help "other" women, but such intentions neither necessarily justify intervention nor justify the forms of intervention that have been preferred. Once it is revealed, for example, that military intervention to save Afghan women leads to vulnerability to new types of forced marriage, the idea that all that is needed is for Western feminists to take a stand becomes less and less plausible. The ability to perceive negative effects of Western interventions can also work against idealization and moralism by revealing the extent to which those interventions have been interest-driven, rather than noble. Missionary feminists, as moralists, see the world in ways that purify Western political activity. The Enlightenment teleological narrative, according to which the West is an agent of natural progress, rather than an agent that benefits from "others'" subjugation, will likely not survive attention to the realities of contemporary neoliberalism and militarism. It is difficult to maintain about the Afghanistan case, for example, that a history of self-interested action by the United States is irrelevant to the contemporary oppression of Afghan women.

Call the second epistemic prescription in the normative framework I propose the "justice-enhancement prescription." According to it, feminists should remember that strategy choices in specific contexts are partly case-specific judgments about how to improve conditions. I borrow the term justice enhancement from Sen (2009), who contrasts it with justice achievement; the former aims at making the world better, and the latter aims at making it ideal.[30] Remembering that feminist praxis aims at justice enhancement means recognizing that strategy choice is rightly shaped by, and can be criticized for failing to take account of, concerns about context and effectiveness. It does not require a highly specific end goal (as the ethnocentric justice monist believes), and strategies should not be evaluated only or primarily as statements about what would achieve ultimate gender justice. Whereas the Enlightenment teleological narrative suggests that the same strategies will bring about feminist change in every case (because "others" are in the past of the West), and moralism discourages taking the costs of change into account, the justice-enhancement prescription calls for rich and longitudinal empirical attention to contexts and asking case-specific questions about what will make a difference. The strategies that will make a difference are usually different from those that involve just "doing something" about gender injustice, and they can rarely be identified without context-specific knowledge.

Indeed, contrary to missionary feminist assumptions, a focus on justice-enhancement suggests that context variation in feminist strategy choices is not merely to be expected; it should be affirmed as part of the shared feminist goal of opposing sexist oppression. The missionary feminist assumption that all forms of veiling in Afghanistan must stop immediately, for example, refuses to countenance questions relevant justice-enhancement: such as about the compatibilities of values in the local moral vernacular that could be interpreted in ways compatible with feminism (such as, for example, the possibility of a reconstruction of Islam that places the same modesty requirements on women and men) and the possibilities for strategies based on incremental change.

Remembering that strategy choices concern justice enhancement can also counteract the moralist tendency to treat Western intervention as the feminist solution. Whereas it and the Enlightenment teleological narrative provide reasons for Westerners to think that their knowledge about "other" contexts is sufficient, thinking that feminist praxis is about justice enhancement makes clear that many of the types of knowledge necessary for feminist change are not ones Westerners can easily access. A role for context-specific knowledge and authority displaces the claim by missionary feminists that Westerners are uniquely positioned to make change. In other words, once transnational feminist praxis appears to be about justice enhancement, the case for feminist activism "from below" becomes very clear—and clear in a way that is fully compatible with universalism.

Beyond Missionary Feminism: The Freedom without Fear Platform UK

I have tried to open conceptual space for a feminism that is universalist but not missionary—and to describe a nonideal universalist framework fits within this space. Since I began with a picture of missionary feminism in practice, I end with a sketch of what political strategies motivated by nonideal universalism might look like. After the much-publicized 2012 gang rape, torture, and death of Jyoti Singh Pandey (popularly known as Nirbhaya), activists in India organized the Bekaouf Azadi (Freedom without Fear) movement. Thousands marched in the streets, and teach-ins and advocacy efforts aimed to influence the government-appointed Verma Committee to reject victim-blaming and honor-focused responses to sexual assault (Singh 2012–2013; Carty and

Mohanty 2015; Krishnan and Wilson 2013). A solidarity movement led by Black and South Asian women in the United Kingdom, the Freedom without Fear Platform UK, will be my focus here. A point of departure for the UK activists was recognition of the ways the rape in India would be used opportunistically by the UK government to highlight contrasts between a "backward" India and a civilized Britain, despite the UK government's drastic cutting of resources from efforts aimed at reducing violence against women (Freedom without Fear Platform 2013).

Whereas missionary feminists begin from idealizations of global structures that portray the West as gender-just and associations that presume the West is an agent of morality, the Freedom without Fear Platform foregrounded similarities in the government responses to gender violence in India and the United Kingdom. Kavita Krishnan, an Indian activist, describes having been bombarded with questions from the Western media, friends, and relatives along the lines of " 'we are concerned about you because you live in such an unsafe place, how bad is it in India, it must be terrible in Delhi' etc. When I would tell them that rape culture and the kinds of things we were raising show up in different forms in different countries, then there would be this response, 'yes but, it's worse in India isn't it?, it must be worse there' " (Krishnan and Wilson 2013). To offset the imperialism-legitimizing effects of such notions, the UK activists highlighted the prevalence of rape culture in United Kingdom and agitated against the government's withdrawal of financial support and community-led resources for women victims of violence. They publicly drew attention to a concomitant shift toward racializing violence against women. The government's focus on forced marriage and incarcerating its supporters was a way of stigmatizing minorities more than it was a way of demonstrating support for violence against women, they argued (Freedom without Fear Platform 2013).

The Freedom without Fear Platform's approach to discussing the similarities in rape culture in both countries can be understood as involving a focus on sexist oppression rather than an ethnocentric monist idealizing and moralizing approach, as well as a recognition that contextual information is important to determining which strategies would be justice enhancing. In this case, contextual differences in indicators of advantage and disadvantage did not come into play, since the platform and the Indian activists agreed that patriarchal violence against women was an urgent border-crossing feminist issue, one that could not be understood in either context without an analysis of patriarchal control over women's bodies (Press Trust of India 2013). At the same time, the activists were attentive to contextual differences in the ways sexual victimization harmed and disadvantaged women, often through context-specific intersections with race and class. In India, it was important to draw attention to the ways in which the rape of Dalit girls and women was a tool of caste violence (Freedom without Fear Platform 2014) and in which discourses about rape that articulated its wrongness as a symptom of men's inadequate ability to control women (Krishnan and Wilson 2013). In the United Kingdom, in contrast, it was important to mobilize against the ways in which criminalization and the gutting of the refugee regime were reducing women's (and LGBTQ people's) access to services to protect them from patriarchal violence (Kumar 2014).

Central to the platform's work have been strategies consistent with the justice-enhancing and imperialism-visibilizing prescriptions. Much of its activism focused on debunking attempts by UK actors to depict themselves as on the right side of morality by publicly denouncing violence elsewhere, and violence committed by Muslims internally. Against the moralizing idea that such denunciations were correct or sufficient, and consistent with the justice-enhancement prescription, the platform drew public attention to inconsistencies between this grandstanding and allocations of the kinds of resources that would actually contribute to decreasing gender violence. Existing resource allocations and the increasing criminalization of forced marriage, in their view, more clearly demonstrated commitments to treating gender-based violence as caused by "others" than they did any genuine feminist commitments. I have already mentioned that activists organized around the UK government's withdrawal of support from refugee and immigrant women and the ways in which the focus on violence against women by brown and Black men was a way of appearing to take a stance against violence while actually withdrawing resources from it. In another effort, the UK activists organized a write-in campaign and a protest against a government poster that featured a black hand over a white mouth to draw attention to child sexual abuse (Freedom without Fear Platform 2015b).

The Freedom without Fear Platform also acted consistently with the imperialism-visibilizing prescription by organizing against UK contributions to violence against women in India. One of the things they did was to organize forums on the ways neoliberalism exposed Indian women to rape and rendered them vulnerable to dowry violence. For example, multinational mining companies used rape to silence Adivasi women who resisted their incursion (Wilson 2013) and recruited women to do exploitative factory work with the promise of a one-time dowry payment at the end of the job (Krishnan and Wilson 2013). They also gave a platform to Indian activists who argued that the perception of women as men's property in India was a result of colonial law (Krishnan and Wilson 2013). Additionally, in response to calls from Indian activists, they protested the visit of India's Prime Minister Modi to the United Kingdom. The rationale was that in hosting him, the UK government was legitimizing the types of religious fundamentalism that fueled violence against women, such as the use of rape as a tool of control in Kashmir and in the attacks on thousands of Gujarati Muslims (India Tomorrow 2015; Wilson 2015). The Freedom without Fear Platform was also part of a team that issued a public open letter, signed by UK organizations, to Modi about these facts, as well as the fact that sexual assault cases were pending against many members of Modi's cabinet (Wilson 2015). They also pressured local Members of Parliament who had provided financial support to celebrate Modi's visit to withdraw their support (Freedom without Fear Platform 2015a).

Conclusion

Missionary feminists suppose that there is a single endpoint of gender justice embodied by the West and employ idealizing and moralizing schemas that preserve the notion that the West is primarily or exclusively an agent of moral progress. Underlying their point of view is a cluster of associations between the West and moral rightness. The idea that anti-imperialist feminisms oppose universalism conveniently, and sometimes perversely, protects these associations. My aim has been to undermine the missionary feminists' perceived monopoly on morality by showing that anti-imperialist feminisms need not be conceived as opposed to universalism. The core concerns raised by missionary feminism's opponents can be addressed through a new type of universalist feminism, a nonideal universalism that recognizes that sexist oppression is the central feminist normative concern, encourages Western feminists to add historical and structural explanations to their repertoire of explanations of "other" women's oppression, and that considers transnational feminist praxis to be about justice enhancement rather than moralist grandstanding. Anti-imperialist universalist feminisms are possible, I have argued, because missionary feminism is not driven by universalism per se; it is driven by universalism combined with an excessively thick and culturally specific notion of gender justice joined with ideological ways of construing nonnormative information.

Yet recognizing the possibility of redeeming universalism is only the beginning of a conversation. Whereas the universalism/relativism framing of debates about transnational feminisms forces anti-imperialist feminists into a corner, I hope the possibility of anti-imperialist universalisms opens the door to discussing of the moral merits of specific values, histories, and interventions. One question to which we must turn our attention if anti-imperialist universalist feminisms are to be possible is that of which values feminists who wish to also oppose imperialism should endorse. Which values are central to conceiving and practicing opposition to sexist oppression, and which are not? How and when do "other" women's movements and criticisms of Western values illuminate reasons to revise them, recognize their parochiality or context-specific applicability, or abandon them altogether? When values that seem central to transnational feminist praxis also seem to be vehicles for imperialism, can such conflicts be avoided or overcome? These are the questions I take on in the rest of this book.

2 INDIVIDUALISM

BEYOND OKIN'S ULTIMATUM

Some women living in patriarchal non-Western cultures "*might* be much better off if the culture[s] they were born into were . . . to become extinct," Susan Moller Okin (1999, 14) wrote in the now-classic "Is Multiculturalism Bad for Women?" Though Okin explicitly preferred cultural reform to extinction, it is what Abdullahi An-Na'im (1999, 53) called Okin's "ultimatum" that has become notorious. The ultimatum, whether or not it accurately describes Okin's overall view,[1] discloses a view that seems to tacitly underwrite many feminisms that become complicit in imperialism. According to this view, cultural, familial, and communal associations can hamper the self-realization of individual women, so taking a blithe attitude toward their destruction is just what feminism requires.

Many anti-imperialist feminist critiques of individualism can be understood as responses to this ultimatum view that underestimates the harm of associational damage and treats somewhat indiscriminate associational damage as required by feminism. Anti-imperialist feminists worry that the form of individualism that devalues cultural, communal, and familial associations is a Western parochial value and that it breeds moral insensitivity about the value of such associations in "other" women's lives. Since the relevant associations are often non-Western cultures or impediments to neoliberal projects, this moral insensitivity often amounts in practice to the justificatorily imperialist view that "other" women benefit from projects of Northern and Western domination.[2] Anti-imperialist feminists worry that individualist commitments wrongly make associational losses seem like feminist benefits. Saba Mahmood (2005, 198) puts the worry thus: do feminists "ever run up against the responsibility [they] incur for the destruction of life forms so that 'unenlightened' women could be taught to live more freely"?

But the feminist response to these imperialism charges cannot be to simply reject individualism. We know that sexist oppression is frequently enacted through relationships and justified by appeals to familial love, cultural preservation, and religious adherence.[3] We also know that the interests of individual women are routinely subordinated to the interests of groups. The way to take the anti-imperialist critique of individualism on board while remaining feminists, then, has to involve narrowing the range of cases in which associational damage is called for rather than suggesting that it is never justified.

I argue that the specific form of individualism that is the object of the anti-imperialist critique need not, and should not, be central to transnational feminist praxis—though many advocacy discourses concerning "other" women suggest that it is. The objectionable form of individualism, which I call "independence individualism," is conceptually unnecessary for feminism (conceived as opposition to sexist oppression) and gets much of its supposed connection to feminism from idealizations of modernity and Western late-capitalist life. Moreover, independence individualism is a parochial Western value, which, when applied under nonideal conditions, actually impedes transnational feminist projects by promoting the worsening of gendered labor burdens and rendering invisible the transition costs of proposed feminist change. The chapter proceeds as follows: I begin by explaining the types of harms to women anti-imperialist feminists think are caused by individualist commitments and show how the portrayal of these harms as necessary for feminism is caused by two nested mistaken assumptions: (a) the assumption that feminism just is treating women as individual persons and (b) that treating women as individual persons means turning them into "modern" subjects of late capitalism. I then turn to arguing that independence individualism interferes with transnational feminist praxis under nonideal conditions by encouraging interventions that promote Western parochial values, worsen women's gendered labor burdens, and obscure the transition costs of feminist change by denying the objective value even patriarchal forms of relationship can have in women's lives in the real world.

Individualism and Imperialist Associational Damage

To motivate the anti-imperialist critiques of individualism I hope to take on board, and to forestall the objection that anti-imperialist feminist critiques value groups to the exclusion of individual women,[4] we need to get clearer about just what the harms to "other" women associated with individualism are and how these harms come to be perceived as *feminist*. I distill four distinct harms from the anti-imperialist feminist literatures, all of which are harms to individual women that come about through failures to apprehend the value of their existing attachments. Each of these harms, which I will collectively refer to as caused by "imperialist associational damage" are connected to imperialism in at least one of three ways besides their issuing from Northern- and Western-driven policies: they weaken local cultural attachments, they increase women's vulnerability to material forms of harm that serve the interests of Northern and Western actors, and they enact cultural domination by foisting parochial Western values on "others."

Neoliberal Governmentality Harms

Call the first set of harms enacted through imperialist associational damage "neoliberal governmentality harms." They are governmentality harms in a loosely Foucaultian (1997) sense; they occur through incentives to internalize and act in accordance with the values that motivate official policies. According to transnational feminists, neoliberal economic agendas increase women's vulnerability to poverty and gendered exploitation, partly by encouraging their divestment from communal associations.[5] There is evidence from many contexts that the poor rely heavily on social networks for survival (Narayan 2000). Such practices as lending to one another without the expectation of receiving interest, caring for one another's children, and sharing food provide support in lean times and enable poor women to survive precarious situations. Though poor communities are not without conflict or competition, the existence of certain goods depends on strong cooperative norms.

Lamia Karim's work on microcredit offers an example of how development interventions can erode these norms. According to her, microcredit in Bangladesh encourages women to conceive of themselves as individual small-business owners. Each woman now needs to compete with other women in her community who are operating similar businesses. She also now knows that loans should be conceived of as sources of profit rather than of informal mutual aid. Karim (2011) sees this as creating a "usury culture" in which women start to view others' demands for loans as parasitic or as opportunities for financial gain (101). A more comprehensive study suggests that the phenomenon Karim describes is common: microcredit brings about a "culture defined more by the maintenance of discipline and distrust as the marker of relationships between the women members" (Sharma and Parthasarathy

2007, 117).[6] The loss of protective associations has also been documented as a potential harm for women who migrate to cities to become factory workers; for example, loss of family makes such women vulnerable to trafficking (Guilmoto and Loenzien 2014).

Transnational feminists also argue that women thinking of themselves as individual entrepreneurs increases their vulnerability to capitalist exploitation. In many cases, pro-poor social movements and policies preceded neoliberal interventions. For Karim (2011), microcredit replaces women's understanding of themselves as members of a dominated laboring class with the idea that they are individual owners of petty capital. Similarly, Kalpana Wilson (2015, 809) argues that the focus on individual gain causes poor women to focus more on how to move up economic hierarchies than on how to dismantle them. Whereas previous self-conceptions permitted forms of class solidarity that might enable pro-poor social change, the self-conceptions encouraged by neoliberalism are of the every-woman-for-herself kind.

The loss of such associations and their protective power does not tend to figure in neoliberal accountings of what will benefit or harm women. Instead, what we see in the justificatory discourses surrounding development policies that promote neoliberal governmentality harms is the idea that entrepreneurship is the way of transforming traditions that force women to be use objects for men (Kabeer 1994, 17–19). As I will discuss in the section "Feminization-of-Responsibility Harms," when women's existing associations appear at all in development discourse, they are associations with cultures and male family members that are portrayed as causing women's oppression by preventing their entrepreneurship. W. Arthur Lewis, an early development theorist, argued that economic growth had feminist potential because it would allow women to cease to be third-world men's "beasts of burden" and be acknowledged in their "full personhood" (see Kabeer 1994, 19).

Feminization-of-Responsibility Harms

Another set of neoliberal harms to women occurs through increases in the inequality of (already unequal) household relationships, and a failure to apprehend the ways existing relationships shape women's lives. Sylvia Chant (2008) argues that, because of failures to look at women's existing unrecognized labor and at the benefits women gain from marriage in managing that labor, interventions aimed at increasing women's income through work increase their workloads while reducing their household negotiating power. The amount of time poor women spend on tasks such as cooking, carrying water, caring for dependents, and, in many cases, growing food—often in addition to paid activities such as agriculture, trading, or piecework—leaves little time or energy for additional work. One study in India showed that women worked fourteen to eighteen hours a day—and yet recommended that these women use their remaining time to "earn more and live better" (quoted in Wilson 2015, 805).

Transnational feminists argue that the income-generation focus, absent a change in received gender roles, can also decrease women's status relative to men. Income can subsidize men's withdrawal from household responsibilities (by refusing to pay children's school fees, for example) while preserving their disproportionate household authority (Chant 2008; Mayoux and LaCoste 2005). Paying school fees for example becomes another low-status feminized job. Development interventions that focus only on income through work also encourage men to see women as points of access to financial gain (Ahmed 2008; Chant 2008; Hoffman and Marius-Gnanou 2007), and in some cases, they subsidize polygamy (Chant 2008; Mayoux 1999). Women may also perform subservient household roles more scrupulously or take on additional household labor to manage the tensions that are created by the fact that they now generate income (Khader 2014; Chant 2008; 2006; Adato et al. 2000).

The justificatory apparatus behind the feminization of responsibility is multifaceted,[7] but I isolate the role individualism plays in producing its harms. Designers of exclusively income-focused interventions seem to fail to appreciate women's reasons for having relationships with men, or they ignore those relationships altogether. Instead of recognizing that a fairer allocation of labor and household authority requires negotiation within relationships, the interventions seem based either on the assumption that relationships will magically change or that women will exit them because they are harmful. Images of poor, racialized Southern men as the main cause of women's oppression are common in development discourse. I have mentioned the men's "beasts of burden" representation. More contemporarily, Wilson (2011) argues that the Nike commercials that extol the "girl effect" present cultures, local communities, and families as the forces that drag women down—and capitalism as the force that brings women up.[8] According to Naila Kabeer, standard approaches to women in development, whose assumptions continue to affect policy, saw the problem as women's status as housewives, passive recipients of the household goods that would arrive through development. Making women economically self-sufficient was supposed to demonstrate respect for them as agents whose individual potential equaled men's (Kabeer 1994, 6–20).

Kinship Harms

A third type of harm through imperialist associational damage occurs when existing kinship forms are weakened.[9] Such bonds are, of course, sources of goods with intrinsic value, such as care, love, friendship, and belonging. But kinship also provides access to other important goods, such as social recognition, wealth, reductions in one's dependency work burdens, and access to care in times of dependency. Recognition and wealth attach to kinship because a society's system of kinship, especially its marriage practices, is a key means of transferring and growing wealth.[10] Dependency concerns attach to kinship because in most societies, it is the first resort for access to care in times of dependency.

Changes in kinship structures can reduce women's opportunities for wellbeing. A frequent claim about educational interventions aimed at reducing early marriage is that if they do not also expand the economic opportunities associated with education, they may worsen girls' life prospects. For example, Caroline Archambault (2011) argues that one of the reasons Maasai fathers may promote early marriage for their daughters is that education is unlikely to provide them with economic opportunities.[11] In contrast, marriage is a gateway to a pastoral livelihood. Without denying that early marriage exposes girls to significant harms, we can note that education interventions that reduce early marriage to a cultural practice and overlook the economic benefits associated with it can reduce women's prospects for well-being, or simply fail to increase them in the desired way.[12]

Lila Abu-Lughod's (2013) recent ethnographic work shows how Bedouin women can be harmed through changes in kinship structures that remove supports for care in times of dependency and increase individual women's responsibility for dependency work. One of her examples is a widow named Gateefa, who expresses nostalgia for a time when she lived in an extended multigenerational household, despite at the time having disliked elements of it, such as the presence of co-wives (205).[13] Now, partly as a result of economic changes, changes in educational expectations, and the physical displacement of her Bedouin community, her sons live in separate households, and her daughters-in-law (selfishly, in her view) focus on the needs of their individual children. In other words, Gateefa's support system for care (and power) in old age, one she had invested in when she was younger by fulfilling household commitments, including commitments for dependency work, had dissipated.[14] The same in the kinship structure might have harmed another, younger woman differently; she might, for instance, have lost access to an extended family with whom share the burdens associated with dependency work.

Western advocacy discourses surrounding both types of kinship harms paint kin relationships as impediments to women's self-actualization. Archambault (2011, 635) notes that the justificatory discourses surrounding the Maasai case follow a familiar logic; attachments are ignored, but when they are mentioned, they take the form of Southern men (in this case, fathers and uncles), who are imagined only as detractors from women's well-being. This view contrasts with the actual view of many Maasai people that education empowers girls *and* the community (639). The changes in Bedouin kinship forms are not the result of explicit Western-driven policy, but Abu-Lughod (2013, 211–213) argues that human rights discourses suggest that what women need is the right to exit and refuse marriage, when in fact, the demands of dependency work and care make such choices unbearably costly to them, and to other members of their communities.[15]

Cultural Harms

A final familiar type of harm occurs when women's attachments to cultural groupings are weakened. Discussing the weakening of and damage to cultural groupings is complicated, because cultures are not static or monolithic, and changes to them need not constitute cultural *damage*. However, we do not need to regard all cultural change as damaging to be able to identify harms to women that come through incentives to exit cultures or changes to practices that mark membership.[16]

Feminist strategies can harm women by expecting them to exit, or weaken their ties to, communities that have protective functions under conditions of cultural domination. Harry Blagg (2008) offers a useful example of this concerning family violence in Australian Aboriginal communities. Blagg argues that many interventions, designed with domestic violence against white Western women in mind, assume that women want to leave their communities of origin (149) and ignore the role the settler colonial state has played in causing family violence. Aboriginal women often do not want to leave and treat shelters only as temporary safehouses (149). Interventions that make exit the only option ignore the fact that women gain well-being from participating in kinship networks, communal associations, and from symbolic, cultural, and relational resources for navigating the intergenerational trauma of colonialism (see Sotero 2006). They also ignore the fact that the world outside the community may have little to offer women (in

Anne Philips's [2009, 133–158] words; when considering the value of exit, it matters what women would exit *to*). Aboriginal Australians have reason to distrust the state's incursions in the family because of policies of erasure, such as the stolen generations, that used the family as a fulcrum for cultural domination and destruction. Once this history is in sight, policies that provide only the opportunity to exit rather than helping women live free of violence in their communities, can be seen not just as missed opportunities, but as the continuation of generations of harm to indigenous women.[17]

Policies that stigmatize cultural membership and participation in cultural practices can also reduce women's ability to be seen as equal citizens by the state.[18] Mairead Enright (2009) argues that policies surrounding forced marriage in the United Kingdom, because they blur the line between arranged and forced marriage (see also Phillips 2009) and occur against a backdrop of criminalizing South Asian and Muslims, infringe on the autonomy of young women who seek arranged marriages and reduce the likelihood that they can expect equal treatment from the state. A policy raising the age at which one could migrate a foreign spouse in the United Kingdom to twenty-one threatened to prevent adult women who chose arranged marriages from being able to engage in them.[19] The policy materials surrounding this change, which focus on freedom from the backward South Asian family are, according to Enright (2009), likely to have negative effects on women's ability to seek public services. Fears ranging from stigma to deportation may reduce the likelihood that women who are victims of domestic violence will seek services (348). Women and girls who do flee forced marriage and other forms of gender violence often experience religious and racial harassment as, for example, in domestic-violence shelters (Khanum 2008). The assumption that culture is the source of the problem also causes the underfunding of culturally specific domestic-violence services (Enright 2009, 350).[20]

The justificatory discourses surrounding both types of policies associate women's liberation with the ability to leave one's cultural grouping behind, and they assume that the latter is the proper exercise of choice. Though one can of course choose to retain one's cultural membership and practices, the discourses strongly suggest that a woman only has choices when she exits her culture or reduces participation in its practices. Blagg (2008) argues that many advocates view the "*Aborginality* of Aboriginal women as an obstacle" (149). The desirable path for escaping domestic violence is, according to Blagg, widely thought by the designers of Western feminist interventions to be to "repackage and reconstitute one's identity as an autonomous individual in a new location" (149). Enright (2009) argues about the forced marriage case that, though the key risk factors are educational deficits, age disparities, language proficiency, and lack of time spent in the United Kingdom, policy materials present the harm of forced marriage as a lack of choice (352). Lack of choice is presented primarily as the lack of the ability to strike out for one-self as a career woman, who may choose a husband but not an extended family, or as freedom from South Asian culture (Enright 2009); what it would mean to reject forced marriage is to transition from "symbol of primordial culture to modern individual" (357).

Two Types of Individualism

A distinct argumentative and rhetorical strategy that promotes feminist com-plicity in imperialism emerges in the justificatory discourses surrounding im-perialist associational damage. In it, harms to women are recast as benefits, and individualist commitments are what permit the recasting. If existing relationships have a generally negative valence (or are ignored altogether), losses of these relationships (or inadvertent worsenings of them) do not count as losses. As I said in the introduction, this fact seems to place feminism and anti-imperialism at odds with each other, because, as Naila Kabeer (2011) puts it, "injustices are ingrained in the social relationships that construct women's sense of self and security within their communities" (503). Yet this apparent tension between feminist normative commitments and the anti-imperialist critique is much shallower than it seems, or so I want to suggest.

The justificatory discourses slide between two forms of individualism. They reduce feminism to respect for individual women's personhood and take economic independence and freedom from traditional attachments to be requirements for such respect. Consider the following moves in the justif-icatory discourses:

> Economic growth, through women's entrepreneurship and work-force participation "allows women to be emancipated from the seclu-sion of the household and gain at last the chance to be a full human being . . . for women to doubt the desirability of economic growth is to debate whether women should have a chance to cease to be beasts of burden and join the human race." (Lewis, quoted in Kabeer 1994, 19)

Consider also Archambault's description of why it seemed to defenders of Maasai girls' education that the fathers of girls who saw pastoralism as a safer bet were villains:

The story line is usually framed by a set of prevailing binaries that distinguish violators from victims, patriarchy from female empowerment, tradition from modernity, and collective culture from individual rights. . . .

. . . There seemed to be only one way to secure the well-being of the daughters of Ektorp, through education, [where educated girls are defined by having been given] the right to decide on the timing of their marriage and choose their own partners [in contrast to] girls of the home whose futures are determined largely by parents. (Archambault 2011, 632, 635–636)

Finally, consider these descriptions of what is wrong with forced marriage from the UK Home Office:

Valuing individual citizens, their dignity and the contribution they have to make to society in their own right is a central part of our drive for strong, active communities. The appalling practice of forced marriage represents the opposite extreme. (UK Home Office 2004)

Young British citizens must never be forced in relationships they do not want at a time when they could be establishing themselves as adults through further education or through work. (quoted in Enright 2009, 357)

According to these discourses, feminism means caring about women as individual human beings, "valuing individual citizens" and "their dignity," not treating them as "beasts of burden," and so on. This, I suggest next, is true, though we must be careful not to reduce feminism to this. At the same time, however, the justificatory conversations happening in advocacy and development discourses say more than that women are individual persons; they prescribe liberating women into "relationships of choice" and portray economic self-sufficiency as the feminist solution.

Personhood Individualism

The justificatory discourses correctly associate something we might call "personhood individualism" with feminism.[21] Personhood individualism is the view that people have interests of their own that are not reducible to the interests of others.[22] It is a normative view—that is, a view about what matters morally and politically.[23] To be clear, personhood individualism does not entail two forms of descriptive individualism that feminists have criticized. Many non-Western moral views, and feminist care ethical views, reject the individualistic social ontology of crude forms of liberalism that conceive persons as separate and self-interested long-term planners.[24] Personhood individualism can be embraced without this ontology; as Martha Nussbaum (2001) argues, one might coherently hold that the individual self is illusory and also hold that in the realm of moral and political action individuals matter (58). It is also possible to hold that what matters deeply is the good of a whole, but that we cannot achieve the good of the whole without seeing others and ourselves as individual loci to whom duties are due (see Dhand 2002; Bilimoria 1993). Personhood individualism also does not entail methodological individualism, the view that we can explain social phenomena, including how well individual human beings are doing, by referring only to interactions among individual human beings. Feminists simply cannot do without two concepts that methodological individualism removes from our explanatory toolbox: social groups and social structures.[25]

We now know what personhood individualism is, but what does it have to do with feminism? From the perspective of proponents of the harmful interventions described in the first section of the chapter, personhood individualism just is feminism, and societies that respect personhood individualism will make it possible to live a specific independence individualist (a term I will explain in a moment) kind of life. But the relationship between personhood individualism and feminism is not straightforward. Recall that feminism is opposition to sexist oppression and that oppression characterizes social structures in which some groups systematically benefit from the disadvantage of others (Frye 1983).

Because oppression describes relationships between groups, personhood individualism and feminism do not imply one another. Accepting personhood individualism, and even accepting that women count as persons, is *insufficient* to render a society or doctrine opposed to sexist oppression; widely held beliefs in the contemporary United States, for example, say that everyone has an equal interest in living as they choose, cast women's situations as the results of their choices, and thus deny that the social relations constitutive of sexist oppression are a problem. More important for our discussion of whether feminism requires individualist commitments, it is theoretically possible to imagine a society in which there is no intragroup oppression that does not respect personhood individualism. If no one is treated as having separable basic interests, then lacking this sort of treatment will not track group membership—and thus cannot count as evidence of the specific form of injustice known as oppression.

Feminist reasons for caring about individual personhood must refer to the ways in which it functions in a social context as a prerequisite for power or a currency for advantage. The empirical reality seems to be that in the vast majority of societies, the ability to count as an individual exists[26] and is gender-differentially distributed so as to disproportionate harm to women. Nussbaum (correctly, in my view) argues that many of the practices most widely (and cross-culturally) criticized by feminists, such as rape, forms of marriage that take women to be men's property, and notions that women's well-being only matters as a vehicle for the well-being of families, are perpetuated through ideologies that deny that women are persons in their own right (Nussbaum 1999, 57–79).[27] Sara Ahmed adds that personhood individualism is particularly important in contexts where imperialism has turned some into use objects for others: "When you have been owned, being your own can be radical" (quoted in Carty and Mohanty 2015, 87). At the same time, however, we need to be careful not to assume that all forms of sexist oppression are caused by failure to respect women's status as individual persons. Women can still have lesser status in societies that say no one counts as an individual. We can imagine a society in which people all matter insofar as they fulfill their role in the group. But the content of gender roles may still cause women as a group end up worse off; for example, everyone may be encouraged to think of themselves primarily as a contributor to a family, but women's role may be defined so as to include more labor hours than men's, and so result in lower well-being outcomes for women.

Most real-world contexts do include norms according to which individual persons matter because they are persons, and we also should be careful not to conclude from a society's communal orientation that no one in it is thought to count as an individual. Patterns of treatment that regard people in advantaged positions as having some interests that are basic and inviolable and others as expendable suggest that individual personhood matters, whether it is widely articulated that way or not. When being treated as having individual and equally important interests is actually a part of a society's practices, lacking it will be a fundamental harm different from lacks of other goods. Lacking it will typically justify vulnerability to losses of other goods, and exposure to harms ranging from cruel treatment and subjection to violence to lack of political voice. In chapter 1, I argued that some things are universal, or fairly universal, and widely recognized indicators of access to advantage or disadvantage. The idea that one's basic interests count in their own right, which underlies the notion of human rights, may be one of these. The relationship between feminist commitments and personhood individualism is thus best understood as very strong but contingent—that is, conceptually unnecessary. My reasoning for universalizing, or at least highly generalizing, feminist value for personhood individualism differs from that of some liberal feminists who take opposition to sexist oppression to require a worldview that places a high value on personhood individualism (see Nussbaum 1999 for an example of such a view).

Conceptualizing Independence Individualism

Our discussion of personhood individualism revealed a fact that will also be important for understanding the relationship between feminism and independence individualism: the fact that opposition to sexist oppression is not conceptually linked with any specific description of what goods are important in human life, or in human societies. Feminism is a view about how goods should be distributed, or about how the social power dynamics underlying their distribution should be shaped, but not what the goods are. For any good to be seen to be worthy of universal promotion by feminists, a case must be made that it is a universal good in human life that might accrue in gender differential ways.

Independence individualism, the form of individualism I see as motivating imperialist associational damage, does not meet these criteria. To get clearer about what it *is*, we might say as a first pass that it is the view that people's lives go better when they are unencumbered by ties to others. But that is not quite right. Take the discourses surrounding forced marriage in the United Kingdom; it is not marriage that is seen to be undesirable, it is arranged marriage and multigenerational families. Similarly, "strong communities" are considered desirable, but they seem to be defined by economic productivity more than filial ties. Another reason independence individualism should not be conceptualized as the view that all relationships are impediments is that the harms it motivates are not always caused by the devaluation of relationships. Sometimes, as in the case of feminization of responsibility harms, it occurs through *ignoring* them. More specifically, the justificatory discourses seem to assume away the existence of certain attachments, rather than assign a negative valence to them; it is not really that children or communal associations are seen to import negative value; it is that the effects of their existence on women are not considered at all.[28]

What seems to unify the justifications of imperialist associational damage is the idealization of a certain form of life in which some types of attachment are acceptable and others are not. The forms of attachment that are unacceptable are economic dependence and what I will hereafter call "relationships of custom," relationships entered into and maintained with social and cultural pressure (in which social pressure and cultural pressure operate as racialized notions[29] and are thought to exist very disproportionately in the lives of non-Western people) and because of concern for the interests of others.[30] Independence individualism overlaps with, but is not identical with, the form of individualism that is the object of familiar feminist philosophical critique. The independence individualist ideal is not merely androcentric; it is imperialist in the sense that it treats the form of life characteristic of Western late capitalism as universally desirable, and in the sense that it hierarchizes relationships of choice and relationships of custom, while associating the former with moral progress.[31] Though supporters of policies that produce imperialist associational damage see independence individualism as a feminist value, clarifying its content reveals that it is not obvious what independence individualism has to do with feminism, if anything at all. If economic independence is not distributed gender differentially, or if it is not valuable at all in a context, it is unclear why feminists should be bothered by its absence. And though feminism undoubtedly requires the absence of coercion in relationships, it is unclear why making relationship decisions with the interests of culture and kin in mind is a feminist problem, unless this capacity is gender-differentially distributed.

The most plausible explanation of why independence individualism seems to proponents of the harms described in the first section to be required for feminism pertains to its role in ideological Western narratives about moral progress. I argued in the first chapter that Western feminists often appeal to an "Enlightenment teleological narrative," one according to which the moral and economic superiority of the West is caused by endogenous factors and embodies the ultimate destiny of "other" societies. Part of this narrative is the idea that modern societies freed people from the bonds of tradition and family. Naila Kabeer (1994) offers a clue to how Western ideas about modernization link economic independence to freedom to choose one's relationships, as well as how the combination of these becomes linked to feminism: "pre-modern societies" needed to be transformed so that a variety of differentiated roles were available, and the statuses associated with them should be "achieved as a consequence of purposeful individual effort rather than ascribed by custom" (16).

In other words, reductions in people's tendencies to value relationships whose origins they did not choose, and in which they are expected to consider the needs and desires of others, are beneficial for success under capitalism. Shifts from agrarian to industrial societies, and to transnational global economies, require mobile workforces. Additionally, the notion that economic independence is possible offers a narrative about how it is possible for individuals to meet their needs under capitalism, and deflects responsibility for ensuring people's survival from communities, kin, and the state. As Nancy Fraser and Linda Gordon (1994) note, the valorization of independence was historically linked to industrialization in the West; independence only became a property of individuals in the eighteenth century and was valued positively only when used to describe the condition of the wage laborer in the nineteenth. The underlying logic connecting independence individualism to feminism seems to hold that the cause of women's oppression (or maybe just lack of personhood) is relationships characterized by custom and a high degree of consideration for the needs of others, and that individual economic independence is the way to escape it. Sexist oppression is an artifact of premodernity, and it will ostensibly disappear once the trappings of modern capitalism allow people to move from "traditional" to market-dictated roles. One of the major arguments I am making in this book is that Western feminists often mistakenly think that universalizing the values of what I call Enlightenment liberalism[32] is the feminist solution; the idea that tradition causes sexist oppression and that capitalism is beneficial because of its ability to decrease the hold of tradition lays bare an important Enlightenment liberal line of thought.

A potential alternative explanation of the ascent of independence individualism is the familiar one from Western feminist philosophers in the care and dependency traditions. These philosophers argue that independence is an androcentric ideal that obscures the value of dependency in human life (see Baier 1995, Kittay 1999; Friedman 2000, 2013; Fineman 2005). I am sympathetic to this view, and in the last section of the chapter, I adopt a key care ethical insight: that the ideal of economically independent citizens impedes feminist change by refusing to offer a vision for gender-just allocation of dependency work. However, androcentrism on its own cannot explain either (a) why economic self-sufficiency and opposition to relationships of custom become fused together in a single ideal (this fusion seems to require background commitments about the value of choice and specific empirical assumptions about the context in which the ideal is to be pursued) or (b) why independence individualism seems, not merely desirable, but also necessary for feminism. The idea that economic independence is supposed to erode the hold of "backward," traditional practices, and not merely increase women's ease of exit from bad relationships—and the idea that this in turn will constitute women's liberation—draws on the colonial idealizations about modernity I describe below (see pp. 67–68).

Independence Individualism as Unnecessary for Feminism

But perhaps it just seems true that women's possession of economic independence and relationships that are not influenced by custom will reduce sexist oppression. This claim is at best only true about certain contexts. (At worst, it is based on failures to acknowledge the feminist need to redistribute dependency work and the well-being women gain from even oppressive relationships, but this is the topic of the next section.) The most plausible argument in defense of a link between independence individualism and feminism goes like this: the ability to exist only or primarily in chosen relationships and to be economically independent of others is necessary for well-being, so gender-unequal access to it constitutes sexist oppression. A variant of it would hold that because relationships of custom are the cause of women's oppression, and because women are trapped in relationships of custom because of lack of economic independence, financial independence is the path to reducing sexist oppression. Versions of both arguments are plausible about Western late-capitalist contexts. But as Margaret Urban Walker (2007, 158) argues in her influential discussion of individualism, we need to remember that the ability of moral ideals to impart "gifts" to those who enact them is dependent on the contexts in which they are lived out.

Many of the examples in the first section discuss contexts where independence is not a gift, where well-being is secured by forms of life that do not embody the independence individualist ideal.[33] Consider the women in rural communities who rely heavily on sharing and informal lending in communal associations to access food, money, and help with dependency work discussed in the section on neoliberal governmentality harms. It is unclear that refusing to depend on others economically, or ignoring their interests in one's personal decisionmaking, would make the women better off—especially given that there is little evidence that short-term development interventions will make them cease to be poor and plenty of evidence that farmers and informal sector workers in rural South Asia lead precarious lives. Or consider a society, similar to the Maasai one described by Archambault, but in which economic opportunities tied to education are genuinely absent and pastoralism is a clear path to income and food security. In this society, marrying into the right family, and doing so influenced by the alignment of economic interests of the relevant families, is likely to be in a girl's best interests. Remember also Gateefa's society, wherein, like many of ours, access to care in old age depends on having close kin; it is unclear that economic independence is possible for or beneficial to her, and likely that arranged marriage was the best bet for ensuring well-being when she was a child, and that the intergenerational household is the best bet for her now. These latter two examples are not meant to deny that choices about who to marry and divorce are not important components of well-being. But we should not assume that well-being consists *only* in the ability not to be influenced in one's marital choices (as the reduction of feminism to independence individualism inclines us to do) since goods like access to food or care in times of dependence also matter. Acknowledging this fact, some indigenous people even go so far as to describe people who lack kin relationships as poor (Hunt 2010). These points about context are consistent with the claims of more sophisticated Western feminist defenders of economic independence. For example, Marilyn Friedman (2013, 118) argues that much of the value of economic independence for women is *prudential*; its importance derives from how it allows specific goods to be pursued within specific contexts.[34]

Perhaps it seems unfortunate that these relationships are women's best options for well-being. About some of the cases, this is clearly so—but the reason is that the societies are gender *oppressive*, not that they are *communal*. The fact that people rely on one another is not itself obviously unfortunate; the problem for feminists is that some societies, communal and not, expect women to sacrifice more than men or to be subordinate to them in other ways. In fact, the forms of affiliation in the first and third examples provide women protections from vulnerability that more independence individualist societies have difficulty providing. The reasons for the assumption that independence individualism is the universal answer to women's oppression, then, seems inextricable from ethnocentrism—and, perhaps more perniciously, Northern and Western interests. The form of ethnocentrism may be as simple as the assumption that all contexts are like the contemporary West. Refusal to recognize context variation is undoubtedly why economic independence, rather than, say, the possibility of being absorbed into households besides the one has married into, seems to be the one solution to women's domination by husbands. But it seems noncoincidental that the Western way of life seems like the feminist solution, and this suggests that the Enlightenment teleological narrative is operating in the background of independence individualist arguments.[35] After all, it is false that the West has ended sexist oppression.

Another, related possibility is that many feminists who embrace independence individualism think it just is the moral truth that a human life goes well when a person is economically independent and chooses her relationships free of social influence. But this argument would at least need justifying, and feminism itself—at least as I have defined it as being independent of any specific cultural view about what matters in human life—does not provide a justification.

One might attempt to counter that the universal value of independence individualism in liberating women has been empirically shown. Some economic theories, such as modernization theory, the principal theory of development through much of the twentieth century, have held that women's liberation is a byproduct of modern capitalism (Kabeer 1994, 16). But this line of thinking does not avoid the ethnocentrism charge. Methodologically, much of what modernization theory did was describe (what were assumed to be) stages in the development of Western societies, and then assume that all societies would necessarily develop in such stages; in other words, it just assumed the Enlightenment teleological narrative (Pieterse 2001; Escobar 1994). The empirical and moral claims underlying this theory are suspect, and not because of any particularly romantic view about agrarian societies. I cannot tackle all the problems here, but the empirical claim that Western nations followed a path from traditionalism to independence individualism and industrialization is disputable, given cross-country variation (Pieterse 2001, 29). The feminization of responsibility and kinship harms described in the first section provide evidence of a broad phenomenon in contemporary development studies—failures of income-generation activities to empower women (see Mayoux 1999; Alkire 2007; Molyneux 2006). A plausible empirical correlation may exist between independence individualism and economic growth, but even mainstream development economists now doubt that this leads to greater justice within countries—and feminism is a set of concerns about justice.

Though ethnocentrism plays a role in motivating the belief in the universal desirability, and gender-justice-achieving potential, of independence individualism, there is a danger of culture-washing (or, in the term I used in the first chapter, moralizing) Northern and Western investments in it. Northern and elite economic and geopolitical *interests* surely play a role. If leaving one's family and community is not a burden, neither is relocating to the city, or even transnationally, for work—even multiple times over a lifetime. If one sees oneself as personally responsible for one's own and one's family's well-being, one is more likely to attribute one's exhaustion at work to one's personal failures than to unjust labor conditions or inadequate state support. Such concerns clearly operate in many examples in the first section of the chapter; if South Asian women cannot immigrate spouses, there will be fewer drains on the welfare state in the United Kingdom; if women become less attached to family roles, they can become entrepreneurs and better consumers of credit, and so on.[36]

Against Independence Individualism

Should feminists who are engaged in transnational praxis value independence individualism? I have argued that feminist visions that harm women through imperialist associational damage confuse personhood individualism (which is contingently important for feminism) with independence individualism (which is not) and that the latter gains much of its appeal from Northern economic interests and Western ethnocentrism. The upshot of my argument so far is that feminists should only value independence individualism in certain contexts—contexts where crude forms of liberalism and capitalism prevail, or ones in which access to economic independence and relationships of choice, rather than relationships of custom, are the predominant, and gender-differentially distributed, paths to well-being. Recommending context-specific employment of the value would be consistent with familiar anti-imperialist feminist arguments that Western strategies do not work everywhere, and that Western moral languages often impede Western feminist activism in postcolonial contexts.[37]

I think the value of independence individualism is even more limited than this. To see why, we need to take into account a certain feature of transnational feminist praxis—one that shapes the vision I offer in this book. As I argued in chapter 1, transnational feminism is a nonideal, or justice-enhancing, project.[38] It aims, not at envisioning a gender-just world, but at attempting to reduce or end gender injustice. Thus, as with all nonideal theoretical concepts (see Sen 2009; Anderson 2010; C. Mills 2005): feminist normative concepts should encourage us to act in ways that reduce injustice. Independence individualism actually gets in the way of struggles to achieve gender justice in both Western and "other" contexts—or so I will argue.

Independence Individualism Worsens Gendered Labor Burdens

One reason independence individualism is likely to produce political strategies that fail to reduce women's oppression stems from the way it individualizes economic responsibility. Part of the independence individualist ideal is the notion that individual people can and should meet their own economic needs. This individualization of responsibility, adopted under the gender-unjust conditions we actually inhabit, is likely to worsen, or do nothing to change, the disadvantageous gendering of labor burdens. As feminists have pointed out for generations, women in most societies are assigned labor that is not only unpaid but also low status, unseen, or not considered to be labor at all (Davis 1983; Glenn 1992; Waring 1988; Beneria and Sen 1981; Folbre 2001). The clearest example is the work of caring for dependent people, such as children, the ill, and the disabled (Kittay 1999). However, other related tasks, such as cooking—a role that is demanding and somewhat cross-culturally intransigent (see Sen 1990)—also fit the bill. Some typically gendered but low-status and invisible tasks that may be less known to Northern audiences include the cultivation of food, the collection of fuel (such as firewood and dung) and water, and care of the natural environment (Desai 2002).

The low-status character of this labor and its association with women is a source of women's oppression across many contexts. To acknowledge this does not require committing to the claim that role differentiations are inherently oppressive or that roles are cross-culturally identical. Instead, it seems clear that imperialism historically spread oppressive gender divisions of labor and that militarism and neoliberalism contemporarily add to feminized labor burdens. Evelyn Nakano Glenn (1992) shows that the notion of the household as a space of nonlabor has been promoted in the West by the shifting of many forms of household labor onto women of color. The idea that African women were harmed by having to work in the fields or through their trading duties reduced the power associated with women's role in many cases (Mikell 1997; Nzegwu 1995). Neoliberal cuts in social spending on childcare and healthcare, and environmental degradation brought about by the deregulation of corporations, for example, are often subsidized by women's labor (Desai 2002) and attach new burdens to labor that might otherwise not have resulted in oppressive outcomes (see Whyte 2013). As Chandra Talpade Mohanty (2008) argues, neoliberalism as a transnational economic system continues to produce new forms of gendered and racialized labor.

But the gendering of labor burdens will seem to some like a reason to support independence individualism; is not the solution to the devaluation of feminized labor simply to make women independent from men? Two nonideal theoretical considerations can help us see why independence individualism will not solve the problem of unjust gendered labor burdens. First, normative ideals that are useful under nonideal conditions should be consistent with the limitations of human nature and with facts about the world. But the independence-individualist ideal assumes something impossible—that it is possible for all of us to meet our own economic needs. As Eva Feder Kittay (1999) argues, all human beings require care from others because we are all dependent at some point. A large chunk of the labor with which women are disproportionately charged, and which causes them to have less power and worse welfare outcomes than men, is thus ineluctable. In fact, the popularity of the idea that anyone can meet their own economic needs over a lifetime seems causally related to the social invisibilization of the labor of marginalized, typically feminized but often also racialized, others. This is often observed about men's gains from the oppression of women, but the ability of the affluent Northern woman to work a full-time job outside the home is typically subsidized by people of color and immigrants (Hondagneu-Sotelo 2007; Salazar Parrenas 2000). Though dependency work is particularly ineluctable, other goods produced by feminized labor, such as environmental protection, are also likely to consistently need to be performed, and unlikely to get produced through individual economic self-sufficiency.

Still, an ideal might be unrealistic while still being worth approximating. A second nonideal strike against individualizing economic responsibility is that attempting to adopt the ideal would likely worsen women's lot. Because neoliberalism is our contemporary global reality, we do not need to look very far to see what the results of attempting universal individual economic independence are. One is increased vulnerability to poverty as women have to compensate for cuts in social expenditures and economic deregulation with increased labor (see Desai 2002). Another is the feminization of responsibility described earlier (pp. 53–54). So long as independence individualism aims at individual economic self-sufficiency in a world where women are disproportionately tasked with labor that the ideal assumes does not need to be performed, women are likely to continue doing the labor without supports, or to find supports removed. The fact that the independence-individualist ideal does not have any views about gender written into it is beside the point, given existing gender relations, the fact of human dependency, and the fact that much of the relevant labor is not assigned a market value. None of this means that women do not benefit from incomes of their own or that feminists must reject markets altogether. But it suggests very strongly that societies in which women's liberation is possible will be ones that visibilize and support dependency work and other forms of feminized labor, rather than ones that expect each individual to support herself.

Independence Individualism Neutralizes Transition Costs

A second reason independence individualism is an undesirable ideal under gender-unjust conditions has not been discussed in the existing feminist literature on individualism. Independence individualism makes it difficult to perceive the transition costs of proposed feminist change. Changes from any set of social conditions to another, the kinds of change that feminism requires, demand that those invested in existing conditions bear costs or unless those costs can be offset. Many of those rendered most vulnerable by such investments are women. Feminists should care about the costs women have to bear as parts of transitions to greater gender justice, for several reasons. Although this is not the place to list them, we can note that strategies for change that require women to make major well-being sacrifices are unlikely to be effective, that there are moral reasons not to expect women to sacrifice their basic well-being for changes that are risky and long term, and that transferring the costs of change disproportionately onto vulnerable women can itself constitute an injustice. As I argued in chapter 1, one way Western feminisms are particularly likely to go wrong is by ignoring the costs of change.

Independence individualism is unhelpful in drawing attention to transition costs for reasons of both form and content. Formally, independence individualism shares a feature with all ideal theoretical ideals—it offers a vision of what the world should look like but no notion of how to get there. It thus says nothing about what the costs of the transition to greater justice might be and how to manage them. More troubling than silence, however, is the fact that the content of independence individualism actively neutralizes transition costs by suggesting that losses to relationships of custom are not losses at all.

The idea that such relationships can be genuine sources of value for women while also being appropriate targets of feminist change may need some explaining. We must recognize two facts about how relationships, especially relationships to kin and culture, operate in the world in order to see what is at stake in recommending changes to them. First, such attachments have a *nodal* quality. They have intrinsic value, but they are also sites of the expression of, and have instrumental value for the attainments of, other goods constitutive of well-being. Consider a person's membership in a religious grouping. By participating in its practices with its members, she can experience goods such as love, friendship, and artistic and intellectual expression. The religion likely provides some of the meaning-creating goods typical of culture, such as a framework within which to attribute meaning, and value or disvalue, to opportunities (see Raz 1988, 307–313; see also Kymlicka 1991).

Assuming that practices marking religious membership exist across domains of life, a person may also experience goods such as nutrition, play, and education in religiously inflected ways. Declaring one's membership in a religion may allow access to social status, friendship, and other goods.

Second, the nodes that bundle relationships with goods are often tied together by forces that are out of the control of individuals (Narayan 2002) and gender-differentially structured. Narayan illustrates part of the point with an example about Pirzada women who engage in body veiling and seclusion. The women say these practices offer benefits, such as the ability to move in public unseen and the social status that comes with being seen as morally pure. The practices also expose them to losses, ranging from being sweaty to having limited access to education. According to Narayan, these women want certain elements of the practices and reject others, but they "lack the power to undo the bundle." A woman who wants not to be hot cannot make it the case that nonveiling will communicate superiority to women of other classes and religions. This inability to undo bundles of goods with relationships and affiliations is not specific to "other" women or conditions of oppression; it is a general feature of living in a social world.

The problem for feminists is not the inability to undo the nodes, which affects all persons living in complex social structures, but rather the frequent gender-differential stakes of maintaining the relationships as they are. Oppressed individuals will generally find their societies structured so that the terms on which they must interact to access benefits are unfair to them. Women, in particular, are likely to find that access to many goods depends on participation in forms of relationship that render them vulnerable to men, or worse off as a group than similarly situated men. This means that participating in sexist forms of affiliation may genuinely be the most self-interested thing women can do. Many of the cases in the first section involve this kind of situation; women's existing attachments have sexist elements, but participating in them in their current forms is also women's best available course of action. Consider women's nonexit from relationships in which responsibility is feminized and their bargaining power low. Women who do not exit are often simply expressing the realistic judgment that their prospects for well-being would be worse without male partners—even as it would be better for women as a group for some different, more egalitarian, type of kinship to exist.[39]

The upshot—and the tragedy—of this is that feminist change is typically going to require changes to relationships women are genuinely self-interestedly invested in. In other words, strategies for feminist change confront women with transition costs. Facing this reality raises important moral and political questions that are relevant to choices among potential feminist strategies. Among these are questions about who has to bear the costs and whether they accrue disproportionately to vulnerable people, whether the costs to women's well-being can be offset, and what time horizon feminist change should happen in. To ask any of these questions, we need to be able to see the losses that women stand to incur through changes in the relationships in which they find themselves.

Unfortunately, independence individualism encourages the opposite. It either encourages us to ignore certain relationships in women's lives or asserts that elements of the relationships women stand to lose as a result of proposed feminist change were never really of valuable at all[40]—so that there are no reasons to worry about eliminating them, and women's objections to losing them are motivated by confusion or false consciousness forms of adaptive preference.[41] Lack of attention to the nodal quality of relationships under nonideal conditions causes "other" women, to borrow Narayan's image, to appear as either "prisoners of patriarchy," dying to escape, or dupes, valuing the oppressive character of relationships for its own sake.

Losses to two types of interests are especially likely to disappear from the scope of independence-individualist analysis: identity interests (interests women have in the preservation of a cultural grouping) and kinship interests. In many cases, goods experienced through cultural attachments are irreplaceable or extremely costly for the people who inhabit them to replace; as Will Kymlicka (1995, 84) puts it, changing one's culture is not like changing one's job. For members of culturally dominated groups, beyond the intrinsic and instrumental value typical of cultural attachments, there are symbolic and community resources for managing and resisting the experience of domination. Additionally, as we saw in the UK forced marriage and Aboriginal family-violence cases described earlier, in cases of cultural domination, being absorbed into majority cultures or Western culture may be difficult and place one at risk for subjugation and abuse. For an example of how independence individualism obscures transition costs to identity interests, we can return to the case of the Australian Aboriginal women. Independence individualists encouraged the women to exit the community in the name of feminism, seeing their cultural attachments as causes of harm to be superseded. As a result, the women were left without important public resources for ensuring their freedom from family and gender-based violence. Organizations that have recognized women's identity interests have produced strategies that allowed feminist change while preserving the elements of well-being added by cultural membership. Krushil Watene (2016) argues that developing a cultural infrastructure for healing is central to strategies for justice for indigenous people, and Aboriginal groups have sought ways of reducing family violence that simultaneously build up Aboriginal culture. Aboriginal community organizations in Australia have developed programs for survivors that connect them to services noncoercively through the sharing of stories during craft activities like beading or weaving, and through attending retreats in culturally significant locations (Karahasan 2014). But such strategies are unavailable to those who can only see the negative effects of existing relationships with patriarchal elements.

A similar point can be made about kinship interests. Strategies for feminist change that propose simply abandoning existing forms of kinship risk worsening women's lives or recommending changes that women do not endorse, but if relationships of custom or economic dependence were never worth having in the first place, we cannot see this. Recall the case of Gateefa, the Bedouin woman in Abu-Lughod's (2013) work whose husband died, and whose daughters-in-law left the multigenerational household. Abu-Lughod expresses puzzlement when this woman who, at a younger age, stood up to her husband in favor of her own equal rights; laments the new generation; and reports "you need a man who knows how to rule" (204). After wondering whether Gateefa is more supportive of patriarchy than she had thought, Abu-Lughod lands on the explanation that she is nostalgic for the love, care, and mutual support that a multigenerational household would provide—and the status that would come from being an elder woman in such a household.

Abu-Lughod (2013) argues that Western feminist attempts to bring about gender equality often fail to apprehend the realities of women's lives in societies that value "relationality and mutual concern above individualism and where gender is closely tied to social power" (208). But I think the upshot is broader than this; it is not merely in more communal societies that women's fates are likely to be bound up in loving and caring attachments and that a failure to understand the value of such attachments can impede feminist politics. Women's lives across contexts are particularly likely to be affected by changes to kinship forms because of their common roles as dependency workers, and in cementing communities through marriage. Strategies for feminist change that refuse to imagine relationships of custom as losses, or simply minimize those losses—that is, the types of strategies independence individualism recommends—can increase their vulnerability in unnecessary or morally unacceptable ways. The challenge for feminists in such situations is, of course, to figure out how the sexist elements of the relevant kinship forms (including, in Gateefa's case, polygamy, lack of household decision-making power and access to income, and unilateral emphasis on sexual purity) can be reformed in ways that minimize costs to the women affected, or that make the costs of exit ones the women are willing to bear.[42] But this type of change is impossible from the independence-individualist perspective—which denies that costs to relationships of custom are even costs.

Conclusion

It may seem that, since women's oppression often occurs in and through relationships, promiscuous associational damage is just the feminist cost of doing business. I hope to have shown that this ultimatum view overstates the need for associational damage, because opposition to sexist oppression does not require—and is in fact practically at odds with—commitment to independence individualism. There is a strong but contingent relationship between feminism and personhood individualism, but independence individualism is a value transnational feminist praxis can do without. Independence individualism encourages dangerous and ineffective strategies by ignoring the fact that pathways to well-being are often context specific, by recommending interventions that worsen women's gendered labor burdens, and by suggesting that transition costs to women's kinship and cultural interests that result from proposed feminist change are not really costs at all.

Once we recognize this, we can see why the protection of cultural and kinship groupings is more consistent with feminist goals than it seemed to be to Okin. Even when women are invested in cultural and relational forms that are sexist, concern for women's well-being and concerns about effectiveness under nonideal conditions often weigh in favor of political strategies to reduce oppression that do not expose women to high levels of risk. Even though economic dependence in the West can reduce women's domination by men, it is less clear that it can reduce any women's subjugation through unregulated capitalism and unjust gender divisions of labor. If feminists are to avoid ethnocentrism, then to take women's well-being under nonideal conditions seriously and to create more just divisions of dependency work, our visions of emancipation must look beyond independence individualism.

AUTONOMY AND THE SECULAR

DO MUSLIM WOMEN NEED FREEDOM?

Post–September 11 cultural discourses present the fate of Muslim women as tied to the fate of civilization itself. Muslim women are oppressed by a barbaric, medieval religion, and "Islamland" represents a sort of final frontier in humanity's struggle for freedom from the bonds of the past.[1] A body of scholarship on Muslim women (Abu-Lughod 2002, 2013; Alexander 2006; Mahmood 2005; Mahmood and Hirschkind 2002; Maira 2009; Puar 2007; Razakh 2008; Volpp 2011) claims that this cultural imagery draws much of its appeal from the values of freedom, autonomy, and the secular. According to it, these values play what I call a "justificatory" role in imperialist projects that range from unjustified war to the marginalization of Muslim populations in the West.[2] As Sherene Razakh (2008) puts it, "The secular/religious divide . . . functions as a color line, marking the difference between the modern, enlightened West, and people of color, notably Muslims" (148). If adherence to religious traditions both marks the absence of modernity and causes women's oppression, feminism appears to authorize the destruction of "other" traditions.

Yet feminists cannot simply refuse to criticize traditional dictates. People often see women's inferiority as part of their religious or cultural inheritance. This produces a version of the anti-imperialism/normativity dilemma described earlier in this book.[3] Since the same value that seems necessary for feminist critique (anti-traditionalism of some kind, often justified with reference to the values of autonomy or the secular) also seems to motivate feminist complicity in imperialism, we face a choice between a feminism that licenses cultural domination and other imperialist harms and, rejecting feminism altogether. Adding fuel to the anti-imperialism/normativity dilemma, many anti-imperialist feminists suggest that the solution is to abandon normative judgment as such. Some caution that moral judgments are inextricable from imperialist notions of "progressive and backward, superior and inferior, higher and lower" (Mahmood 2005, 198) or suggest that what we need is universals that are "not normative" (Abu-Lughod 2013, 201–229).[4] This chapter develops a way out of the dilemma and suggests that a critique of women's oppression is compatible with a much greater degree of respect for traditional and religious worldviews than is often supposed.

I argue in this chapter that feminism and traditionalism, even the sort of traditionalism that takes some dictates to be beyond question, are not necessarily at odds with one another. The idea that they are incompatible arises from a mistaken sense that the oppressiveness of traditions is a function of their inheritedness, or so I will attempt to show. The mistaken view that externally dictated practices are inherently objectionable stems from the value I call Enlightenment freedom. Although both liberal and anti-imperialist feminist theorists connect feminism to Enlightenment freedom, I claim that the link is conceptually unnecessary. I propose that the conception of feminism as opposition to sexist oppression directs feminism to oppose practices with certain objectionable *effects*—irrespective of their perceived origin. The upshot of my analysis is a view according to which feminism can be grounded in worldviews that value orienting human lives around tradition, and even ones that take certain traditional dictates to be beyond question. I discuss the moral epistemologies of Islamic feminist movements to show that this possibility, rather than being merely theoretical, is pursued by real-world feminist theorists and activists.

I begin by explaining what Enlightenment freedom—the value that makes antitraditionalism seem appealing—is, why it has been seen as an imperialist value, and why it seems to some to be necessary for feminism. Second, I show how the idea that traditions are inherently patriarchal, an idea surprisingly shared by many liberal and postcolonial feminists, motivates the view that feminism requires Enlightenment freedom. Third, I consider an alternative view about the feminist importance of opposition to tradition that takes traditions to be problematic only insofar as they prevent individuals from questioning their social roles. I contend that this alternative reflexive distance view retains vestiges of Enlightenment freedom and is unnecessarily hostile to what I call "metaphysically traditionalist" worldviews that hold certain inherited dictates to be beyond question—that is, the worldviews that have been posed as challenging for feminism in Saba Mahmood's work. Finally, I argue that elements of the nonideal universalism I have developed here allow a feminist perspective that is genuinely normative without being thoroughgoingly antitraditionalist. I claim that the view of feminism as opposition to sexist oppression makes the question of whether beliefs and practices are inherited orthogonal to the question of whether feminists should reject them, and I show how the moral epistemologies of some Islamic feminist movements demonstrate the compatibility of genuine feminist commitments with traditionalist worldviews.

Three notes about the scope of my argument are in order before I continue. First, I use the terms "religious" and "traditional" relatively interchangeably. I do so not because the terms are interchangeable in all contexts but because a single shared feature makes them problematic for feminists who enjoin "other" women to come into modernity. This shared feature is the perception of inherited external dictatedness. In other words, for many feminists, the problem with traditional and religious dictates is that they gain their authority from a communally recognized source that is antecedent to and outside any individual agent. Second, I focus on Muslim women, not because my argument applies exclusively to them, but because the scholarship on them is an important site of feminist theoretical conversations about the relationship between the secular, autonomy, and imperialism. My ultimate argument that it is possible to be a traditionalist and a feminist can be logically extended to apply to those who subscribe to other worldviews that place a high value on traditional adherence. Third, by "secular," I refer to moral ideals according to which structuring one's life and the life of one's community around religious dictates is harmful or undesirable. Talal Asad's (2003) distinction between secularism and "the secular" is useful in denoting the attitude toward religion I am interested in distancing from feminism here; for Asad, the secular is way of thinking about what it means to be human that, among other things, situates authority, agency, and responsibility in individual human agents and human law, rather than in the divine will or religious traditions. Proponents of the secular often associate freedom or autonomy with the ability to reject religious traditions. Secularism, in contrast, is a view about the relationship between religious institutions and the state and is outside the scope of my analysis. My interest is in showing that one need not be a secular person, or lead a secular life, to be a feminist—not in defending religious social institutions.

Enlightenment Freedom and Its Dangers

Value for liberation from tradition appears to some liberal feminists as women's only hope and to some transnational feminists as the cause of imperialism. Liberal feminist public intellectual Ayaan Hirsi Ali, in her celebrated memoir *Infidel,* describes her literal and metaphorical journey from Africa and the Middle East to Europe. She describes having been a victim of female genital mutilation, having worn the hijab, and having developed sympathies for conservative Islam during a youth spent in Kenya, Ethiopia, Saudi Arabia, and Somalia. After moving to the Netherlands, Hirsi Ali read voraciously, became an author and politician, and codirected the film *Submission*—a film whose reception included death threats to her and the murder of her collaborator, Theo Van Gogh. Her life's lesson, in her words, is that "it is possible to free oneself from one's faith, to examine it critically, and to understand the way in which faith itself is at the root of oppression" (Hirsi Ali 2007, 350). Not only is faith itself oppressive but clinging to faith is Muslims' way of miring themselves in prehistory. "I moved from the world of faith to the world of reason . . . We in the West would be wrong to prolong the pain of that transition unnecessarily, by elevating cultures full of bigotry and hatred toward women to the stature of respectable alternative ways of life" (348).

French philosopher and public intellectual Elisabeth Badinter advocates banning headscarves in public schools in strikingly similar terms. In a pamphlet cowritten with Régis Debray, Alain Finkielkraut, Elizabeth de Fontenay, and Catherine Kintzler, she writes:

> To tolerate the Islamic veil is not to accept a free being (in the form of a young girl); it is to open the door to those who decided, once and for all, to try to bend her to their wills. Instead of offering her a space of freedom, you send her the message that there is no difference between the school and her father's house. . . . It is no longer the equality of the sexes, or free decision making—that is the law of France . . . [You want] a school in which each student is always reminded of her parents, riveted to her roots—a school of social predestination. (Badinter et al. 1989; translation mine)

Badinter refers to a number of different justifications in the passage, but the last sentence is particularly noteworthy. "Being riveted to [one's] roots" is presented as incompatible with freedom, so much so that it is equivalent to being bent to another's will. What (liberal) education is supposed to offer is the ability to question veiling (which Badinter casts as oppressive[5] largely *because it is traditional*).[6] The central worry seems to be that traditions—embodied here in the homes of "others"—are hotbeds of patriarchy. The only way to protect "other" women from patriarchy is to reduce the power of their roots over them.

Hirsi Ali and Badinter both suggest that adherence to a faith or a tradition is incompatible with two other values: feminism and freedom. More precisely, they argue that traditions promote women's subordination by making a certain type of freedom unavailable. For Hirsi Ali, a free person is one who recognizes that "faith itself is the source of oppression"; for Badinter, even being "reminded" of one's tradition by seeing others follow it constitutes a "riveting." Ali and Badinter use the term "freedom" in a loose, nontechnical way. If we map their concerns onto the language of contemporary political philosophy, we can characterize Ali and Badinter as endorsing a particular variant of positive freedom. Positive notions of freedom allow that impediments to freedom can exist within the self (see Hirschmann 2002).[7] For Hirsi Ali and Badinter, an individual agent's desire to follow tradition constitutes an internal barrier to her excavating her true will, and traditional practices are barriers to her executing it.

Yet Hirsi Ali's and Badinter's conception of freedom will strike many as implausible. Dictating appropriate beliefs and behaviors is just what human cultures do. As Diana Meyers (2000) puts it, "The fact is that we are all immersed in a culture at a historical moment" (469). It is thus worth asking why such a suspect concept of freedom is embraced by Hirsi Ali and Badinter. The answer, I believe, is a submerged descriptive assumption that only "others" have traditions. Asad (2003) argues that the secular has its own myths, and perhaps one of them is the Enlightenment teleological narrative I discussed in the first chapter, according to which the West achieved its preeminence because of its preference for reason over tradition, rather than because of its global political and economic domination. Homi Bhabha (1999) ironically calls the idea that Western cultures are not cultures "liberalism's sacred cow." The notion that the West has no traditions lurks behind Badinter's description of what is wrong with veiling in public schools; it is difficult to imagine her suggesting that encountering girls with *uncovered* heads in school, or encountering French cheese in the school cafeteria for that matter, would "rivet" white French teens to their roots. Indeed, Badinter argues elsewhere that teenagers who dye their hair blue are rejecting tradition but hijab wearers are not (quoted in Mahmood and Hirschkind 2002, 352). In Hirsi Ali's stronger iteration of the assumption that only "others" have traditions, tradition is more or less synonymous with "patriarchy." The move is almost metonymic—the part stands for the whole. Non-Western cultures are defined by their "bigotry and hatred towards women."

The value that Hirsi Ali and Badinter are describing is what I call Enlightenment freedom. Enlightenment freedom is a form of positive freedom according to which the acceptance of traditional dictates constitutes an impediment to self-realization. This value is conceptually distinct from the belief that only "others" have traditions. However, the value is likely to be unappealing to those who see the inheriting of external dictates as an inescapable part of all human socialization.[8] I have named the value Enlightenment freedom partly to make plain that it is not the only possible conception of freedom, nor one to which all liberals subscribe. I will return to alternative liberal interpretations of freedom in the section "Moderating the Feminist Relationship to Tradition"; here I wish only to point out that Hirsi Ali's and Badinter's understanding of freedom, though widespread in popular culture, is idiosyncratic in contemporary political philosophy—and the appropriate target of contemporary transnational feminist critiques of freedom, secularism, and autonomy seems to be this pop-cultural notion of freedom rather than any contemporary philosophical notion.

A second reason for the term "Enlightenment freedom" is to make explicit that the type of autonomy Badinter and Hirsi Ali value borrows from, even if it is not identical to, the ideas of some eighteenth- and nineteenth-century European philosophers who cast tradition as quelling human freedom. Immanuel Kant's "What Is Enlightenment?" mobilizes some of the very same background assumptions that seem to motivate Hirsi Ali and Badinter— even if, as I note in the next section, Kant stigmatizes traditional adherence far *less* promiscuously than they do.[9] Kant's essay takes religious authorities who demand unthinking adherence to be enemies of freedom par excellence. Traditional authorities demand obedience and discourage independent thought as a way of maintaining power. To be free, then, is to refuse to obey simply because one has been told to obey; it is to excavate one's own will and reasons instead of acting according to reasons given from outside (Kant 2010). Offering a different justification for a similar idea, John Stuart Mill (2002) argued that traditions stifle the expression of human individuality: "Human nature is not a machine to be built after a model, and set to do exactly the work prescribed for it, but a tree, which requires to grow and develop itself on all sides, according to the tendency of the inward forces which make it a living thing" (64). Third, the term "Enlightenment freedom" highlights the fact that many of its exponents, such as Hirsi Ali, support what I called the Enlightenment teleological narrative in chapter 1—the view that contemporary Western culture represents the epitome of human progress and has managed to do so because of endogenous factors such as commitment to reason.

A look at the types of harms transnational feminists think are caused by the Western focus on freedom suggests that the object of their critique is Enlightenment freedom.[10] I have mentioned that transnational feminists suggest that vocabularies of freedom, autonomy, and the secular have allowed concern for women to become a pretext for what they see as imperialist acts—ranging from the wars in Afghanistan and Iraq (Abu-Lughod 2002, 2013; Alexander 2006; Mahmood and Hirschkind 2002; Razakh 2008) to the denial of civil liberties to Muslims living in the West (Maira 2009; Razakh 2008) to the rendering of public institutions inaccessible to Muslims (Mahmood and Hirschkind 2002; Razakh 2008; Scott 2010; Volpp 2011) to the desire to eradicate Muslim women's movements (Mahmood 2005).

Saba Mahmood offers the most extended argument for the view that freedom is an imperialist value that encourages harm to Muslims. In addition to making the same arguments about justificatory imperialism that I attribute to Abu-Lughod in the next paragraph, she suggests that autonomy is a *constitutively* imperialist value[11]—one that is parochial and valuable only to Westerners, and whose spread is part of a regime of cultural domination. She argues that Western feminists will have to want to erase the worldview of the Salafist women's *da'wa* movement in Cairo, because they hold that traditions and "pious practices [are] scaffolding" (Mahmood 2005, 148). The meaning of this idea about scaffolding varies in Mahmood, sometimes meaning just that traditional dictates are worth following, and at other points meaning that such dictates cannot be questioned. Debates within the *da'wa* movement are always over the content of what is dictated, not whether what is dictated is worth doing. For the da'wa women, the ineffability of divine commands means that the significance of religious practices can often only be understood *after* one has made habits of them; attempting to rationally weigh their costs and benefits before engaging in them is not only impious; it is fruitless and prevents the practices from having their intended edifying effects on individuals. For example, Nama, a da'wa participant, describes having felt hypocritical when she started veiling because she did not feel "shyness" in her heart. However, according to her, "you must first wear the veil because it is God's command, and then, with time, your inside learns to feel shy without a veil, and if you take it off, your entire being feels uncomfortable about it" (157).

Lila Abu-Lughod's (2002) concern with the *justificatory* role vocabularies of freedom play in imperialism also seems to have Enlightenment freedom as its target. Those in the thrall of the freedom vocabulary, for her, believed Afghan women in the early 2000s were longing to "throw off" their burqas, waiting for Westerners to liberate them from the shackles of religion. According to Abu-Lughod (2002), the problematic notion of freedom, besides promoting imperialism, cannot accept that "humans are social beings, always raised in certain social and historical contexts, and belonging to particular communities that shape their desires and understandings of the world" (787). Freedom, as Abu-Lughod understands it, is incompatible with traditional adherence—and is enhanced by the destruction of the traditions of "others."

Such worries about the justificatory role of Enlightenment freedom in imperialism boil down to the idea that Enlightenment freedom breeds a form of moral insensitivity in Westerners (see especially Mahmood 2005, 198). Mahmood argues that value for Enlightenment freedom breeds this insensitivity in two ways: first, if desire for freedom is naturalized, it may seem that all women are yearning to be free of their traditions—that they are, to use an image from Uma Narayan (2002), "prisoners of patriarchy," chafing at traditions and longing for their elimination—waiting to throw off their burqas, as it were. Second, insensitivity to the harms of cultural destruction may manifest as the view that, whether women *want* freedom from their traditions or not, they would be better off if their traditions were destroyed. Mahmood expresses this concern when she suggests that feminists would want the da'wa women to learn to see their traditions as an impediment to excavating their true wills.

Traditions as Inherently Patriarchal: Why Feminism Seems to Need Enlightenment Freedom

If Enlightenment freedom is a parochial Western value, and if adopting it justifies promiscuous destruction of "other" lifeworlds, an anti-imperialist feminism must find its grounding in another value. But extricating Enlightenment freedom from feminism is easier said than done. A single fact about the world threatens the possibility of a feminism not founded in Enlightenment freedom: people often see women's subjugation as traditionally dictated. Is it possible to take an affirmative or neutral stance toward traditional adherence without becoming an apologist for patriarchy? Transnational feminists have often attempted to answer this question by reminding us that what are called "traditions" are political products—often of colonial marginalization (Abu-Lughod 2002; Jaggar 2005; Narayan 1997; Nzegwu 2006; Song 2008; Phillips 2009; Volpp 2011). For instance, Narayan argues that *sati* (widow immolation) only achieved the status of cultural practice in India through the British colonial fascination with it. But this type of answer does not vitiate the feminist need to criticize traditions. Although it is certainly true that imperialism has deepened existing patriarchal practices and created new ones, it is not their only source. Even if it were, it might not matter—because many people *believe* that their traditions demand the subordination of women. It is unclear that there is an authenticity criterion that allows sorting "true" from false traditions. A view or practice can gain the status of a traditional or religious dictate merely from being widely perceived as such—regardless of whether this perception is based on a selective or distorted history.

Enlightenment-liberal feminists are thus responding to a genuine problem when they cling to Enlightenment freedom. As Sindre Bangstad (2011) points out in a critique of Mahmood, feminism has to be a normative doctrine in order to be anything at all; feminism is literally meaningless if it is compatible with *all* dictates and practices (42–43). Ali and Badinter see straightforward rejection of relativism as an advantage of their view; for them, if "imperialism" is a bullet feminists just have to bite, so be it. Some transnational feminists have inadvertently buttressed such Enlightenment-liberal self-satisfaction by expressing skepticism toward the idea of normativity itself. For instance, although Abu-Lughod and Mahmood claim to eschew moral relativism and political passivity, they also claim, somewhat contradictorily, that normative judgment is indistinguishable from imperialism.[12] We thus seem to face a choice: embrace Enlightenment freedom and criticize sexism or embrace sexism and criticize Enlightenment freedom. It is difficult to formulate an anti-imperialist response to this dilemma, but luckily, it is a false dilemma. It arises out of a questionable assumption that many transnational and liberal feminists share: the assumption that traditions are defined by patriarchality.

Perhaps the most famous defense of the view that feminism requires a critique of traditions is Susan Moller Okin's (1999) essay "Is Multiculturalism Bad for Women?" Okin argues that policies designed to preserve cultures can undermine gender justice. Although Okin restricted her initial argument to questions about the toleration of the patriarchal practices of (mostly immigrant) minority cultures within liberal states, her response to her critics defends the general idea that the subjugation of women is wrong, regardless of who practices it. She argues against the idea that "others'" support for patriarchal gender roles justifies the perpetuation of those roles. I believe this normative claim is correct, but her descriptive claims are problematic in ways that are relevant to our current discussion. Okin has a particular view of the source of patriarchal oppression. For her, all cultures have patriarchal pasts—but "other" cultures are closer to those origins.[13]

The idea that the *origins* of Western culture are patriarchal and that "other" cultures remain so suggests a particular understanding of the relationship between tradition and patriarchy, one that makes Enlightenment freedom seem like an appealing value for feminists. Consistent with the Enlightenment teleological narrative, patriarchy belongs to a past shared by Western and non-Western cultures; it is just a past in which "other" cultures remain more stuck and out of which Western cultures have progressed. Okin (1999) is quite explicit on this point: "Most cultures are patriarchal, then, and many (though not all) of the cultural minorities that claim group rights are more patriarchal than the surrounding culture" (17). "While virtually all of the world's cultures have distinctly patriarchal pasts—some, mostly but by no means exclusively, Western liberal cultures—have departed further than others" (16).

The logical coherence of Okin's view that Western cultures are more removed from traditions than others rests on the idea that *what makes the past the past* is its patriarchality. If her understanding of the past were merely temporal, the idea of Western culture as further removed from the past would be unintelligible—all cultures in 1999 would be similarly situated with regard to pastness. Traditions typically gain their authority from their extension into the past, so what makes something a tradition for Okin seems to be, at least partly, its association with patriarchy. Okin (1999) argues that a central *purpose* of traditions is to control women (13) and cites no examples of traditional practices that are not sexist. She consistently describes existing sexist practices in the West as vestigial and attempts to mitigate them as openings into the future—rather than, say, developments of existing nonpatriarchal elements within cultures.

This nexus of associations between the past, patriarchality, and tradition does not occur at the level of explicit argument in Okin and is not logically necessary for her defense of moral universalism. Yet the idea that traditions are almost by definition patriarchal helps us make sense of Okin's more justificatorily imperialist statements. In a sentence that seems to embody exactly the insensitivity to traditional destruction Abu-Lughod and Mahmood worry about, Okin (1999) remarks that women may not have an interest in the preservation of patriarchal cultures and that sometimes women "*might* be better off if the cultures they were born into were . . . to become extinct . . . ." (22). In the same sentence, she argues that cultural reform is preferable to extinction, but as I discussed in the last chapter, the glibness of the remark has struck many transnational feminist commentators. Okin's framing of the question of whether cultures ought to be preserved as a core feminist question suggests that she understands tradition to be a key source of patriarchy.

One might expect transnational feminist scholarship on Muslim women to reject this characterization of tradition, but Mahmood inadvertently accepts it. As a result, instead of disputing the idea that traditions are patriarchal, she ends up being skeptical about whether patriarchy is really bad. As we have already seen, Mahmood's ethnography emphasizes the fact that Egyptian revivalist women see submission to traditional, conventional, and/or divine dictates as the path to self-actualization. Beginning from the assumption that respect for the da'wa movement is a good thing, Mahmood argues that Western feminists cannot respect the da'wa women *because they are feminists*.[14]

But this conclusion is somewhat bizarre. To see why, we need a clearer picture of the traditional dictates to which the da'wa movement prescribes unquestioning deference. Among these traditional dictates are that women's capacity to arouse men is so strong as to justify a prohibition on mixed-gender worship (Mahmood 2005, 65), that women should refrain from divorcing even immoral husbands (69), that women should either not interact with unknown men at all or severely limit their interaction with them (107), that women should submit to their husbands' authority (177), and that unmarried women should not protest scorn they receive from others (172–173). Also among these dictates are the ideas that women's education is necessary and worth pursuing (101), that there is a higher moral court of appeal than the commands of one's husband (180), and that weeping, covering one's head, and prostrating oneself during prayer help one become closer to God (147). According to Mahmood, the reason feminists have difficulty respecting women who submit to these dictates is that they are indebted to "an imaginary of freedom." Interestingly, Mahmood uses the terms "feminism" and "liberalism" (and occasionally, the words "secularism" and "individualism") nearly interchangeably. This is imprecise but coherent because she sees feminism as requiring the view that women need *liberation from* oppressive traditions and norms.[15] What she calls "liberalism" and feminism are so conceptually intertwined that Mahmood suggests that feminists who question value for the sort of freedom she is criticizing must become skeptical of feminism itself.[16]

But Mahmood's conclusion comes too quickly. Note that there is a key difference between the two sets of dictates I have just described—the former subordinates women, whereas the latter does not. Once we recognize this, a logical puzzle emerges. How, if Mahmood mentions features of the da'wa movement that are not sexist, does she arrive at the claim that feminism is altogether incompatible with tradition, rather than the claim that some traditions are compatible with feminism? The answer, I believe, is by making the same move that Okin makes—by tacitly building patriarchality into her definition of tradition. This comes out most clearly in Mahmood's indictment of the work of Janice Boddy (1989), whom Mahmood sets up as the paradigm of objectionable Western feminist scholarship. Mahmood (2005) writes about Boddy, "When women's actions seem to reinscribe what appear to be 'instruments of their own oppression,' social analysts can point to moments of disruption of, and articulation of points of opposition to, male authority . . . Agency, in this form of analysis, is understood as the capacity to realize one's own interests against the weight of custom, tradition, transcendental will, or other obstacles, individual or collective" (8).

Yet Boddy's explicit argument does not criticize custom or tradition as sweepingly as Mahmood suggests. Boddy describes the healing and spiritual practices of the centuries-old, women-dominated *zar* cult in Sudan. Boddy's explicit claim is that the cult is an arena in which women can assert their value against the background of a sexist dominant ideology. Does this really amount to the view that feminism means value for the rejection of "custom" and "tradition"? Only if opposition to sexism and asserting women's value in spite of it requires flouting, or stepping outside of, tradition. But Boddy seems to show the exact opposite—that some traditions are feminist vehicles, even if they are restricted to certain spaces. After all, the practices of the zar cult are *themselves traditions.* In another example, Mahmood argues that feminists will have difficulty understanding the behavior of a woman named Abir, who tries to get her husband to allow her to develop her personal relationship with God by exhorting him to become a better Muslim. Mahmood (2005) argues that feminists will puzzle over the fact that Abir's exhortation relies on the "perfection" of a religious tradition and occurs within "Islamic norms" (79). Mahmood fails to make clear whether the puzzle originates in the tradition subjugating Abir or its being a tradition at all.

Mahmood concludes from her inquiry that we should perhaps give up on feminism if we want to oppose imperialism. Okin concludes from hers that if we must be called "imperialists," so be it. But for the purposes of our discussion of Enlightenment freedom, what they agree about is more important than what they disagree about. They both attribute a patriarchal valence to tradition. Because of this, they see Enlightenment freedom—or perception of tradition as an impediment, especially when its dictates are internalized—as necessary for feminism.

Moderating the Feminist Relationship to Tradition: Reflexive Distance

If the confluence between feminism and imperialism comes from the idea that feminists should object to views and practices *because they are traditional,* an anti-imperialist feminism will need to conceive the normative commitments of feminism differently. Liberal rehabilitations of communitarianism may seem useful for this re-articulation of the normative commitments of feminism, since they explicitly seek to define freedom in ways that acknowledge that inherited beliefs and practices can add meaning and value to human lives.[17] However, the existence of patriarchal inherited practices has made the tension between communitarianism and feminism more difficult to resolve than that between communitarianism and liberalism.[18]

Reflexive Distance from Traditional Commitments

Liberals who accept communitarianism's social ontology, including many feminist autonomy theorists (see Friedman 2006; Meyers 2000; Christman 2018), have argued that there is inherent value, not in rejecting traditions, but in being able to *ask whether one wants to* reject them. Like Hirsi Ali and Badinter, these contemporary liberals are inspired by Kant's argument that tradition can interfere with the living of a life guided by one's own reasons. Unlike Hirsi Ali and Badinter, these contemporary liberals claim that only certain types of subjective relationships to tradition are incompatible with freedom.[19] Will Kymlicka, who advances one example of such a contemporary liberal view, argues that, although traditions can be important to individuals' flourishing and development of self-respect, individual freedom requires that agents have the ability to reflectively evaluate their relationship to traditions. As he puts it, "People can stand back and assess moral values and traditional ways of life and should be given, not only the liberal right to do so, but also the social conditions which enhance this capacity" (Kymlicka 1995, 92). Kymlicka (1991) sets high standards for what constitutes the attainment of this capacity: "no end or goal should be exempt from possible re-examination" (52).

Kymlicka's view seems at first blush to make room for feminist criticism of traditions without accepting Enlightenment freedom's implausible assumptions about human socialization. In the eyes of Enlightenment freedom's defenders, traditions prevent agents from developing their own views merely by offering guidance that originates outside agents themselves.

For Kymlicka, in contrast, traditions have to do more than just be traditions to discourage autonomy. They must discourage or prevent individuals from being able to reflectively evaluate traditional dictates.

Yet even if Kymlicka's view renders some traditional adherence objectionable, it is unclear that these instances of objectionable traditional adherence are the ones *feminists* should find objectionable. Kymlicka's view suggests that traditional adherence is unfree in any case in which the agent cannot, or refuses to, raise the question of whether she wants to identify with a particular tradition. It thus renders unfree, for instance, a person in a society that values filial duty who is incapable of asking whether she could identify as anything but the child of her parents and the case of a person who cannot countenance the question of whether her religiously forged dietary preferences are appropriate.[20] We may (or may not) find such views about vegetarianism and filial duty objectionable, but it is not obvious that the reasons behind such objections would be *feminist*.

Reflexive Distance from Social Roles

If the value of reflexive distance is going to sort feminist and nonfeminist traditional adherence—not just autonomous and nonautonomous adherence—we need to say more about the *types* of traditions from which people need reflective distance. Seyla Benhabib, another rehabilitator of communitarianism, suggests a potential feminist addendum to Kymlicka's view. Although Benhabib agrees that we need the capacity for reflective distance from all traditional dictates, she also identifies a more specific problem for feminists: communitarians need to "distinguish their emphasis on constitutive communities from an endorsement of social conformism, authoritarianism, and, from the standpoint of women, patriarchalism." She thus suggests that it is particularly important to develop a capacity to criticize social *roles*, or to be capable of asking whether I am separable from what F. H. Bradley refers to as "my station and its duties" (Benhabib 1992, 74). The type of view Benhabib advocates in this passage resonates heavily with Okin's (1999) more moderate comments in "Is Multiculturalism Bad for Women?" Women need to be able to question "our place within our culture," especially "to the extent that our culture is patriarchal" (22).

Can this reflexive role distance view move us beyond the dilemma that pits feminism against anti-imperialist critiques of autonomy and the secular? Recall that the anti-imperialist feminists whose concerns I am trying to accommodate hold that feminists promote imperialism through their inability to apprehend the harms of traditional destruction. Benhabib's view very clearly rejects the idea that the destruction of traditions always benefits women. Instead, what needs to be eradicated are specific traditional forms and dictates—those that prevent people from asking whether they want to identify with traditions and, more specifically, whether they want to accept their traditionally defined roles. Ali and Badinter are committed to a much stronger view—one that takes women to benefit from the eradication of even those traditions that allow the questioning of social roles. Even a chosen "faith" belongs to Ali's "world of faith," and merely being "reminded" that some members of one's religion want women to cover their hair is, for Badinter, an objectionable "riveting to one's roots." Benhabib's view offers a principled reason to reject such views: being exposed to, or being expected to follow, traditions is not itself harmful.

Reflexive Distance as Unaccommodating of Metaphysically Traditionalist Views

However, Benhabib's reflexive role distance would still be found insufficiently accommodating by some transnational feminist critics of autonomy and the secular. Up to this point, I have focused on the fact that Abu-Lughod and Mahmood defend worldviews that find meaning in practices that are inherited and externally dictated. But on a closer look at some of the putatively Islamic practices they want to defend, we notice that many of them have a feature beyond being seen as externally dictated. The practices appear to their adherents as worth doing *because* they are externally dictated. In many of these cases, questioning a given inherited external dictate would prevent the dictate from having its intended effect on the agent. To distinguish them from worldviews that merely *value* traditional adherence, let us call worldviews to which one cannot adhere unless one treats certain dictates as *beyond question* "metaphysically traditionalist."

To be clear, metaphysically traditionalist views do not hold that it is desirable to lead an unreflective life (the da'wa women are highly reflective), but rather that some views that are externally dictated should not be questioned— and that one should orient one's life around them. For an example of metaphysical traditionalism, we can examine the belief of Mahmood's da'wa women that one can only understand the meaning of certain dictates by engaging in them first. One becomes modest *through* veiling. Asking whether one wants to veil, or whether female modesty is the right end, is inconsistent with veiling for the right reason. Veiling for the right reason means beginning from trust in the divine will and desire to surrender to it, so evaluating the practice without identifying with it is impossible. Religious worldviews are not the only metaphysically traditionalist worldviews, but they are particularly good candidates because divine will is readily understood as something one is not in a position to question. Religion is seen by many to require faith precisely because reflection cannot provide reasons for adherence or nonadherence.

Benhabib's reflexive role distance suggests that metaphysically traditionalist worldviews are antifeminist, or at least ones that are metaphysically traditionalist about certain social roles. Consider Mahmood's example of a woman who is socially ostracized because she is unmarried. A woman named Nadia counsels this woman that the virtue of *sabr*, or bearing hardship correctly, means that she should not try to persuade others that her marital status is irrelevant to her social value. For Nadia, the reason one must accept suffering rather than question unjust social conventions is that "divine causality . . . cannot be deciphered by human intelligence" (Mahmood 2005, 172–173). In other words, in cases of disidentification with what are seen as religiously dictated roles, one is supposed to try harder to identify with social roles. Whereas Benhabib would argue that it is important for the woman to be able to decide whether she identifies with a doctrine that attributes lesser status to unmarried women, the da'wa women's worldview says that this is a type of hubris that gets in the way of leading a pious life.

I believe Mahmood is wrong that feminists should respect this particular metaphysically traditionalist view. The idea that unmarried women should believe that they are damaged goods or do not deserve social benefits, unaccompanied by the idea that men should be exposed to similar penalties, is simply incompatible with feminism. But Mahmood may still be pointing out something important—that *some* metaphysically traditionalist acceptance of social roles may be respectworthy. Let us consider another example of a view that is metaphysically traditionalist about a social role—a view that Benhabib's reflexive role distance would have to prescribe rejecting or modifying. Islamic feminists have devoted significant energy to discussing the type of love between husbands and wives dictated by the Qu'ran. For instance, Asma Barlas (2002, 162) argues that part of the Islamically dictated role of a husband involves repudiating sexual violence. It is not difficult to imagine such a conception of husbandhood being plugged into a metaphysically traditionalist view similar to that of the da'wa women. A man may believe that it is not up to him to ask whether he wants to believe sexual violence is wrong, or whether he wants to believe the verses of the Qu'ran that stipulate it are true. Such a man lacks Benhabib's reflexive role distance, but it is not clear that his views are antifeminist.

If I am correct that such a man's views are potentially feminist, two important points about whether reflexive distance offers a helpful anti-imperialist recasting of feminist normative commitments come to light. First, the reflexive role distance view does not pick out the feature of traditionalist views and practices that determines whether they are objectionable *to feminists.* On the reflexive-role-distance view, the content of roles is irrelevant; what matters is a person's ability to raise the question of whether the roles are worth fulfilling. This should be unsurprising; reflexive distance is a conception of autonomy, not a conception of what makes something an appropriate or feminist political goal. Autonomy, at least according to procedural conceptions, is a feature of agents' relationships to views, rather than their content. Relational conceptions of autonomy, though they conceive autonomy differently, cannot on their own explain what makes views and practices feminist, either. They hold that a person's ability to make choices that are genuinely her own depends on certain features of her social context; making feminist views the same as those that promote relational autonomy closes off the possibility that contexts within which women exercise agency can be oppressive.[21] Once we have recognized that the question of whether an agent identifies with a role is distinct from the question of whether that role promotes feminist ends, we can see that reflexive role distance shares an important feature with Enlightenment freedom. Both, when taken to explain what feminists' normative commitments are, identify the *external dictatedness* of practices or views as the feminist problem. The difference between them is the stringency of the requirements for objectionable external dictatedness; for the reflexive distance theorist, certain subjective attitudes toward practices can make them no longer externally dictated.

Second, the possibility of the externally dictated and inherited feminist view in the husband example suggests that the *perceived source* of a view or practice is not what determines its compatibility with feminism. Assuming that patriarchality is a defining feature of traditions, á la Okin and Mahmood, prevents us from apprehending this fact. I now turn to showing how the nonideal universalism I have developed does not locate feminist moral concern in the inheritedness of practices, but rather in their *effects.* My view allows feminist respect for some metaphysically traditionalist worldviews and thus does a better job than reflexive role distance at responding to anti-imperialist concerns. It refuses to suggest that secular or antitraditionalist worldviews are the only ones hospitable to feminism.

From Inherited Sources to Oppressive Effects: Making Conceptual Space for Traditionalist Feminisms

Up to this point, I have relied on our intuitions to determine which practices are objectionable to feminists. However, to see why feminists should worry more about the effects of dictates and practices than about their sources, we need an explicit definition of feminism. As I argued in my defense of nonideal universalism in chapter 1, the early work of bell hooks offers what I hope is a noncontroversial one: feminism is opposition to sexist oppression.[22] According to Marilyn Frye's (1983) now-classic essay, oppression is a social system that subordinates one social group to another. An oppressive practice must have three features: it must target its objects on the basis of social-group membership; it must be part of a system or network of forces that work together to produce similar effects; and one of those effects must be the subordination of the targeted group. So, for example, the expectation that Western women wear high heels is oppressive because it applies only to women; it is one of many expectations that tie women's access to social benefits to their sexual availability to men, and the overall function of this system is to subject women to sexual violence, reduce their ability to participate as equals in public life, and so on.

My analysis of the high-heels example presupposes that freedom from violence and participation in public life are goods to which people deserve access as a matter of justice. As I argued in chapter 1, nonideal universalists believe that the indicators of advantage differ from context to context, so to find out whether sexist oppression is happening in a given case, we need context-specific information about which goods are important.[23] What I am about to say about the relationship between feminism and tradition, however, holds true irrespective of what the goods in human life are, so long as strong Enlightenment freedom is not taken to be one of them (and given Mahmood and Abu-Lughod's suggestions that the value is parochial, and my claim that it is implausible, an argument that Enlightenment freedom should be seen as a universal good in human life is not forthcoming). If it is possible to imagine gender-just social conditions under which human beings are not encouraged to abandon tradition or to stand back and criticize every single inherited belief (or both), Enlightenment freedom is not necessary for feminism.[24]

Conceiving of feminism as opposition to sexist oppression clearly separates the question of whether views and practices are feminist from where they are perceived to come from, and this is where its anti-imperialist feminist potential lies. We know that inherited dictates and practices can have oppressive effects. However, we can also identify oppressive expectations whose force does not stem from historical or religious inheritance. Consider the expectation that North American women shape their genitalia to simulate those in pornography—an expectation that is both oppressive and new. More importantly for responding to imperialism allegations, we can identify views that are nonoppressive or anti-oppressive and yet perceived as externally dictated. Contemporary Muslim feminisms, for whom navigating tradition is often a central concern, suggest that this possibility is not merely theoretical.

According to the nonideal universalist perspective I developed in the first chapter, transnational feminists should reject justice monism, the idea that there is, or that they need a single model of, the gender-just society. Instead, in addition to recognizing that the indicators of advantage and disadvantage vary from context to context, nonideal universalists recognize that the conception of sexist oppression as wrong underdetermines what should happen to reduce oppression in any particular case. Thus, nonideal universalism suggests that looking more closely at "other" women's political strategies can reveal *genuinely feminist* possibilities that would otherwise be difficult for Western feminists to imagine. Many Muslim women organize in contexts in which there is, at the very least, strategic value to framing arguments against patriarchal oppression in religious terms. The incentives to frame feminist arguments in "Islamic" terms are varied and context dependent but are often put in place by some combination of the following: (a) historical or current Western cultural and/or political domination, (b) the widespread belief that acting in accordance with religious dictates is morally obligatory, (c) the presence of religious dictates within existing legal frameworks, and (d) the association of secular feminisms with the upper classes. However, it would be a mistake to suggest that all women advocating feminisms in Islamic terms do so for purely instrumental reasons; many of them would offer first-personal reasons that have to do with deeply held religious convictions (Moghadam 2002).

Barlas's feminist rereading of the role of husbands in the previous section is one example of an Islamic feminist interpretation of tradition—though not an example of Islamic feminist adherence to a metaphysically traditionalist worldview. To illustrate the compatibility of feminism with metaphysically traditionalist worldviews, we can look at contemporary Islamic feminisms. Although there is no agreed-upon use of the term "Islamic feminist," I use it here in Margot Badran's (2009) sense to mean a feminism "that derives its understanding and mandate from the Qu'ran" (242). It is important to note that not all Muslim feminists are Islamic feminists; many are overtly secular or ground their opposition to patriarchy in a variety of sources. Additionally, some Muslim feminists adopt Islamic feminist argumentative strategies without committing themselves to the idea that the Qu'ran is the only or primary source of moral truth. For instance, the Collectif 95 Maghreb Egalité (2005) combines doctrinal arguments against sexist practices, such as child marriage and the expectation of obedience from wives, with human rights and sociological arguments.

Islamic feminists who see the Qu'ran as the ultimate moral truth that cannot be questioned by humans affirm a traditionalist worldview, one that affirms the value of living according to traditional dictates. They take as a point of departure that living consistently with Islam is worth doing. Yet they interpret gender equality as Islamically dictated. Movements with such understandings of Islam have participated in reducing women's oppression. For example, Islamic feminist agitation in Iran advocated for such reforms such respecting unmarried women's rights to study abroad and married women's rights to claim wages for housework in divorce proceedings (Moghadam 2002). Movements that ground opposition to sexism in religious dictates also organize in countries with more secular histories than Iran. Some Egyptian feminists use religious argumentation to argue that women should be able to serve as *muftis*. Turkish Islamist feminists claim that Islamist politicians have failed in their own purported goals by failing to improve women's status (Badran 2001). Some Indonesian feminists oppose polygamy and support increases in the marriage age on theological grounds (Robinson 2006). According to many Islamic feminists, those who believe the Qu'ran accepts sexist oppression are misinterpreting the Qu'ran. Enlightenment-liberal feminists might argue that the fact that such "misinterpretations" are in circulation at all is evidence that tradition is oppressive. But this misses the point of the Islamic feminist moral epistemology. Islamic feminists are not inventing new traditions; they see themselves as returning to the true meaning of their inheritance. Further, some Islamic feminists see the authority to reinterpret the Qu'ran as issuing from *within* Muslim traditions (Moghadam 2002, 1144). The right to *ijtehad,* or independent reasoning about religious texts, was historically well-established in Islamic jurisprudence.

I do not focus on Islamic feminism to suggest that it is the only legitimate feminist approach for Muslim women. Nonideal universalism, with its emphasis on context specificity and the (nonidentical) roles imperial legacies play in shaping contemporary contexts, must acknowledge that Muslim women face different contextual challenges, have different priorities, and hold different metaphysical commitments.[25] Islamic feminisms are just especially relevant to the question of whether one can value traditional adherence and be a feminist; they demonstrate the possibility of worldviews that are simultaneously feminist and grounded in submission to certain inherited external dictates.[26]

But if my oppressive effects view is going to be more helpful than reflexive role distance in respecting traditionalist worldviews, we need to know whether it is possible to oppose sexist oppression from within worldviews that are *metaphysically* traditionalist—that hold that some traditional dictates to be beyond question. Mahmood's da'wa women are clearly not feminists, but is it possible to reject sexist oppression from a worldview like theirs, one that values unquestioning submission to certain inherited dictates? Many existing Islamic feminists do not accept the *metaphysical* version of traditionalism. For instance, Mohsen Sa'idzadeh states, in an interview with Ziba Mir-Hosseini (1999), that he opposes "unquestioning obedience" and that "humans have the capacity to understand the reasons for God's commands" (256).

However, some Islamic feminists insist that it is in principle unacceptable for believers to question the truth of the Qu'ran or other divine dictates. For instance, Amina Wadud (2006) writes in her early work, "As believers in the faith and tradition of Islam, we cannot rewrite the Qu'ran . . . As an historical record of the word of Allah revealed to Mohammed, those words are unchangeable" (204).[27] Wadud defines the word "believer" so that the identity of believer precedes questioning and restricts the types of questions one is allowed to ask. Whereas Sa'idzadeh suggests it would be possible to come to a reason to accept divine dictates without antecedent faith, Wadud suggests no such thing. Yet the metaphysical traditionalism of Wadud's view grounds rather than undermines her opposition to sexist oppression. Those who believe that Islam is fundamentally patriarchal, in her view, not only misinterpret the Qu'ran; they are guilty of instrumentalizing divine dictates for human power struggles. Wadud (2006) argues that the metaphysical traditionalism of her feminism is actually a moral advantage; human reason is fallible and excessive reliance on it will actually get in the way of feminist causes. "I chose the literary tradition of Qu'ranic exegesis . . . to sustain my faith by equipping me with the tools to determine how the master's house has been constructed, without limiting the sacred potential to human tools" (81).

Wadud's underlying stance toward tradition is strikingly similar to that of Mahmood's da'wa women. This is especially clear when we return to Mahmood's (2005, 174–177) story of Abir. Abir is married to a "Westernized" man who drinks and expects her to entertain male houseguests. To prevent her religiosity from impeding his lifestyle, he tells her that she is flouting her Islamic wifely duties by focusing more on the women's mosque movement than on him. Her response is to exhort him to be a better Muslim, often praying loudly in front of him for the fate of his soul. The parallels between Wadud's relationship to tradition and Abir's are triple. First, both assume that certain Islamic dictates are beyond question and worth following; they exhort others to change based on the idea that they share this assumption. Second, Abir and Wadud both see religious dictates as offering a normative standard that allows human practices to be judged, rather than vice versa. Third, they suggest that the views and practices they find objectionable are objectionable because those who engage in them have failed to successfully submit to the divine will.

The parallel between Wadud and Abir makes clear that acceptance of sexism does not directly track attitudes toward tradition. What makes Wadud a feminist and Abir not, I contend, is the type of social relations each takes to be divinely dictated. In other words, feminism (or sexism, as the case may be) pertains to the *content of their tradition* (as they understand it) rather than to their attitudes toward it or understanding of the source of its normative authority. Feminism is a stance about the normatively acceptable effects of social practices rather than their perceived origins, and once this becomes clear, traditionalist feminisms are no longer a contradiction in terms.

Conclusion: Feminism without Enlightenment Freedom

Feminism does have genuine normative requirements, but contra those who would ground feminism in Enlightenment freedom, hostility to tradition *because it is tradition* is not among them. Feminism does not require the view that traditions are patriarchal (as Okin and Mahmood inadvertently suggest), the belief that people must reject all inherited external dictates (as Hirsi Ali and Badinter suggest), or even the belief that they must *question* all of them or the roles those dictates assign (as Kymlicka and Benhabib do). Feminism does require reshaping a subset of traditional dictates and practices—but because of their sexist effects, not their perceived source. Feminism is thus compatible with worldviews that place a high value on acting on inherited external dictates, including some that are metaphysically traditionalist.

Enlightenment liberal feminists must acknowledge that their reasons for wanting to *spread* Enlightenment freedom do not originate in feminism alone.[28] Their support for Enlightenment freedom seems instead to originate in adherence to an ethnocentric justice monist view, according to which the cultural forms they associate with the contemporary West are imagined as the only ones that can support gender justice. But as Collectif 95 Maghreb

Egalité (1993) argues, "universality does not in any way signify Western monopoly" on the concept of gender justice (10). Feminist concerns militate against sexist oppression, but not in favor of exporting any specific understanding of where human beings should find meaning. Given concerns about the effectiveness of making change in neo-/postcolonial contexts and the history of cultural domination, Western feminists need to recognize that being attentive to the harms of traditional destruction is not the same thing as abandoning feminism. Feminism, though it requires a stance about sexist oppression, does not require a stance about the appropriate human orientation to tradition. Feminism can be thought of as what Rawls (1996) would have called a "freestanding" doctrine—capable of being defended from within a variety of different understandings of the ultimate ends of human life. As Badran (2009) puts a similar point, feminism can be a "plant that grows only in its own soil" (243).

As I discussed in the first chapter, Abu-Lughod (2002, 788) encapsulates her objection to "saving" Muslim women by noting that it involves, not just saving them *from* something, but saving them *to* something. For her, the attitude of saving demands rescuing someone from one (inferior, traditional, religious) lifeworld and transporting them to a (superior, modern, secular) one. One of my broad points in this book is that feminist normative judgment does not require the view Abu-Lughod associates with saving—the view that there is a single correct feminist endpoint (typified by the trappings of Western "modernity") at which all societies must arrive. In a world characterized by imperialist domination, the demand that "others" abandon their entire worldviews and adopt those of Westerners cannot be presumed innocent. Sweeping judgments about the sexist valences of the traditions of "others" end up aligning feminism with cultural domination, economic exploitation, and imperialism. Feminists need to criticize sexist oppression without trading in a discourse about destroying and replacing lifeworlds or bringing "others" out of the bonds of tradition into the light. We need a feminism that, as Allison Weir (2013) puts it, addresses "the reality that we are all embedded in and attached to specific cultural identities, within which we value different ways of flourishing; and they must confront the possibility that feminism itself may be wedded to particular cultural identities" (2). Mahmood (2005) rightly ends her book with a wish for a feminist "vision of coexistence that does not require making the lifeworlds of others extinct or provisional" (199). Untethering feminism from Enlightenment freedom makes it possible to oppose sexist oppression without surrendering that hope.

4 GENDER-ROLE ELIMINATIVISM

COMPLEMENTARIAN CHALLENGES TO FEMINISM

Many women, and women's movements, embrace worldviews according to which men and women should occupy different social roles.[1] These worldviews are often cast as alternatives to Western feminism, a doctrine whose dominant strand insists that gender is morally irrelevant, and whose exponents have supported harmful and ineffective interventions in "other" women's lives. Can complementarian worldviews furnish feminist ideals? What roles can they play in transnational feminist praxis? The answers to these questions are not straightforward. For one thing, claims about difference are often used to justify sexist oppression, and suspicion of complementarianism on these grounds is not unique to feminists in the North and West. As Aymara feminist Julia Paredes (2006) writes of the same chachawarmi[2] ideal Lugones celebrates in her well-known article on decolonial feminism, "The woman cooks and the man eats—what lovely complementarity" (quoted in Maclean 2014, 79).[3] Moreover, the demands of transnational feminist praxis suggest that the relevant questions are not merely conceptual. According to a nonideal universalist perspective concerned with justice-enhancement, those engaged in transnational feminist praxis need to know, not just whether complementarian doctrines are compatible with feminism, but also what allegiances women have to them and what roles they play in women's lives.

This chapter and the next take on questions about whether transnational feminist praxis requires gender-role eliminativist commitments.[4] I argue in this one that a particular type of complementarianism I call "headship complementarianism" cannot furnish feminist ideals, but that concerns about women's well-being and the demands of political praxis weigh against flatly dismissing political strategies based in it. I make this argument largely by responding to claims that headship-complementarian societies provide women with agency and offer men role-based reasons to promote women's well-being, and by showing that, in spite of this, headship-complementarian views cannot generate certain moral judgments that feminist views should be able to generate. Such views cannot explain why patriarchal risk and the devaluation of women's labor (which I here refer to as intrahousehold-inequality-supportive norms and practices) are wrong. I consider two defenses of headship complementarianism, one from Usha Menon's work on high-caste Oriya women and one from the Jamaat-e-Islami women activists in Pakistan described in Amina Jamal's work, and show how these defenses fall short of being feminist or showing that headship complementarianism offers feminist ideals. Feminism requires a critique of sexist oppression, and not just the beliefs that individual women matter and should be able to pursue their interests within oppressive social arrangements.

Unfortunately, headship-complementarian views can only generate concern about the latter two. Because headship-complementarian worldviews treat asymmetrical vulnerability between men and women as a good thing, they suggest that gender-oppressive arrangements are ideal. Nevertheless, movements based in headship complementarianism may, in limited ways, contribute to feminist goals without themselves offering ideals of gender justice. Though they cannot proclaim the value of a world free of sexist oppression, they can offer arguments for increasing women's basic well-being under conditions where it is not available and by increasing women's aspirations and political voice.

Before proceeding to the argument, it is worth recapitulating the nonideal universalist vision that guides it and this book. As I argued in the first chapter, nonideal universalism combines a view about what the normative core of feminism is with a view about what the aims of transnational feminist theorizing are. The normative core of feminism is opposition to sexist oppression. Sexist oppression is present when social structures systematically disadvantage members of some gender(s) in relation to others (see Frye 1983). Opposition to sexist oppression does not imply any culturally particular view about which goods and powers constitute advantage and disadvantage in different societies. Though nonideal universalism does suggest that there are some universally important goods (see chapter 1), it does not hold that feminism requires adopting any specific cultural form, or any specific set of indices of advantage and disadvantage. To offer a simple example, food and social recognition are universally important goods, but whether having land to farm is the best way to access these goods is context dependent. My nonideal universalist conception of the goals of transnational feminist theory also takes the central task to be developing theories and concepts that enhance justice in an unjust world. This focus on justice enhancement allows nonideal universalists to avoid articulating a culturally specific endpoint of gender justice and to take questions about what will produce effective and meaningful political strategies as morally relevant.

The Anti-imperialist Case for Complementarian Feminisms

Given that some Western feminists are complementarians and many non-Western feminists are not,[5] and given that gender-role eliminativism has been used to many genuinely feminist ends, the connection between eliminativism and imperialism may need some motivating. Readers who are already familiar with the fact that noncomplementarian understandings of gender are often understood as a harmful Western imposition can feel free to skip this section. We can begin to motivate the connection by noting that imperialist projects have often assumed Western gender regimes would emancipate women. The most radical decolonial critics claim that gender was absent in many societies prior to colonization (Lugones 2010; Oyewumi 1997).[6] Others make the more modest claim that attempts to replace local gender regimes with Western ones often worsened the lives of women victims of colonialism. For example, feminized roles in some sub-Saharan African contexts had distinct forms of political power built into them (Nzegwu 2006; Amadiume 1998). Europeans introduced the idea that men and women occupy different spheres, and that the masculine public sphere was a source of power (Mikell 1997). British objections to "heavy labor done by African women" in agriculture also promoted the colonial relegation of some classes of women to domestic roles, seclusion in the home, and inferior access to education (see Akyeampong and Fofack 2014, 55). A similar point has been made about indigenous women in North America; settlers negotiating treaties only with men and instituting their conceptions of land rights meant that women's abilities to influence the conditions of their lives decreased (Lawrence 2013).

Western regimes of gender also seem to have played justificatory roles, not only in perpetuating or instituting sexist oppression, but also in simply causing harm to women. British colonial fascination with the harem fomented support for British colonial rule of North Africa and South Asia (see Grewal 1996). Income-generation projects for women in the Andes that focus on bringing women into male-gendered activities have not merely increased their labor burdens in ways that decrease their access to health, sleep, and leisure time; they seem to have diverted attention from women's traditional environmental land-management tasks, and this in turn promotes environmental degradation, which in turn affects the entire community, including women (Paulson 2016, 125).

Some of these interventions, such as preventing African women from receiving educations, were undoubtedly motivated by Western forms of *complementarianism* rather than eliminativism. But is worth noting that gender eliminativism can promote Western feminist complicity in imperialism today without having been its original cause. Given that eliminativism, not complementarianism, is the dominant strand in contemporary Western feminist thought, we can expect Western feminists to sometimes see exporting it as the solution to "other" women's oppression, irrespective of the origins of that oppression. Some contemporary Northern and Western interventions that have questionable effects on women's lives seem to be the product of gender eliminativist commitments—or at least worldviews that do not recognize the value created by tasks associated with culturally specific feminine roles. The example of women's environmental roles in the Andes is a case in point.

There are also reasons to worry that gender eliminativism might play a constitutive role in imperialism.[7] Many indigenous and Southern women's movements[8] emphasize gender difference and complementarity, and some worry explicitly that gender eliminativism is part of a regime of cultural domination. Some African women accept "symbolic gender distinctions and identities that incorporate naturist assumptions about 'femaleness' and 'maleness,' but nevertheless challenge the subordination of women as an accompanying feature of these cultural constructs" (Mikell 1997, 7). Some indigenous feminists describe men's domination as an example of failure to acknowledge complementarity rather than failure to acknowledge similarity (Lugones 2010, 743). "The philosophical principles that I would recover from my culture [to support feminism] are equality, complementarity between men and women, and between men and men and women and women," says Alma Lopez, a Quiche indigenous woman in Guatemala (quoted in Castillo 2010, 539). Concerns about colonialism arise in discussions of "other" women's conceptions of gender, not merely because of cultural differences in gender regimes, but also because the idea that "other" women's gender roles are oppressive has participated in motivating imperialist interventions.

To say that gender eliminativism has played justificatory and constitutive roles in imperialism is not yet to say anything about whether it has reduced or will reduce sexist oppression. Of course colonialism impacts women. Yet it remains conceptually possible for a gender regime to institute cultural domination and simultaneously improve the status of women relative to men. There are nonetheless good reasons for Western feminists to avoid assuming out of hand that gender eliminativism is the single solution to gender inequality. First, even if gender eliminativism or Western gender regimes had the potential to improve gender justice, it would not follow that they ought to be instituted. As I have argued throughout this book, the fact that any particular strategy is likely to reduce gender injustice is not enough reason to adopt it; given that there are likely many strategies for reducing it, questions about how the strategy fits with existing forms of life, how effective it is likely to be, what sacrifices it asks women to make, and how it accords with other values come into play.[9]

Second, many common Western feminist arguments against considering the feminist potential of noneliminativist gender regimes are flawed. It is sometimes argued that defenses of other regimes romanticize precolonial gender relations.[10] But not all defenses of complementarianism do this. As I argue in the next chapter, many defenders of anti-imperialist complementarianisms explicitly claim that they are creatively reinterpreting their traditions or trying to improve on current ones, not returning to some perfect past state. It is also often objected that seeing any complementarian roles as nonoppressive requires denying that the women who inhabit them face gender oppression. This, too, is an unnecessary inference. One reason is that cultural roles are not the only potential sources of sexist oppression, and structural conditions can transform the effects of cultural roles. For example, Kyle Whyte (2013) argues that environmental degradation adds new costs and time demands to North American indigenous women's traditionally prescribed labor. A final objection is that complementarianisms are necessarily harmful because the roles they prescribe are rigid and harmful to gender nonconforming people. Again, though they may do this, they need not. It is frequently argued that some non-Western complementarian societies allow multiple gender groupings and a high degree of movement between or among groupings (see Smith 2010; Amadiume 1998). Such facile objections to complementarianism seem to reflect missionary feminist commitments to the idealizations of history and Western culture I described in chapter 1 rather than a serious examination of actual complementarianisms.

Defenses of Household Headship Complementarianism

This chapter addresses the limitations of one type of complementarianism, what I call "household headship complementarianism," or "headship complementarianism" for short. Complementarian views in general hold that the functioning of society or the cosmos, as well as the well-being of individuals, depends on distinct masculine and feminine roles being fulfilled by the people appropriate to them. They irreducibly include the normative claim that it is good *for* certain people to fulfill certain roles. The term "complementarianism" is sometimes invoked to claim that a given conception of gender roles that is criticized for being unjust or harmful is actually beneficial. This has led some feminists working within traditions that some define as complementarian to claim that the term "complementarian" is a sexist term of art.[11] My use of the term, however, is intended to be neutral about sexism; complementarianism on its own does not entail sexist oppression. My ultimate view will be that some complementarianisms will probably turn out to be capable of becoming feminist ideals while others will not.

Complementarian views can differ in many ways, but three types of variation are particularly important for the argument of this chapter. First, they can differ about whether persons matter in their own right or only insofar as they are useful to others. I will assume here that all complementarianisms that might reasonably count as feminist hold that individual people have value beyond their usefulness to others. Second, complementarianisms differ about whether the basic needs of each gender are different. The complementarianisms I consider here treat men and women as possessed of the same basic human needs, even if what is important to their well-being differs above a basic-needs threshold.[12] Third, complementarian views differ about the content of the prescribed gender roles; they may differ over which tasks are gendered or how tasks should be divided among genders.

Headship complementarianisms, the ones I am interested in here, define the feminine role around specialization in household labor and dependency on, and deference to, men; they define the masculine role around preferential and direct access to goods that are necessary for survival. In other words, they build asymmetrical vulnerability into the roles.[13] This role differentiation is typically justified with claims about how women's one-way dependency on men enhances women's own well-being,[14] as in familiar claims that women need men to be their providers or protectors. Headship complementarianisms exist in traditions inside and outside of the West. Complementarians who believe that the appropriate gendering of responsibilities does not track the household/public divide do not count as headship complementarians.[15]

Arguments that headship complementarianisms can be feminist usually point to the fact that the doctrines value individual women's well-being. Usha Menon (2012) offers one such defense of a headship-complementarian doctrine, claiming that fulfilling its roles gives women agency and self-esteem. Based on an understanding of "multicultural feminism" as commitment to recognizing sources of meaning "other" women find in their lived worlds, Menon argues that high-caste Oriya Hindu women in India gain power and self-worth by fulfilling headship-complementarian roles. A number of asymmetrical vulnerabilities are built into these roles: women are cut off from their natal households; men alone can earn income (though household spending is decided upon by older women); and women live in seclusion while men have more freedom to move from place to place (Menon and Schweder 2001).[16] According to Menon (2000), the women gain self-worth from their religious metaphysics, which, instead of completely devaluing the feminine, suggests that women are as important in reproductive processes as men, valorizes the household, and includes myths in which men depend on women for their self-realization (84–85). Additionally, according to Menon, cultivating the virtues associated with femininity, including those of chastity and self-denial, gives them a sense of personal accomplishment (87).[17]

A second defense of headship complementarianism contends that it ensures women's well-being, not directly by promoting agency and self-esteem, but indirectly by prescribing guardianship duties to men. The Jamaat-e-Islami women described in Amina Jamal's (2013) ethnography advance this view. The Jamaat-e-Islami is a long-standing political party in Pakistan whose goal is to reform society in accordance with Islamic principles. It frames this agenda partly in terms of rejecting Westernization. Jamal argues that because the Jamaat women operate in a public space in which women's rights talk is common and incentivized, they frame their vision of complementarianism as doing a better job of securing women's well-being than feminist agendas do. The Jamaat-e-Islami women are in favor of women's political participation and oppose violence against women, but they argue that the way to avoid it is "not economic independence but rather economic protection" (Jamal 2013, 193). Women's optimal position is specialization in household labor, with a male provider who is also a "manager" with "some level of priority" in decision-making (Jamal 2013, 201); violence against women is largely a result of men's failure to fulfill the moral demands of this role. The Jamaat women recognize the existence of some cases where male guardianship is unavailable, as in the case of widows, and argue that in such cases women should not be prevented from earning a living. They explicitly reject feminism, arguing that the notion of women's equality is a colonial imposition that is hostile to the family (Jamal 2013, 176–177). They see class oppression as the true moral concern and think feminism is unnecessary.[18]

A Feminist Desideratum: Criticizing Patriarchal Risk and the Devaluation of Women's Labor

To show that the above-mentioned defenses of headship complementarianism are not enough to make such views feminist, I argue that neither defense goes far enough in showing what is wrong with a set of norms and practices that are intuitively objectionable to feminists and whose objectionable quality has achieved a strong transnational consensus. My hope is that this argumentative strategy will allow us to identify problems with headship complementarianism from premises that are relatively noncontroversial to feminists. The set of norms and practices I focus on here, which I think most feminists will find objectionable, I call "intrahousehold-inequality-supportive norms and practices" (IISNPs). There is currently a strong transnational feminist consensus on the wrongness of intrahousehold inequality. Intrahousehold inequality is unequal resource allocation within households. It rose to prominence as an issue in development studies when it became clear that household-level data omitted important deprivations women faced (see also Iverson [2003]; Sen [1990]; Papanek [1990]). Women and girls tended to receive lesser benefits from household income, and resources such as nourishing food tended to be disproportionately allocated to men. The human rights and development communities use research and advocacy methodologies that treat intrahousheold inequality as a problem, and the class of practices and norms objected to under that classification has broadened beyond unequal resource allocation within households.[19] Discussions of intrahousehold inequality now include, but are not limited to, allocation of superior nutrition to males, disproportionate spending on men, women's dependency on male patronage for access to basic goods, men's seizure of women's earnings, male-dominated household decision-making, and cultural views that devalue women's labor.

IISNPs are widespread beliefs and practices that contribute to women's accessing lesser shares of household goods. The two I focus on here are high levels of patriarchal risk and practices that invisibilize and devalue feminized labor. "Patriarchal risk" refers to situations wherein women face risks to their social status and, consequently, risks to their access to many basic goods if they do not have the patronage of a man (Cain, Khanam, and Nahar 1979; Kabeer 2011). The greater the risks to a woman's well-being absent male patronage, the greater the level of patriarchal risk. By practices that invisibilize and devalue household labor, I mean linguistic and evaluative practices, as well as practices of organizing roles and social space that cause men to (a) be unaware of the amount of feminized labor that needs to be practiced for the maintenance of their societies or (b) assume that the labor is not labor (including by not rewarding the labor).

I have said that what is objectionable about patriarchal risk and the devaluation of women's labor is intuitive and widely agreed on, especially by feminists. But for those for whom the objectionable quality of these IISNPs needs motivating: nonideal universalist feminist normative concepts I have developed here support the intuition that they are wrong. Recall that oppression is the systematic disadvantaging of one social group relative to another (Frye 1983) and that feminism is opposition to sexist oppression. Patriarchal risk meets the criterion, first by tracking social-group membership: women bear the risk and men do not. The normative significance of the risk, helpfully theorized by Okin (1991) in contexts in the global North, involves vulnerability to poverty and abuse. In societies in which income is a primary source of access to goods constitutive of well-being and advantage, dependency on another person for access to income not only enables the dependent person to receive lesser income (and the goods attached to it) at that person's will, it also creates disincentives for the dependent person to seek freedom from violence, the ability to do what she wishes with her time, and so on, because of the potential threat of losing access to income and the goods attached to it. Bina Agarwal (1997a) frames a similar insight with reference to women's access to goods within households: what a women will be able to demand in a family where patriarchal risk is high depends heavily on whether she has a credible ability to exit.[20] Put simply, in societies with high levels of patriarchal risk, women's bargaining power and their ability to subsist on their own is low, and this causes women to have lesser access to goods like food, the ability to have discretion over their time use, and freedom from violence.

The devaluation of household labor also leads to systematic disadvantage for women. A key reason is that in contexts where cash is a source of access to other goods through income, those who specialize in labor that is paid have advantages. (When those doing unpaid labor access income through relationships, concerns about patriarchal risk are triggered.) Other reasons are more directly tied to the labor itself. If a person's labor is unrewarded, the costs of the labor on health, discretion over time use, and leisure go un-compensated for; and if the labor is gendered, women as a group suffer lower access to these goods. The content of feminized labor, under circumstances in which it is devalued, also often directly transfers advantages to men. A number of feminists have argued that the formal economy is effectively subsidized by women's nonmarket activities. For example, the tasks of pro-viding care for people in periods of dependency and of preparing food are essential to the sustenance and (literal and figurative) reproduction of the paid labor force (Kittay 1999; Schutte 2003; Beneria and Sen 1981; Waring 1988; Folbre 2001). More to the point, benefits like cooking and care con-tribute directly to men's income-generating capacity and protect men from labor burdens that would inhibit their ability to earn income, participate in political life, and so on.[21]

Can the Wrongness of IISNPs Be Explained in a Headship- Complementarianism-Compatible Way with Reference to Agency or Self-Esteem?

If I am right that feminists should reject the devaluation of women's labor and high levels of patriarchal risk, then any doctrine capable of constituting a feminist ideal must have resources for showing that these IISNPs are wrong. Menon argues that headship complementarianism fosters individual women's agency and self-esteem. If headship complementarians value women's agency and self-esteem, perhaps the path to headship-complementarian feminisms is to show that patriarchal risk and the devaluation of women's labor com-promise them. Unfortunately for headship complementarians, however, an argument that IISNPs get in the way of agency and self-esteem is not forth-coming, or so I will show.

How might one argue that patriarchal risk and the devaluation of women's labor interfere with women's agency? That depends on what we mean by agency, and whether our conception of agency is value neutral. A well-known value-*laden* conception appears in Amartya Sen's (1999), "Women's Agency and Social Change." Instead of offering an explicit definition of agency, Sen contrasts agency with welfare. He seems to have in mind a distinction be-tween women as objects of change initiated by others and women as subjects of self-initiated change. Yet his examples suggest more than this; they import normative content into what counts as agency.[22] All of Sen's (1999) examples of increased agency, except for his description of child-rearing as an "agency role" (196), involve women adopting traditionally male-gendered tasks.[23]

Women become agents, according to Sen, through increased awareness of alternatives to traditional family arrangements (192), economic productivity, land ownership, and political participation.

Patriarchal risk and the devaluation of women's labor undoubtedly interfere with women's agency on this value-laden definition of agency, but reductions in this type of agency cannot register as a harm in the eyes of headship complementarians. Women's ability to be economically productive is undermined by the devaluation of women's labor, and both economic productivity and land ownership are genuinely undermined by patriarchal risk. The problem is that headship complementarians reject the values with which this conception of agency is laden. The value-laden conception of agency assumes that that women's lack of land ownership, access to their own incomes, and so on, are bad things. Headship complementarians, in contrast, think these things are good, and more precisely good *for* women.

Perhaps a value-neutral definition of agency can yield the conclusion that IISNPs are wrong in a way that is more compatible with complementarianism. On a value-neutral conception, agency is the ability to pursue what one values and affect the world consistently with one's own values. A value-neutral account avoids the risk of being laden with values that headship complementarians reject. Unfortunately for the project of imagining a headship-complementarianism-compatible objection to IISNPs, however, a value-neutral conception of agency cannot yield the conclusion that IISNPs are bad. Here is why: women can embrace the ideas that their labor is worth less than men's and that women must depend on men for access to basic social goods. In a social context where the devaluation of women's labor and patriarchal risk are prevalent, women can advance their ends, and even their own well-being, by internalizing and acting in ways that support these IISNPs.

I have argued elsewhere (Khader 2014) that women can achieve high levels of value-neutral agency by accepting norms and practices that undermine gender justice. Women can develop adaptive preferences whereby they accept or perpetuate practices that subordinate them (Bartky 1990; Sen 1990; Nussbaum 2001; Kabeer 1999; Khader 2011; Papanek 1990; Nagar and Raju 2003), including IISNPs. Some preferences to participate in such practices are motivated only by prudential or strategic reasons.[24] For example, Agarwal (1997b) argues that women living under conditions of patriarchal risk accept lesser shares of food, not because they endorse the view that they deserve less food or endorse patriarchal risk itself, but rather because it is a well-being-maximizing strategy to retain their male relatives' favor. Women adherents of headship complementarianism are especially likely to find higher-order, moral reasons to support IISNPs, however. Menon's cases seem to provide concrete examples of this. The Oriya women see themselves as especially morally worthy when they practice self-sacrifice, purity, and chastity. Some of these norms are intertwined with patriarchal risk and the devaluation of women's labor; not earning and income and living in seclusion are valorized as expressions of these values. Though I am sure that for many women the internalization of such beliefs is partial, I see no reason to doubt that some women really believe self-sacrifice is morally required—and thus exercise value-neutral agency by subordinating themselves. Moreover, it is highly plausible that they are able to influence their social worlds (and even gain some level of objective well-being) by coming to believe patriarchal risk and the devaluation of women's labor are good things. After all, the Oriya women receive social recognition for exercising the values of "good" women and wives, and it is probably most effective for them to advocate for the meeting of their own needs in terms of what they need to meet the demands of socially shared standards of femininity. Thus, instead of turning up the conclusion that patriarchal risk and the devaluation of women's labor are wrong, concern with value-neutral agency seems to produce the conclusion that IISNPs can be good, as long as women believe in them and make participating in them a condition of social recognition. In fact, it seems that in some cases, the most value-neutral agency-maximizing thing for women to do is to internalize the norms behind IISNPs and effectively comply with them to gain the rewards that accrue to "good" women.

It may be objected either that self-subordination cannot be a person's own goal (i.e., genuinely autonomous or agentic) or that accepting IISNPs undermines agency instrumentally by decreasing women's ability to do other things they value. To the first objection, I reply that most theories of what it means to take a goal as one's own are procedural. A goal becomes one's own through certain reflective processes, not through the adoption of specific values. Some conceptions of autonomy, particularly those developed by feminist theorists, hold that a person cannot actually endorse subservience (MacKenzie 2008; Stoljar 2000). However, John Christman (2003), Marilyn Friedman (2006), Meyers (2000), and I (Khader 2011) have all argued, such conceptions of autonomy saturate autonomy with controversial views about the importance of independence from others. They thus seem to draw on values that headship complementarians reject in the same way value-laden conceptions of agency do. To the second objection (about women's ability to achieve other values), I point out that the likelihood that internalizing one's oppression or complying with oppressive norms interferes with one's ability to achieve other ends depends heavily on context. Some social structures, especially ones characterized by high levels of patriarchal risk, make accepting inequality a welfare-maximizing strategy. Agarwal's claim about women needing the favor of male relatives is a case in point. The point seems extensible to the Jamaat women (or at least women living according to their prescriptions) and the Oriya women (though currying favor with old women who make household decisions is also strategic for them).

But perhaps we can find a headship-complementarianism-compatible objection to IINSPs by claiming that they reduce self-esteem rather than agency. As Rawls (1971) observes in defending the idea that (the social basis of) self-respect is a primary good, it is difficult to pursue any plan of life if one does not believe oneself or one's projects to be of value—or if one thinks one will be incapable of pursuing them effectively. Self-esteem would seem to be a motivational prerequisite for both complementarian and noncomplementarian lives. We thus may be able to argue that IISNPs reduce headship-complementarian women's self-esteem in ways that prevent them from pursuing their complementarian ends. Unfortunately, it is difficult to find a reason that IISNPs reduce women's beliefs that their projects are of value, unless they already value projects that headship complementarians would morally condemn. The argument that treating one's well-being as less important than that of others definitionally means denying one's own status as a person is well-known (Superson 2005; Hill 1995), but such a position is not available to complementarians, who likely think that maternal self-sacrifice is morally desirable and that self-sacrifice need not involve the involuntary surrender of one's own needs.

Alternatively, we may say that headship complementarianism itself, because it claims that women are ill-suited for certain tasks, causes women to feel shame about their own perceived inferiority. But this ignores two facts. First, as both Menon's and the Jamaat-e-Islami women's defenses show, many headship complementarianisms officially send the message, not that women are inferior, but rather that they are different—or even, as I say in the next paragraph, morally superior. Second, even if we accept for the sake of argument that complementarianism sends women messages of inferiority, it is unclear that this would result in individual women feeling shame. Inferiority might attach to all women by birth, and individual woman need not blame themselves for this.

But does being subject to IISNPs not require felt humiliation? Though I believe it often does, we should not ignore what Papanek (1990) calls the "compulsory emotions" and "compensatory beliefs" involved in inegalitarian socialization. Many, if not most, patriarchal societies characterize submission as a *discipline*—a skill that can be perfected, and whose perfection is often rewarded. Papanek (1990) argues that in some cultures, women learn that they need to eat less because of women's ostensibly morally superior ability to control their appetites.[25] The notion that self-abnegation can cause self-esteem if it is cultivated as a discipline actually seems to be one of Menon's main points; ideas about the superiority of the household to the public and the value of self-denial help women feel that their participation in IISNPs is valuable. This seems true enough (and I will say more about why feminists should care about self-esteem gained from objectionable practices in the final section of the chapter), but it cannot provide support for the intuition that something is wrong with the devaluation of feminized labor and patriarchal risk. Unless we are willing to abandon the view that these IISNPs are bad, we will have to reject the idea that a headship-complementarian view's ability to secure some level of individual agency for women is enough for it to count as a feminist ideal.

Can the Wrongness of IISNPs Be Explained with Reference to Men's Duties of Guardianship?

A second type of argument that might offer headship-complementarianism-compatible objections to IISNPs is role based. Headship complementarians believe it is part of men's role to promote women's well-being; perhaps it can be argued that patriarchal risk and the devaluation of women's labor get in the way of men's abilities to discharge this role. The Jamaat-e-Islami women draw on such a role-based argument to diagnose the problem of violence against women; they understand men who perpetrate such violence to be failing at fulfilling the religiously dictated duties of husbands. Though I find this argumentative strategy more fruitful than the agency strategy I described in the preceding section, it does not go far enough in explaining what is wrong with IISNPs. It furnishes arguments only against *severe* patriarchal risk, and only against *some* of the harms caused by the devaluation of women's labor.

An application of the role-based argument to patriarchal risk could begin by drawing attention to the incentives it creates. Unchecked power increases the likelihood that people will act selfishly. Conditions under which anyone has sole access to a good, and their authority about how to allocate it cannot be challenged, encourage action that is self-enriching at the expense of others. By definition, very patriarchally risky conditions confront men with few penalties for engaging in self-enriching acts that cause women to be deprived of goods such as food, income, and leisure time. Though headship complementarians support moral injunctions against depriving women, women who are under extreme patriarchal risk cannot enforce these injunctions against the men in their lives. This situation of severe patriarchal risk means that men's bargaining position is strong and women's is weak; men can exit with relative ease if they are harmed, and women cannot. The inequality of fallback positions likely both ups men's perception of what they deserve and discourages women from asking for (or even adequately perceiving) what they need (Sen 1999a).

Headship complementarians might draw on these facts to claim that reducing patriarchal risk will encourage men to better discharge their duties to promote women's well-being. The argument might be that increased bargaining power and exit options for women, and legal penalties on men, discourage men's abuse of otherwise legitimate power. Naila Kabeer's work on South Asian women shows that some women's groups in highly patriarchally risky societies draw on the arguments of this sort. Kabeer shows that women in Bangladesh deploy newfound abilities to enforce men's complementarian roles to publicly shame men for allowing selfishness to interfere with their duties to protect women. For example, Kabeer recounts the response of women activists in rural Bangladesh to a man who repudiates his wife in a fit of anger. The women generally oppose divorce. But now that they (after an NGO intervention) know that verbal divorce is not legal, they use his decision's lack of legal sanctioning to show the community that he is a bad guardian and persuade him to take her back (Kabeer 2011, 520). In another strategy in the same community, women activists persuade a man's family to allow him to marry a woman he previously attempted to elope with. They argue that men who promise marriage must follow through, and that they ruin women's honor when they do not (521). In both cases, activists argue that women's utter dependence on men, coupled with (and embodied by) lack of regulation, encourages men to violate their duties to secure women's well-being. In other words, women's well-being becomes precarious when men have the power to act as they will without facing the possibility of penalty or even reprimand from women.

Though such arguments have undoubtedly improved women's lives, they can only recommend moderate reductions in patriarchal risk, because patriarchal risk incentivizes behavior headship complementarians see as *good for* women. Eliminating the asymmetrical vulnerability altogether would require transforming headship-complementarian views about gender or denying that society should be designed in ways that incentivize the discharging of headship-complementarian roles.[26] The Jamaat-e-Islami women believe women are worse off when they earn incomes than when they are supported by men. Because specialization in household labor is part of the desirable feminine role, eliminating incentives for women to become economically dependent on men would be a bad thing; it would encourage women to stray from their morally prescribed role, and this would be, not just bad for society, but bad for the individual women.

For headship complementarians, the bad of women being economically independent is similar to the bad of men being selfish. To put this differently, eliminating patriarchal risk is at odds with the headship-complementarian aim of encouraging women to specialize in household labor. The need to retain social incentives for some level of asymmetrical vulnerability is evident in the compromise position about widows the Jamaat-e-Islami women endorse. On the one hand, they agree that widows being prohibited from working poses a risk to their well-being that is unacceptable. But they restrict the opportunity to earn income to widows because they see independent income earning as suboptimal for women, and they do not want economic independence for women to become too widespread.[27]

How well might a role-based argument do at illuminating the wrongness of the devaluation of women's labor? Whereas patriarchal risk tempts men to ignore women's needs, norms that devalue women's labor might be thought to interfere *epistemically*—that is, to interfere with men's capacities to *identify* women's needs. Norms and practices that invisibilize women's labor or obscure the demands of feminized labor get in the way of men (and sometimes women) knowing what women need. Such norms and practices encourage men to be ignorant of women's time use—of the difficulties and bodily demands of household labor. Knowledge about women's time use and the bodily demands of their labor is undeniably relevant to basic welfare outcomes—like health and nutritional status. As has been widely documented, poor health, safety, and nutritional outcomes are strongly related to women's household labor, especially in times of economic change (Jaggar 2013). To be able to respond to women's needs in arenas such as nutrition and health, men need to understand what women do. Sen (1990) argues that ideologies that obscure the demands of women's labor distort the "informational base" about the relative needs of men and women in households. Sen's solution is not compatible with headship complementarianism, since he claims that challenging the gender division of labor is the way to expand the informational base. However, headship complementarians could plausibly argue that learning more about women's labor can expand men's informational base and could do so in ways that make them better guardians. The women activists in Kabeer's work draw on this type of strategy, stating that men become better guardians by becoming better informed about women's day-to-day tasks. One man reports that before his participation in an NGO, "We really had no idea that women worked as hard as we did in running the family. Now I realize that our family is a result of our joint effort" (Kabeer 2011).

This argument against the devaluation of women's labor can only turn up a moral problem with a relatively small subset of cases of the devaluation of women's labor, however. Since the role-based argument characterizes problem with the devaluation of women's labor as located in its effects on men's ability to protect individual women, it only offers reasons to visibilize the observable effects of feminized labor on individual women's well-being. The cases in which the role-based argument is useful are ones in which an individual woman is harmed because of gendered labor burdens; say, her health becomes compromised because she sleeps very little because she spends so much time cooking, engaging in dependency work, and carrying water. But many of the effects of the devaluation of women's labor that feminists should care about do not translate into deficits in individual women's well-being that individual men could prevent. An important problem with the devaluation of women's labor is its effects on women as a group; it seems to leave them with fewer opportunities and worse well-being outcomes than men as a group. But since this overall social outcome need not result in well-being deficits for individual women (individual women can have well-being and still be collectively worse off than men), arguments about what individual men should do for individual women's well-being offer few resources for critique of group-based inequality.

Moreover, the role-based argument cannot provide an argument against the harms of the devaluation of women's labor that come from the failure to compensate it financially. The weaknesses of the role-based argument against patriarchal risk also apply here. Headship complementarians seem committed to the idea that women earning incomes will disincentivize women's one-way dependency on men—a dependency they see as morally valuable. Financially compensating feminized labor, though it would likely be preferable in headship-complementarian terms to allowing women to engage in market labor, would still likely disincentivize women's acceptance of men's household authority. So devaluing women's labor by not compensating it seems actually to support, rather than impede, men's enactment of the duties of guardianship.

What Role Can Headship Complementarian Strategies Play in Transnational Feminist Praxis?

What does the foregoing analysis imply about the role headship-complementarian doctrines can play in transnational feminist praxis? On one hand, I have shown that such doctrines can only provide arguments for modest increases in women's well-being, rather than arguments for feminist change. In other words, headship-complementarian doctrines have conceptual limits that make the end states they prescribe incompatible with gender justice. On the other hand, the nonideal universalist perspective I develop in this book suggests that we should resist concluding from conceptual arguments that headship-complementarian arguments have no role to play in feminist change. Nonideal universalism suggests instead that though (a) headship complementarianisms cannot supply feminist *ideals*, they can (b) supply arguments in favor of increasing women's well-being that are, in some limited contexts, worthy of support by feminists—because women's basic well-being can only be achieved through headship-complementarian strategies in those contexts, or because increasing women's well-being through headship-complementarian strategies is the most likely path to feminist change.

For a view to constitute a feminist *ideal*, the end state of affairs it produces must be compatible with gender justice. I have argued in this book that transnational feminist praxis does not need a single thick vision of the end state that is gender justice and that a number of social ideals can therefore be feminist. But it does not follow from this that *all* social ideals or metaphysical views about gender are compatible with gender justice. Headship complementarianisms, I have shown, fall into the group of doctrines that cannot paint sexist oppression as morally undesirable, or at the very least, cannot portray IISNPs as genuinely bad.[28] They instead claim that asymmetrical vulnerability between women and men, in particular, the devaluation of women's labor and somewhat high levels of patriarchal risk, is morally good—and not just because of unfortunate background conditions.

It may be objected that concern with women's basic well-being, which I have shown headship complementarians can easily avow, is evidence of feminist potential. I have three lines of response to this. The first is just to point out that having "feminist potential" is not the same thing as constituting a feminist ideal. If having "feminist potential" means being capable of motivating strategies that contribute to feminist goals in the long run, the idea that headship complementarianisms have feminist potential is plausible under certain conditions, as I will discuss later in this chapter. But if having feminist potential means "having a vision of genuinely gender-just social relations," headship complementarianisms simply do not offer such a vision. Since asymmetrical vulnerability is morally good for headship complementarians, and since this promotes oppressive practices such as high levels of patriarchal risk and the devaluation of women's labor, headship-complementarian condemnations of sexist oppression are not forthcoming. This is not to deny that people who are now headship complementarians might become feminists at some future point. It is rather to establish that becoming feminist would require changing some definitional commitments of their view; to become feminists, they would have stop being *headship* complementarians.

Second, concern with women's well-being is just not enough to make a vision feminist, in the sense of prescribing the achievement of a state of affairs compatible with gender justice. Of course, caring about individual women's well-being is closer to feminism than believing that women are mere use-objects. But if feminism is just providing individual women the ability to access well-being, then virtually *any* vision of social arrangements can be feminist. Almost any set of social arrangements will provide women opportunities to pursue well-being. The question for feminism is whether the opportunities are sufficient and whether societies are organized such that they are *gender-justly distributed*. Under oppressive conditions, the self-interested thing for individuals to do is often to seek the rewards that accrue to "good" members of their groups, even if the norms that demand it are more harmful and disadvantageous.[29] So to point out that some practice maximizes well-being under existing conditions, or even just that it allows the pursuit of well-being under existing conditions, is not to show very much. It may only show that the practice allows individual women to make the best out of a bad situation or protects them from egregious harm or suffering. Feminists believe that *social conditions* need to be designed in a certain way, one in which gender is not a fundamental determinant of one's access to social advantage and disadvantage. So, though it is true that headship complementarians do not want women to suffer severe harm, this commitment is insufficient for feminism.

What does noting the conceptual limits of headship complementarianism imply for transnational feminist praxis? Nonideal universalism allows us to distinguish feminist *ideals* from ideals that can play a role in organizing to improve women's condition, so there remains room for some headship-complementarian strategies in transnational feminist praxis. The nonideal universalist epistemic prescriptions described in the first chapter of this book can help us get clearer about why normative critique of headship complementarianisms does not amount to a feminist license to indiscriminately attempt to remove headship complementarianisms or strategies based on them. Recall that nonideal universalists, when making case-specific judgments, see political judgments as concerning justice enhancement rather than justice achievement, and that they seek out relevant information about imperialist structures. The imperialism-visibilizing prescription will clarify that in certain real-world cases, headship-complementarian worldviews, on their own, are not the most proximate causes of deficits in women's well-being or women's oppression. The temptation to assume that headship-complementarian worldviews, and not global structural phenomena, are the key causes of women's oppression may in some cases betray the missionary feminist resort to the cultural and idealized social ontology. Roles can become more disadvantageous because of changes to how costs and benefits attach to certain behaviors within a context, and sometimes such changes are brought about by colonialism and neoliberalism. In certain contexts, colonialism and neoliberalism have made complementarian roles more disadvantageous than they used to be. For example, the environmental degradation that results from neoliberalism can increase the disadvantage associated with the often-feminized role of carrying water or fuel (Desai 2002; see also Whyte 2013). Similarly, the disadvantage associated with not earning an income can increase when structural conditions change so that cash is more important.

The justice-enhancement prescription nonideal universalists endorse means that political movements should be judged at least partly in terms of whether they increase the status of women vis-à-vis a historical baseline. This prescription can help us see why saying that headship complementarianisms are not feminist *ideals* is not tantamount to saying that strategies based on these views can never lead to feminist change. There may be cases where movements for increasing women's status on complementarian grounds are prerequisites for feminism, or useful accompaniments to it. This may be true in at least two kinds of cases. One involves contexts in which large numbers of women simply cannot imagine themselves in noncomplementarian terms. In such cases, the real choice may be between deploying complementarian ideas to agitate for improvements in their well-being (or for recognition that their individual well-being matters at all) and doing nothing to advance their own interests. Especially, but not exclusively, because of imperialist oppression, women faced with a choice between abandoning all their sources of meaning and becoming feminists can reasonably be expected to choose the former (see Tobin 2007; Khader 2015). The outlook for women who choose headship-complementarian arguments for their well-being over feminist ones may not be completely pessimistic. Though empirical evidence suggests the path is not as clear as many feminists have hoped, increases in women's perceptions of self-entitlement in one domain of life might increase their expectations in others as well.[30]

A second set of instances in which headship-complementarian movements may be worth supporting include contexts where women's basic well-being is so low, and outlooks for improving it while doing something about gender injustice so poor, that it is reasonable for women to prioritize what Maxine Molyneux (1985) calls their "practical interests" over strategic gender interests. The former are interests related to survival and discharging one's socially assigned role, and the latter are interests related to challenging male domination. Such situations are likely to arise under conditions of severe poverty, especially in cases where both men and women are victims of severe poverty or class exploitation. Though the path is fraught here as well, attaining basic well-being may help women become better poised to fight for gender justice. For example, Barakat and Wardell (2002) argue that women in postconflict Afghanistan are so poorly off that simply involving them in antipoverty and reconstruction efforts through their traditional roles is the best first step that can be hoped for.

Still, feminists must tread very lightly in embracing headship complementarianisms. The fact that headship complementarianisms cannot constitute feminist ideals means that the feminist embrace of them must be limited and strategic—and that it must be based on attention to contextual empirical realities. At the end of the day, the fact that headship complementarianisms can agitate for improving women's agency and well-being but not for an end to sexist oppression means that genuinely feminist movements will have to rely on metaphysical views about gender that are not headship complementarian, and that feminists cannot take the fulfillment of headship-complementarian roles to be desirable in its own right.

Further, nonideal universalist concerns also require feminists to be attentive to the practical dangers that accompany even strategic employment of headship-complementarian strategies. As I have argued elsewhere, the fact that women gain well-being through participation in sexist practices means that improvements in women's well-being can also be increases in women's endorsement of sexism (Khader 2014). Additionally, right-wing women's movements are proliferating (see Bachetta 2002), and feminists, both inside and outside the local contexts in which these movements proliferate, need to be careful about supporting and fueling them. Indeed, feminists in postcolonial contexts often criticize Western feminists, and postcolonial scholarship in the West, for being too open to embracing "other" women's movements with gender conservative ideologies (see, for example, Mojab 2001; Bannerji 2001). The justice-enhancement prescription, instead of assuming that headship-complementarian movements are always parts of paths to improvement because they allow maximal cultural pluralism, recommends rich, context-specific empirical engagement with judgments about how people understand themselves and which strategies are likely to work. Though nonideal universalism allows that there may be many genuine visions of gender-just social relations, headship complementarianisms do not seem to offer one.

5 GENDER ROLE ELIMINATIVISM

FEMINIZED POWER AND THE PUBLIC

In the now classic "Under Western Eyes," Chandra Talpade Mohanty identified a stereotype of the "average third world woman"; part of the stereotype was being "tradition-bound, domestic, and family-oriented" (2008, 22). As Mohanty's phrase attests, Western feminists have long associated feminist progress with women's incorporation into a gender-neutral public sphere.[1] Uncritical valuing of gender-neutral forms of power and the public sphere has, in the eyes of decolonial, transnational, and postcolonial feminists, served justificatorily and constitutively imperialist functions.[2] It has played a justificatory role in imperialism by fueling Westerners' sense that "others" need to be economically, militarily, and culturally colonized—as, for example, in the case of the British suffragists who argued that it was unseemly for a colonial power to stoop to the level of Indians, who needed to be ruled because they cloistered their women (Grewal 1996). It has also seemed to be part of a regime of cultural domination, since it suggests that the potentially parochial Western idea that gender is morally irrelevant ought to be universally adopted. Anti-imperialist feminists often argue that Western feminists, because of their focus on bringing women into the public and because of their emphasis on strategies that that bring women into traditionally male roles in hopes of degendering them, underestimate the importance of feminized forms of power.

A common worry, one that reflects what I take to be genuine dangers, is that such arguments ignore or romanticize women's subjugation.[3] I argue, however, that some defenses of feminized power can be consistent with opposition to sexist oppression. I develop normative guidelines for clarifying when this is the case within transnational feminist praxis. Transnational feminist praxis, though it does require wanting women to have equal power to participate in social decision-making processes, does not require dismissing feminized power, and may not even require hoping for a gender-undifferentiated public sphere. Anti-imperialist feminist calls to valorize feminized power are often claims about what is possible under nonideal conditions or appeals to non-Western visions of gender justice that oppose sexist oppression, but missionary feminist precommitments often obscure this.

I begin with a diagnosis of why Western feminists (not exclusively, but particularly) have difficulty seeing calls to recognize feminized power as anything but regressive attempts to accept patriarchy or play within its rules. I show how the missionary feminist precommitments of moralism, ethnocentric justice monism, and the idealized global social ontology discussed in chapter 1 make it difficult for Western feminists to distinguish exercises of power that contribute to ending sexist oppression from those that embrace Western cultural forms. I identify three specific missionary feminist confusions, the idealization of the territorial public, the idealization of Western cultural forms, and the culturalist category error that stem from these tendencies and get in the way of understanding defenses of "other" women's feminized power. In the second section of the chapter, I develop desiderata for normative guidelines for evaluating "other" women's feminized power that can undermine missionary feminist precommitments and are consistent with anti-imperialist transnational feminist praxis. Appropriate guidelines will underdetermine what counts as a valuable exercise of power and acknowledge that what matters is *resistance* rather than the achievement of gender justice. I show how my nonideal universalist position, which understands feminism as a justice-enhancing practice built on opposition to sexist oppression, meets these desiderata and make clear how the presence of a gender-emphasizing moral vernacular need not signal acceptance of women's oppression. Appeals to gender difference and feminized power may instead signal negotiation with nonideal gender conditions or pluralist agnosticism about whether an ideal of gender justice must valorize gender neutrality. I show this by examining two defenses of feminized power that question some element of the value of a gender-neutral public sphere: Leila Ahmed's defense of the harem and Nkiru Nzegwu's defense of an Igbo gender-differentiated public.

Dismissing "Other" Women's Power

"Feminized power" here refers to power that is exercised through women's fulfillment of prescribed gender roles. Because patriarchal gender roles map onto the public/private distinction in the West, Western feminists often assume that feminized power is an inferior form of power, and that investment in it signals a failure to desire the forms of power that would end women's domination. We will see some specific examples of Western feminist difficulties in arriving at more nuanced views of "other" women's power below. First, however, I want to say something about the missionary feminist point of view of which I take these difficulties to be symptomatic. Missionary feminists assume that the situation of the contemporary West is the gender-just telos toward which all societies must reach and have difficulty raising normative questions about whether Western values and cultural forms are genuinely good. I will be schematic here, but readers interested in a more in-depth discussion of missionary feminism can consult chapter 1.

Missionary Feminist Precommitments

The missionary feminist precommitments that get in the way of accurate Western feminist judgments about "other" women's feminized power are commitments to an idealized global social ontology, ethnocentrism, justice monism, and moralism. The first is an idealized *global* social ontology. Idealization, according to Onora O'Neill (1987), occurs when, in the process of abstraction required by theorizing, we represent objects in ways that falsely attribute or emphasize (putatively) positive features to an object. Charles Mills (2005) argues that social theories are particularly likely to involve idealizations of *society* that serve the interests of the dominant. The missionary feminist social ontology "resorts to the cultural," to use Abu-Lughod's (2002) words, to explain "other" women's conditions. This explanatory strategy constitutes an idealization, because as Uma Narayan (1997) argues, the Western tendency to understand cultures as the cause of "other" women's oppression conveniently precludes analysis of the role imperialism plays in causing harm, sometimes sexist harm, to "other" women. The resort to the cultural also permits the idealization of the West as the moral vanguard, whose current state is morally desirable and caused by endogenous features.

A second missionary feminist precommitment is to ethnocentrism, the notion that what is part of one's culture is morally better. The idealized social ontology I just discussed supports it by offering unacknowledged or argued-for associations between Western culture and moral goodness (or justice) and "other" cultures and moral backwardness. A key way the idealized social ontology supports ethnocentrism is by treating the oppressive practices of "other" cultures to metonymically stand for the cultures as wholes. Instead of understanding Western and "other" cultural forms as constituted by both oppressive and emancipatory strands, idealization attaches a positive valence to all or most elements of Western culture and a negative valence to all or most elements of "other" cultures. This unacknowledged nexus of ethnocentric associations makes it difficult for Western feminists to sort out what is of universal value in their form of life and what is not.

These first two missionary feminist precommitments merely magnify a difficulty that accompanies all normative theorizing. The presence of some thick descriptive content is an ineluctable feature of moral ideals, at least as we encounter them in practice. Ideals are developed and understood within specific sociocultural situations and need thick descriptive content to be capable of being applied. Getting the level of thickness right is especially challenging for cross-cultural judgments. Given the fact that ideals arise, and are usually employed in, specific sociocultural contexts, special problems arise in attempts to make ideals travel from context to context. The prescription to achieve some morally good end may include the morally arbitrary injunction to adopt practices of the culture in which the end was first theorized, or in which the evaluator is accustomed to employing it. Further, it may be impossible to know in advance of cross-cultural encounters whether there is arbitrary thick content sedimented onto a moral ideal. As I have argued elsewhere (Khader 2011), this provides a strong reason for those engaged cross-cultural normative judgment to be hypervigilant about the risk of confusing the unfamiliar with the normatively unacceptable.

What exacerbates this difficulty of all normative theorizing in missionary feminist ethnocentrism is the occlusion of the processes by which ideas about what is just were arrived at in the first place. Missionary feminists assume without argument that what is just or good just is best on display in Western culture. The Enlightenment teleological narrative that they believe is a historical truth,[4] claims that the contemporary West represents what all societies will become if they "evolve." There is thus a sort of settledness to missionary feminist understandings of what human societies should aspire to. The desirability of contemporary Western culture is supposed to be self-evidently demonstrated by history; a careful reckoning about the moral desirability of Western cultural forms and conceptions of justice would be superfluous. The association of Westernness with goodness allows ethnocentric judgments about Western cultural superiority to masquerade as morally correct ones; culturally specific but morally arbitrary material can become *concealed* within normative ideals. I will return to this point, but unacknowledged ethnocentrism makes it difficult or impossible to see rejections of Western *instantiations* of things that are genuinely good as anything but rejections of the goods themselves.

The difficulty of posing questions about whether what is Western is genuinely morally good is worsened by two other precommitments: justice monism and to moralism. Justice monism is the idea that there is a single best form of social organization. Amartya Sen (2009) argues that justice monist views unnecessarily hold moral and political projects hostage, because achieving consensus about an ideal is much more difficult than achieving consensus about what might improve current conditions.[5] Ethnocentrism and the idealized social ontology supply missionary feminists with a particular content for a justice-monist ideal; according to the Enlightenment teleological narrative, the West, or something like it, is the correct vision of a just society.

Moralism, the final missionary feminist precommitment, involves treating political activities as though they merely express moral judgments. Being a moralist is not the same thing as making moral judgments; making moral judgments is something that feminists cannot avoid. Moralism is instead a way of purifying political actions, of emptying them of their practical ramifications. Political actions *can* express general moral judgments, but they also always express judgments that about the particular contexts in which they occur. They also have material and discursive effects—and are often motivated by interests. Moralists treat transnational political action as a sort of theater for sweeping claims about right and wrong rather than a terrain in which practical considerations are at play and power is exercised.

Some readers might find it useful to understand these missionary feminist precommitments as stemming from a type of colonial ideal theorizing. Ideal theory is a style of political philosophy that focuses on imagining just situations; nonideal theory in the sense developed by Elizabeth Anderson (2010), Charles Mills (2005), and Amartya Sen (2009) develops concepts and principles that help us move out of unjust ones. Mills and Anderson also argue that ideal theorists ignore the ways that relations of domination infect the content of their ideals.[6] So one way to think of missionary feminist precommitments is as tendencies to take the West to be the ideal of justice, to not see that one is doing it—and, to add a third dimension, to keep filtering new data about the world in ways that will protect the notion that the West and its cultural forms just embody the single gender-just endpoint.

The Idealization of the Territorial Public

I now turn to three misunderstandings of "other" women's feminized power generated by these precommitments. The first, the idealization of the territorial public characterizes important social decision-making power as located in male-dominated spaces and in spaces outside the home. It stems from the idealization of Western culture but can more specifically be understood as an idealization of Western institutions. Incorporating women into male-dominated public institutions in the West has often increased their power; incorporating women into them in some postcolonial contexts has meant incorporating them into institutions that, at least historically, reduced their power, often by emptying preexisting feminized forms of power of their effectiveness.

Idealizations of the territorial public are difficult to detect, not only because of the idealized social ontology's erasure of colonialism, but also because of ambiguous uses of the term "public sphere." In its most mundane sense, "public" means the world outside the home. Western feminists often deploy the term to refer to the areas of life from which women have been traditionally excluded. Still others use the term to mean formal institutions—institutions supported by official regulatory mechanisms, such as the taxed portion of the market and political decision-making institutions. Democratic theorists use the term "public sphere" to mean the space in which claims about collective political enterprises are made and disputed.[7] In the West, the spaces to which these terms refer often overlap. However, this overlap is historically contingent rather than conceptually necessary. The first few meanings of public are primarily territorial. By this, I mean that these first meanings suggest that the public is defined, not (only) by what happens there, but rather by features of the built environment, institutional environment, or who is allowed to enter and exit. The last meaning of public, in contrast, defines the public by the socially important forms of power exercised within it and enabled by it.

It is possible to imagine spaces (such as women-dominated decision-making bodies) that lack some territorial, contingent features of the public but nonetheless house power and influential discussions of the common good, as well as spaces (such as government offices with merely symbolic power) that bear contingent markers of publicity but are not influential. As I have mentioned, this separation of territorial (or institutional) and moral features of publicity is especially likely in contexts where the present forms of such spaces are partly (or entirely) colonial artifacts. The investing of power in formal, male-dominated structures was often a colonial strategy for increasing the power of elites or men, or both. In addition to allowing Westerners to instate what they saw as appropriate gender relations, new institutional forms empowered local forces who were willing to discharge colonial goals.[8] The view that non-home, formal, male-dominated spaces are the sites of social influence thus obscures what is practically at stake in some cases in which "other" women seem to prioritize feminized power.

Ifi Amadiume offers an example of West African women rejecting institutions of the territorial public to protect themselves from the new forms of sexist oppression caused by neoliberal urbanization. Amadiume (2002) describes a Wakirike coming of age ritual in which young women are prepared for marriage by spending weeks with powerful women in their community, "being pampered and loved like princesses, and they equally have to display their decorated bodies to the community in a public ceremony" (47). The ritual does not include female genital cutting or force feeding, but it does encourage young women to gain weight to meet cultural standards of beauty for marriageability. Amadiume compares two girls—one who wants to stay in the village and one who is home from university in Lagos. According to Amadiume, the young woman who stays in the village chooses the protection of a "matriarchal umbrella." She refuses to subject herself to the "global city"—and forms of violence brought about by neoliberalism.[9] The neoimperialist forms of violence are both literal (economic exploitation, sex work, and the lack of protection from kin) and symbolic (commodification and racist beauty standards). Complicating matters is the fact that sexism is an element of imperialist violence—part of what imperialist violence does is wrest power from the hands of women.

Amadiume (2002) asks, "Which of these girls might more easily find support and protection if confronted with any of these new forms of violence against women? The one under the matriarchal umbrella or the one in the city? Is there a feminist imperative that the rule of law must supersede ritual? Is the rule of law more empowering than ritual?" (48). Amadiume does not answer the question. Without taking a stance about this specific case (we would undoubtedly need more information to do so), we can see Amadiume as showing how the idealization of the territorial public makes it impossible to raise the question of whether the feminized forms of power in the "matriarchal umbrella" can be valuable for feminists. For the young women in Amadiume's example, sexist oppression is embedded in both sets of available options. Amadiume, in my view, is simply asking Western feminists not to assume out of hand that participation in the territorial public is the less sexist option. If it is the case that "the matriarchal umbrella" involves comparative protection from violence, and if women have power to shape official village practices in it in a way they do not in the city (which she suggests they do), the assumption that urban life is better starts to look morally arbitrary.

The Idealization of Western Cultural Forms

Whereas the idealization of the territorial public distorts through an implicit historical narrative that makes colonial histories irrelevant to contemporary exercises of power, the idealization of Western cultural forms arbitrarily imputes a unique ability to instantiate gender justice to Western means and symbolic forms. To be clear, this idealization does not occur every time a Western cultural form is assumed to be required for securing gender justice; it is possible that some cultural forms developed in the West are universally necessary. It occurs through the mistaken assumption that a Western cultural belief or practice that is contingently related to women's political power is necessarily related to it. The result is the valuation of Western trappings of power *only because they are Western*.

One type of idealization of Western cultural forms conflates goods that are of universal intrinsic value with context-specific instruments for achieving them. To understand how this works, it is important to first recognize that the effectiveness of means varies contextually (a car is a better tool for getting around in a society constructed around roads than one constructed around waterways, for example). Universally important goods can be sought through different, differentially contextually effective, means. The idealization of Western means, however, preempts questions about alternative means for achieving universal goods. Consider Naila Kabeer's (2012) characterization of rural Bangladesh as characterized by "the continued centrality of family in social life and the near-universality of marriage" (229). According to Kabeer (1999), some feminists assume that frequency of divorce tracks women's ability to act in their own interests.[10] Yet the divorce focus ignores the differential benefits of marriage and divorce in different types of societies. In societies where family membership is both valued extremely highly and necessary for accessing other goods, casting out one one's own may have little appeal. It does not follow from this that women in such societies are unable to act in their individual interests or distinguish their interests from those of their families. According to Kabeer, a live possibility for asserting individual interests in more communal contexts is what she calls "divorce within marriage." Kabeer argues that the ability to limit interaction with one's husband can be an instrument for identifying and asserting one's interests, but the idea that striking out on one's own is the only way to achieve (or the only possible next step toward achieving) gender justice ignores this.

A second type of idealization of Western cultural forms is the idealization of culturally specific gender protocols. This type of idealization can get in the way of understanding "other" women's feminized power by making it seem that any endorsement of non-Western views about femininity is an endorsement of gender injustice. Though feminism requires the view that oppressive gender relations are unacceptable, it is far from clear that only one understanding of gender is compatible with, or capable of enhancing, gender justice. The assumption that a gender-just society would adopt the same comprehensive understanding of gender roles held by Westerners can function to obscure the meanings of "other" women's power and their investments in feminine roles. Joan Scott's discussion of the mainstream French conceptualization of the hijab offers a powerful example of how idealization of Western gender protocols can produce facile overestimations of "other" women's subjugation. Scott argues that the French desire to ban Muslim headscarves in public schools stems from the assumptions of the non-Muslim French that their gender relations are egalitarian, and uniquely so. One source of outrage about the hijab concerned the supposed tragedy of young women "covering their beautiful faces."[11] According to Scott (2010), this example shows how the underlying French preoccupation was with "girls' refusal to engage in what were taken to be the 'normal' protocols for interaction with members of the opposite sex" (154). The view was that gender equality required "sexual liberation," which in turn required presenting oneself as available for sexual relations with, or sexual evaluation by, strangers. In contrast, one purpose of the hijab is to declare that sexuality only belongs in spheres of intimacy. As Scott notes, some Muslim feminists argue that not having to be sexual in public is empowering (171).

We do not have to take a stance about whether the hijab is empowering in France to see what is foreclosed by the French idealization. If Scott is right, the mainstream French view can only accept as gender egalitarian views that encourage women to permit sexualized interaction with strangers. But surely such interaction is not required for having a political voice or access to education (and if it is, and only required for women, the requirement is sexist). It may be objected that the unilateral expectation that women desexualize public interactions is sexist in ways that do not have to do with participation in public life. However, many Muslim women who advocate veiling do not place the responsibility for sexual self-regulation, or for modest dress, disproportionately on women (Al-Khatahtbeh, Raja et al. 2014). On the French view, however, any way of managing sexuality that does not follow "French" protocols about sexual availability and dating appears as opposed to gender equality. Rejecting a Western protocol about gender marking just means accepting women's subordination; the possibilities of reinterpreting Muslim gender roles and criticizing non-Muslim French ones are both off the table.

The Culturalist Category Error

The third missionary feminist confusion that impedes evaluations of "other" women's power is a form of moralism rather than idealization. It assumes that actions taken to navigate particular political circumstances are statements about ultimate gender justice. Or to put the point differently, it uses the standards of ideal theory to evaluate practices and strategies employed under unjust conditions. What matters for the possibility of social change is the ability to effect a certain type of *transition*, but the moralist overlooks this. I will return to this point in the section on assessing feminized power under nonideal conditions below, but practices that effectively increase gender justice in an unjust society may diverge from those that would exist in a society that was already just. (The familiar example in Western political philosophy is that it is fully consistent to believe both that society should be "color-blind" and that race-based affirmative action is necessary in a society that is not).

The culturalist category error involves responding to claims that "other" women's exercises of power improve their lives by pointing out that such exercises of power occur in unjust contexts (usually understood as cultures). It is a category error because it applies ideal theoretical evaluative standards to improper objects—strategies under nonideal conditions. The anecdote that opens Leila Ahmed's well-known essay about the harem helps explain how the idealized social ontology and ethnocentrism set the stage for the culturalist category error. Ahmed recounts that when she first came to the United States, she saw Muslim women emphasizing the fact that Islam had brought women the right to own property and could not understand their "overly rosy picture of women and Islam." Years later, Ahmed (1992) says she finally understood the need to point out positive effects of the adoption of Islam; "Americans 'know' that Arabs are backward . . . and that Islam monstrously oppresses women" (523). The characterization of Arab culture as necessarily backward prevents the evaluation of particular practices within it.

Ahmed's essay as a whole identifies an instance of the culturalist category error. Ahmed argues that Western feminists have difficulty seeing why Arab women accept homosocial forms of affiliation derivative of the harem.

According to Ahmed, the harem has been a site of "women's culture" that allows women to resist sexist self-interpretations. Yet, Ahmed (1992) argues, veiling and the harem have come to metonymically represent the backwardness of Muslims, so all Western feminists can do when confronted with arguments about the harem is point out that societies with strict sex segregation are less just than other societies (529). Ahmed is not alone in noting such argumentative moves by Western feminists. American scholar of Sudan, Sondra Hale, describes a similar response to her paper claiming that Sudanese women are more liberated than American women. According to her, Sudanese women in the 1960s had a higher level of acceptance in the professions, greater political rights, and access to parental leave. However, Hale (2005) says, as soon an American audience member mentioned the ubiquity of infibulation in Sudan, it became impossible to discuss her comparative claim or the genuinely liberatory forms of power exercised by Sudanese women, because the inferiority of Sudanese culture became a foregone conclusion (211–212).[12]

A relatively straightforward and high-profile example of the culturalist category error occurs in the debate surrounding Susan Moller Okin's "Is Multiculturalism Bad for Women?"[13] Bonnie Honig's (1999) reply to Okin includes the claim, attributed to Ahmed, that veiling can empower women. Okin (1999) replies with the following: "I do not doubt that this is so. But surely to be unable to practice one's profession without being enshrouded from head to toe is not, on the whole, an empowering situation in which to live, unless it is a transition to greater freedom" (124). What I want to draw attention to is how strange it is for Okin to think that she wins the argument by pointing out that a situation in which women have to wear burqas is unjust. Honig (1999) quotes Ahmed as pointing out that the situation is nonideal, " 'a sexually integrated social world is still an uncomfortable social reality for both men and women' " (29). So the only claim made by either Honig or Ahmed was that burqas increased women's freedom by reducing seclusion. Okin does mention an apposite response in the point about transition, but it is rhetorically buried in a minor clause, and the rest of the essay focuses on reminders about the patriarchality of "other" cultures. Indeed, Okin soon after makes very similar point about the nonideality of cultures that allow polygamy in response to the idea that co-wives are capable of benefitting from solidarity.[14]

Why, then, does Okin read Honig and Ahmed as having implied that a society that requires women to wear burqas is just? Part of the answer is that Okin's entire essay vacillates between the question of whether patriarchal cultures are unjust and that of what should be done about patriarchal practices under unjust conditions. When individual practices come into question, her argumentative strategy is almost always to point out that the cultures in which they occur assign women inferior roles—but is this really what matters for deciding which practices should be allowed to persist in the short term? The culturalist category error is bound to distort the meaning of "other" women's exercises of power, because *all* power exercised under nonideal conditions will be subject to this criticism, and the idealization of Western culture guarantees that negative associations will attach to "other" cultures.

Assessing Feminized Power under Nonideal Conditions: Normative Guidelines

Now that we have seen three ways missionary precommitments impede accurate normative judgments about "other" women's feminized power and defenses of it, we can begin to ask what kinds of values, concepts, and epistemic guidelines would permit more clear-sighted judgments. I emphasize that the solution cannot be for Western feminists to simply refuse to make value judgments about instances of feminized power by "other" women. The reason moral judgments are ineluctable is neither that Western feminists are irreproachable nor that it is desirable for Western feminists to have power over "others" who have no reciprocal power over them. Instead, in a world characterized by the injustices of sexism and imperialism, Western feminist refusal to judge amounts to a refusal to take seriously their moral responsibilities to oppose the forms of domination in which their position renders them complicit.[15] Anti-imperialist transnational feminist praxis, including activism designed to simply support "other" women's movements, requires normative judgments. The necessary normative judgments are about the potential of instances of "other" women's power to promote feminist change, but the conceptual tools used in such judgments, if they are to be anti-imperialist, need to be tailored to avoid the idealizations of the territorial public and Western cultural forms and the culturalist category error.

Observations about Resistance

An observation about what the culturalist category error misses can help us begin to arrive at desiderata for better normative guidelines for evaluating "other" women's power. The culturalist category error misses the *type* of thing anti-imperialist defenders of feminized power take instances of it to be: *resistance*. Claims that exercises of power are instances of resistance[16] or empowerment[17] are not identical with claims that such exercises of power express or reflect gender *justice*. The culturalist category error, as a response to claims that specific exercises of power are resistant, is a non sequitur; it directs attention to the baseline of ideal gender justice (conceived as embodied by the West because of ethnocentrism and justice monism) rather than toward the effects of power within a nonideal context. Resistance, by definition, occurs under nonideal, or unjust, conditions; if resistance is anything at all, it must be *against* something. The observation that "other" women's conditions are oppressive is, from the perspective of transnational feminist praxis, banal. It amounts only to the observation that resistance is necessary. To claim that an exercise of power is resistant is to make a claim about its capacity to bring about diachronic change, not about whether we would expect to see it under conditions of gender justice.

Desiderata for Normative Guidelines for Evaluating "Other" Women's Power

We want the normative ideals used in transnational feminist praxis to fit the task. I have intended my remarks about resistance to illuminate the fact that the task of evaluating specific instances of "other" women's power is not, contra the culturalist category error, to point out the nonideality of contexts. This is not to deny that feminism should concern itself with the assessment of contexts (sexist oppression is, after all, a feature of a social context); it is rather to point out that knowing that contexts are gender unjust does not offer useful information for comparing strategies aimed at changing this injustice. Seeing what the idealization of the territorial public and the idealization of Western cultural forms get wrong can help clarify two further desiderata for normative guidelines for assessing instances of "other" women's power. First, adequate normative concepts will recognize that different means are effective in different contexts. This point is mostly mundane; the efficacy of strategies for doing virtually *anything* varies contextually. But cross-cultural normative judgments require special attention to this fact. Different moral vocabularies and material conditions, as well as the fact that changing social conditions requires influencing a large number of actors over time, mean that we should expect actions that reduce gender injustice to look different under different conditions.[18] Further, historical and ongoing imperialism raise particular efficacy considerations of which Western feminists need to be aware. "Other" women often need strategies that combat imperialist oppression and deprivation of basic rights in addition to strategies that combat sexism. Feminist prescriptions that require the adoption of Western cultural forms are likely to have reduced efficacy in non-Western contexts, as are ones that ask women to give up on interests in their own well-being (see chapters 2 and 4 for more on this point about well-being).[19]

The desideratum that normative guidelines for assessing "other" women's power recognize that different strategies will be effective in different contexts is susceptible to an objection—that effectiveness is always effectiveness *at* something. It may thus still seem necessary to use progress toward Western cultural forms as an indicator of just how compatible with feminism any given exercise of power is. On this objection, "other" women's forms of power that do not match Western ones could be embraced, but only as steps on the way to eventual adoptions of Western means and cultural forms. This objection correctly understands that a conception of feminist resistance needs normative ideals. But it operates on the straightforwardly ethnocentric justice-monist, and in my view unfounded, assumption that Western cultural forms embody not only the best *existing* gender arrangements—but also the best *possible* ones.

Even if we granted the ethnocentric, justice-monist point for the sake of argument, the objection would remain based on a misunderstanding of the role of normative ideals under nonideal conditions. The objection presupposes that the best way to determine what will reduce existing injustice is to evaluate the extent to which a state of affairs approximates an ideal. However, in Lisa Tessman's (2015) words, achieving "the best goal in the actual world . . . may require very different actions than the best in the ideal world" (198). Robert Goodin (1995) offers a simple example of this point: whether one wants chocolate sauce or pasta sauce should depend on whether one has pasta or ice cream in front of them (51). Even if one's ideal is ice cream with chocolate sauce, chocolate sauce on pasta is supposed to be worse than fettuccine marinara. To draw this point back to using the presence or absence of Western forms to track feminist progress: even if Western forms were the ideal (ice cream with chocolate sauce), looking for Western cultural forms would risk the feminist equivalent of looking for chocolate sauce, irrespective of what food was available to put it on. A better bet for making more reliable judgments about "other" women's power is to devote attention to the actual effects of, and the contexts within which, exercises of power occur.

But this does not solve the problem of needing normative standards according to which to evaluate feminist progress. A second, related desideratum for normative guidelines for evaluating instances of "other" women's power directly addresses the question of what normative ideals for evaluating feminist progress should look like. The desideratum states that they should be culturally underdetermined; they should articulate the desired changes in social relations generally enough that more than one possible set of cultural forms could approximate them. The idealizations of Western cultural forms and the territorial public rely on the justice-monist idea that achieving gender justice is like assembling an object according to a blueprint. Place every element in its place and the desired social structure will appear, the missionary feminist assumes. One way to avoid the missionary feminist ethnocentric blueprint is to avoid the notion of a blueprint altogether. Sen (2009) argues that most real-world political projects are what he calls "justice-enhancing" and that we should not refuse to engage in some projects on the grounds that we lack a consensus on an ideal of perfect justice. I have argued in this book that transnational feminist praxis is such a justice-enhancing project, one that needs normative ideals, but not a single vision of gender justice.

A third desideratum for normative guidelines for evaluating "other" women's feminized power is that they should acknowledge the diachronic character of resistance—that is, that they look at change over time.[20] According to Sen (2009), justice-enhancing projects "demand comparative assessments, not simply an immaculate identification of *the* just society" (401; see also Walker 2007).[21] The comparative assessments relevant to transnational feminist politics concern states of affairs over time, and not relations among cultures. It is important to know whether exercises of power improve gender justice vis-à-vis current conditions, not whether they match up completely to some ideal—culturally specific or otherwise. A phrase from Maria Lugones (2003) usefully situates feminist judgments about resistance within the register of justice enhancement: "resistance is always in the gerund, resisting" (208).

Nonideal Universalist Normative Guidelines for Evaluating Feminized Power

The nonideal universalist perspective I developed in chapter 1 can provide normative guidelines for evaluating instances of "other" women's power in a way that is consistent with these desiderata. Nonideal universalism couples a normative view with two epistemic prescriptions. The normative view is that sexist oppression is wrong, where sexist oppression is the systematic disadvantaging of members of a certain social group (or groups) based on gender (Frye 1983). For nonideal universalists, there is room for the indicators of advantage and disadvantage to vary from society to society. The epistemic prescriptions are that Western feminists should, when dealing with particular cases, seek information about imperialism and global structures and keep in mind that many transnational feminist judgments are practical ones about justice enhancement.

The view that feminism is opposition to sexist oppression, combined with commitment to a nonexhaustive and underdetermined set of universal goods, permits normative distinctions among types of feminized power that do not make the missionary feminist mistake of assuming that a specific culture is the blueprint of gender justice. As I argued in chapter 1, the objects of human rights constitute a culturally underdetermined list of goods whose possession is likely to amount to advantage in most contexts. A relevant human right is the right to participate in public life. Though this right was initially interpreted as a right to participate in elections (which undoubtedly feminists should support), it is increasingly interpreted as the ability to participate in the decisions that shape one's community. The ability to participate in social decision-making should have especially high priority for feminists, not merely because it is intrinsically valuable and likely to be available gender differentially. It is important because a gender-differential distribution of it is likely to affect women's access to other goods. Not having a voice in social decision-making is extremely likely, in real-world contexts, to result in disadvantages relative to other goods. As Monique Deveaux (2016a) argues, research on even very basic deprivations, such as poverty, now suggests that powerlessness is a major predictor of poverty, and that the poor often see powerlessness as one of the most harmful elements of poverty (see Narayan 2000). The idea that the power to shape social decision-making processes should not be gender-differentially distributed does not suggest a particular gender protocol or shape of social decision-making processes.[22]

Combined with recognition that the judgments that are constitutive of transnational feminist praxis are practical judgments about justice enhancement (often in colonial contexts) a focus on the ability to shape social processes can reveal what really matters for evaluating feminized power—and why it is not the same thing as the adopting Western cultural forms. What matters, under nonideal conditions is whether women's ability to shape the conditions of their action is increasing and increasing in ways that make them less likely to have power exercised *over* them. Participation in many of the institutions associated with the territorial public in the West, such as the market or the city, may not track increases in social decision-making power. This is especially likely to be true in cases in which such institutions are not where the real social power is. This is what I take to be the heart of criticisms of the idealization of the territorial public in sub-Saharan Africa; if the village is a site of the ability to influence social decision-making and the city is not,[23] or if the ability to produce food actually is a superior bargaining chip to the possession of cash, strategies based in rehabilitating traditional roles, and rejections of their alternatives, can be consistent with feminist goals. Or consider once more the example of bans on Muslim veiling practices and Islamic feminist defenses of veiling; the power to influence social life might operate relatively independently of whether people make themselves sexually available in public. My point is emphatically not that power that is outside the territorial public, or that rejects some of its trappings, is always greater than it seems. Nor is it to romanticize "traditional" life. It is to say that a culturally underdetermined ideal of participation in social decision-making encourages feminists to ask how power in different domains *actually operates* within a given context, instead of allowing missionary feminist precommitments to determine the answer.

It may be objected that because feminized power appeals to existing gender roles, it must *reinforce* them. Pierre Bourdieu famously crystallized this point, borrowing a phrase from Lucien Bianco, "the weapons of the weak are always weak weapons." Bourdieu (2002) describes "all the forms of soft violence, almost invisible, that women use against symbolic or physical violence from men" as "rooted in the androcentric view" and thus "not strong enough to really subvert the relation of domination" (32). But saying that feminized power reinforces sexism, rather than merely *risks* reinforcing it, ignores the fact that strategies for change can have multiple effects (some reinforcing, some undermining). It also grants excessive determining power to the logic of symbolic structures, denying that people can intervene in how their actions are interpreted, and denying that changes in how people live together can change dominant representations.

Perhaps more important to our discussion of Western feminists making judgments about "others" is this: knowing whether risks of reinforcement are present and how severe they are in a given case requires rich contextual knowledge about the relevant actors and the local moral vernacular. So the potential for reinforcing sexist oppression while attempting to undermine it offers strong reasons for internal debate among women affected by particular strategies. The argument that Westerners without much context-specific knowledge can make reliable judgments about strategy is relatively weak, given that the relevant judgments, instead of being primarily conceptual, need both context-specific knowledge and context-specific authority to be made responsibly.

An Objection: Why Not Agency?

I have claimed that feminists should valorize resistance that enhances "other" women's ability to shape their societies relative to men's and that it should be measured to a historical or diachronic baseline. I have also claimed that knowing what enhances the power to shape social institutions requires recognizing the forms of power that actually shape advantage and disadvantage within a given context. A popular alternative to my view says that feminists concerned with "other" women's power should simply valorize their agency. In my view, this ideal is too normatively empty to guide feminist politics. If agency is the ability to critically reflect on and affect the world, plenty of actions that reinforce sexism express agency. Some of these are actually actions by women that reduce women's social decision-making power—such as movements led by women that aim to discourage women from having the ability to move from place to place freely or pursue education. The more complicated case involves strategies that increase women's social decision-making power but that use it to increase women's oppression with regard to other goods in other domains—such as movements led by women that seek to reduce women's control over their reproductive lives.[24] Feminists need normative ideals that are capable of rendering such cases at least problematic.

Some have tried to solve this problem and create a conceptual link between feminism and value for women's agency by treating only women's expressions of self-interest as agentic.[25] A problem is that this understanding does not distinguish agency that is individually self-interested from that which makes social conditions more gender just. Consider what Deniz Kandiyoti (1988) famously referred to as "patriarchal bargains"—the presence of situations in which women have self-interested reasons to promote patriarchy. As I discussed in chapter 4, women facing high levels of patriarchal risk have self-interested incentives to appear to be dutiful women; it will keep their husbands' attitudes toward them favorable. Focusing on oppression allows feminists to avoid the conclusion that agentic acts that undermine the status of women as a group should be treated as desirable in the long term. Further, the move to include only self-interested acts as agency in effect builds robust normative content into agency. Some feminists who have recognized this, such as Saba Mahmood (2005), argue that this is a reason to question the normative goals of feminism itself (197). But it is unclear why building normative content into agency is better than my view, which acknowledges that women can increase their agency and well-being without promoting the normative goals of feminism—both views involve normative judgments.[26] My view is just clear about the fact that judgments about what improves individual women's desires and well-being in the short term are distinct from judgments about what improves the status of women as a group. Recognizing that sexist oppression is the core feminist issue, and simultaneously recognizing that we live in a world in which many women are rewarded for complying with its dictates, permits more-nuanced normative judgments about cases where women take advantage of feminized power.

Reinterpreting Defenses of Feminized Power: The Harem and the Gender-Differentiated Public

A nonideal universalist understanding of resistance can facilitate less-missionary evaluations of "other" women's exercises of feminized power. Abandoning the ideas that the West is the exemplar of gender justice, that we need an exemplar at all, and that the presence of Western cultural forms tracks what is morally significant for feminist progress—and shifting instead to the idea of reducing sexist oppression diachronically—can reveal how some postcolonial criticisms of the gender-neutral public might be more compatible with feminist aims than is often thought. We can see this more concretely by applying a nonideal universalist approach to two well-known, and relatively typical, defenses of feminized power: Leila Ahmed's work on Arab women's embrace of homosocial social forms and Nkiru Nzegwu's advocacy of a gender-differentiated public.

Focusing on diachronic resistance and context-specific efficacy can explain why defending feminized power that derives its status as such from nonideal conditions does not entail defending the conditions themselves. Ahmed (1992) argues that Western feminists misunderstand Arab women's reasons for valuing the harem. Women-dominated spaces allow women to "satirize, ridicule, and disrespect male ideals and the male world" (530); further, homosocial cultural forms are important sites of intergenerational bonding (532). Contrary to simplistic readings of Ahmed (e.g., Okin's) that view her as suggesting that there is nothing is wrong with the trappings of the harem in the contemporary world, Ahmed opposes restrictions on women's mobility and sexuality, as well as women's lack of economic independence and exclusion from the professions (Ahmed argues that economic exclusion was not even a historical feature of the harem in many cases).[27]

What seems paradoxical to many about Ahmed's position is that it embraces forms of power that are enabled by sexist oppression.[28] The need for a women's culture that opposes the degradation of women only arises in a society that degrades women. Much has also been made of another claim of Ahmed's—that men's space is more violable than women's; because women serve men, they have intimate knowledge of the goings on of men's worlds.[29] This capacity to violate originates in a servile social role, so it seems to some that Ahmed valorizes servitude. The nonideal universalist's acknowledgment that resistance occurs under gender-unjust conditions, and that potential for justice enhancement irreducibly depends partly on efficacy, can dissolve the apparent paradox. There are clear efficacy-related reasons to mobilize existing servile roles—even if there are good long-term reasons to transform them. Further, asking women who already value homosocial social forms to abandon them may be ineffective in bringing about change, both because of the risks it asks women to incur if the world is incompletely transformed,[30] and because many benefits they gain from it that are not inherently subordinating (such as intergenerational bonding) may be intrinsically and instrumentally valuable.

Recognizing these facts prevents Ahmed's argument that Western feminists must recognize the feminist potential of homosociality from dissolving into the simplistic claim that because Arab women value forms of power associated with the harem, the harem must be part of a gender-just world. Instead, Ahmed's claim is that the only way from contemporary conditions to gender-just ones may be embracing nonideal forms of power. This fits with two of her other key claims—that young women want to keep around certain elements of homosociality but not others (they want to access the professions but to keep intergenerational bonding) and that the women's movement in Yemen had (at the time of her writing) been successful in mobilizing homosociality for feminist ends. It would be a mistake, however, to view Ahmed's desire for the temporariness of certain forms of homosociality to imply a belief that a gender-just world would dissolve all forms of it. My nonideal universalist vision of a feminism that is not justice monist or ethnocentric suggests that Ahmed is not *committed* to supporting the ultimate elimination of homosociality. Absent a guarantee that the only condition without sexist oppression is one without homosocial forms of bonding, there is no reason for Ahmed to suggest that homosociality itself should be transcended—only that oppression should be. The challenge she issues to young Arab women is precisely reimagine homosociality in ways that do not promote sexist oppression, and in fact can be harnessed against it.

Nkiru Nzegwu's defense of a gender-differentiated public suggests a different way that defenses of power can be compatible with feminist ends. Though Nzegwu makes some efficacy-related arguments that are similar to Ahmed's, she goes beyond Ahmed in explicitly claiming that feminized power would exist under gender ideal conditions. Nzegwu advocates "functional sex segregation" in which political duties and tasks are gendered, but in ways that render men and women mutually nondominating (Nzegwu 2006). The interdependence she imagines is not the asymmetrical vulnerability I discussed in the last chapter; some feminized roles are public and have veto power over some masculine public roles. She argues that this form of sex segregation existed in precolonial Igbo society and that Igbo women should work toward reinstitutionalizing it.

According to Nzegwu, women's current subordination is caused largely by colonial reinterpretations of Igbo cultural forms—reinterpretations that removed social decision-making power from women-dominated institutions. However, her reasons for rejecting Western conceptions of gender extend beyond their association with imperialist oppression. She believes that Western metaphysics of gender are inherently oppressive to women because they ignore the importance of maternity in human life. Though she understands her view as complementarian, her complementarianism states that neither sex[31] should be capable of dominating the other, and that women's maternity should be a source of power (Nzegwu 2006, 220). Nzegwu also sees non-gender-related benefits to reinstituting Igbo gender practices; for instance, the idea that different genders have different social contributions secures an additional social benefit; it sustains the ideal of the self as having certain duties to the community in which it is embedded (205).

Nzegwu's criticism is particularly challenging for Western feminist theorists because it seems to impugn the view that the incorporation of women into public life is an acceptable cross-border feminist goal. Nonideal universalism can help us see why the threat is only apparent. Note that Nzegwu's view is fully compatible with the culturally underdetermined understanding of feminism I have suggested; she wants sexist oppression to be reduced and she wants women to have the same amount of control over social decision-making processes as men. She just believes that oppressive gender roles are one *subset* of possible distinct gender roles. Her complementarianism imagines gender heavily affecting men's and women's tasks but not their access to social decision-making power.

Whether Nzegwu challenges the value of incorporating women into the public depends on how feminists should understand the word "public." Nzegwu's goal seems to be to retain normatively important social decision-making power while detaching it from the idea that it must always occur in gender-neutral institutions. My claim that ending sexist oppression is a culturally underdetermined ideal holds open the question of whether it is possible to achieve the underlying aims of publicity while rejecting certain (Western, gender-neutral) institutional forms. Combined with the view of transnational feminisms as a justice-enhancing project, another element of nonideal universalism, the imperialism-visibilizing prescription, can help Western feminists see a reason that Nzegwu prefers returning to Igbo traditions over incorporating women into Western-instituted ones. As I noted in discussing the idealization of the territorial public, the colonial history in parts of West Africa has increased in women's oppression through the institution of institutions associated with publicity in the West. Looking at the imperialist history clarifies why a gender-differentiated public might be more promising in this context, or at least why it might seem to be. West African feminists disagree about whether advocating a gender-differentiated public is a good idea, and their worries about romanticism and the co-optation of feminist complementarianism by antifeminist actors are a crucial part of this debate. My point is merely that Nzegwu's proposal ought not be dismissed as antifeminist or incompatible with women having the power to shape social processes just because it advocates some gender-differentiated decision-making bodies. If my reconstruction of Nzegwu's work is accurate, her rejection of a gender-neutral public sphere does not reduce to either a rejection of the ideal of women's incorporation into public life or an apology for sexist oppression.

I have drawn out the normative implications of these two cases less to endorse their conclusions about their specific contexts (I lack sufficient contextual knowledge about either case) than to clarify the types of considerations relevant to determining whether exercises of feminized power are compatible with feminism—considerations that have routinely been obscured by missionary feminist precommitments. Neither Ahmed's nor Nzegwu's arguments are in principle incompatible with opposition to sexism, but missionary feminists' lack of clarity about resistance and the role of ideals under nonideal conditions has prevented them from seeing why. To recognize that defenses of feminized power need not be capitulations to patriarchy, we need to see that the presence or absence of ideal social conditions or idealized cultural forms, Western or otherwise, does not track feminist progress, that defending forms of power under nonideal conditions is not tantamount to imagining them as part of a gender-just world, that identifying resistance does not require a single vision of ideal/perfect gender justice, and that efficacy considerations dictate that genuinely feminist resistance will often look different in different contexts.

Conclusion

The embrace of feminized power and skepticism about a gender-neutral public sphere may sometimes be parts of political strategies that are compatible with feminism. This has been difficult for Western feminists to recognize, particularly when "other" women's strategies and practices are involved. I hope to have offered a path beyond the missionary feminist precommitments that assume that the attributes associated with social decision-making power in the West, and sometimes the extent to which an entire context is Westernized, are the important indicators of whether "other" women's power is feminist. Nonideal universalism reveals a range of reasons to be skeptical about Western gender eliminativism that have nothing to do with accepting sexist oppression. Gender-neutral social forms may have been agents of colonial (or other) harm, they may not be the most immediate next step on the path to gender justice, and there may be a number of potential cultural gender protocols compatible with ultimate gender justice.

NOTES

INTRODUCTION

1. Contemporary transnational feminist work describes a number of cases in which women in the global South, or in cultural minority groups in the West, are advantaged over men. For example, women may be preferred as factory workers (and thus have greater access to employment) because they are more docile and can be paid less. I do not intend to deny the presence of such cases, though it is worth noting that many of them are made possible by background sexist oppression.

2. My idea that feminists need not agree on a single moral vernacular to support the shared normative project of opposing sexist oppression is similar to Rawls's (1991) notion of overlapping consensus. See Baehr (2004) for an application of the notion of overlapping consensus to feminist disagreements.

3. See Young (1990) for a definition of cultural domination.

4. I see Nnaemeka's (2004) argument that African feminisms are nego-feminisms as making a similar point about the nonideal theoretical character of anti-imperialist feminisms.

5. I am grateful to Monique Deveaux for raising this objection.

6. For example, see Friedman (2013).

7. See Walker (2007) for a lucid discussion of what we can learn about morality by studying morality as a set of social practices. Walker's important discussion predates contemporary discussions of ideal and nonideal theory.

8. Chandra Mohanty (1988) famously argued that most Western feminist theory traded in stereotypes and projections about third-world women. See Uma Narayan (2002) and Jaggar (2005) for discussions of how these projections and stereotypes affect philosophical inquiry.

9. See Zerilli's (2009) criticism of Benhabib and Nussbaum for a discussion of the normative possibilities that are cut off by the search for liberal values in "other" cultures. See also Nussbaum's (2001) own discussion of the shift in her thought toward political liberalism—and away from her claims in earlier work (especially

1999) that women advocating for their own interests was tantamount to their embracing liberalism.

10. The term "relational" is used to refer to many types of conceptions of autonomy, including those according to which one can simultaneously be autonomous and socially influenced, those according to which there are normative constraints on the content of attitudes and behaviors that can be autonomously endorsed, and those according to which certain social conditions must be present for attitudes and behaviors to be autonomous. Conceptions of the first sort are subject to my criticism of Kymlicka in chapter 3. As I have argued elsewhere (Khader 2011, 2012), I see conceptions of the second sort as problematically conflating autonomy and the ability to flourish. See Khader (2011), Madhok (2013), and Mahmood (2005) for discussions of other problems with normatively laden conceptions of autonomy or agency. My problem with the third type of conception of relational autonomy (at least as a tool for identifying which practices and preferences are compatible with feminism) is as follows: making feminist views the same as those that promote relational autonomy by promoting context-specific agency closes off the possibility that *contexts* can be oppressive.

11. For a discussion of the terms "third-world women," "women of color," and "women from the global South," see Fatima, Dotson, Herr, Khader, and Nyanzi (2017).

CHAPTER 1

1. For examples of the accusation that postcolonial feminists are relativists, see Okin's (2000) criticism of Mohanty; Chesler's (2010) critique of Abu-Lughod; Jardine's critique of Obiora in Obiora, Hall, and Jardine (1996); and Nussbaum's (1992) critique of Frederique Apfel-Marglin (though in later works Nussbaum acknowledges the possibility that anti-imperialist feminists are focused on bargaining with patriarchy and her universalism has also substantially changed since her endorsement of political liberalism). Most of the uptake of anti-imperialist literatures in philosophy has been centered around rejecting relativism. See, for example, Jennifer Mather Saul's (2013) discussion of respect for culture in her well-known textbook, as well as Nussbaum (1999, 2001) and Okin (1999). Chandra Talpade Mohanty (2005) argues in "Under Western Eyes Revisited" that her work has been widely read as relativist. For more general discussions of how universalism/relativism debates work to silence critics of imperialism, see Volpp (2001) and Nnaemeka (2004).

2. The term "Western feminist" denotes a theoretical perspective common in the West. It is a perspective that is particularly easy for those who are in positions of global dominance and subject to Western internal ideology to hold. However, the positions associated with Western feminism are also held by some "other" women, and some feminists from the West reject Western feminism. To make clear that the object of my critique is a point of view rather than a set of people who inhabit a particular geographic region, and to avoid delegitimizing the perspectives of "other"

women whose prescriptions happen to match up to popular Western ones, I predominantly use the term "missionary feminism."

3. Khoja-Moolji articulates this critique of human rights discourses, in particular, though at many points in her article her target seems to be universalism as such.

4. See, for example, Abu-Lughod (2002), Jaggar (2005), Jamal (2005), Mohanty (2003), Tobin (2009), Volpp (2001), Zerilli (2009), Alcoff (2007), Ayotte and Husain (2005), Charusheela (2008), Gopal (2013), and Sharp et al. (2013).

5. Though there are a number of straightforwardly antinormative claims, as well as a number of ambiguous criticisms of normativity (such as Abu-Lughod's [2013] endorsement of "universalism without normativity'), I think many pejorative uses of "universalism" in anti-imperialist feminist literatures can be straightforwardly read as rejecting *descriptive* universalisms—that is, claims that women's experiences or the causes of their oppression are the same in all contexts.

6. The idea that anti-imperialists are primarily concerned with respect for culture also distorts their actual concerns—many of which are about physical, political, and economic harm and domination.

7. The AWWP project is funded partly by the US State Department and was founded by a former employee; it enables Afghan women to tell their stories through online workshops and mentorship with US women writers.

8. See the introduction and chapter 3 in this book for further discussions of Enlightenment liberalism and the ways in which it does and does not overlap with liberal doctrines in contemporary political philosophy.

9. A teleological view of human history as moral progress, complete with Western vanguardism and the association of Western political activity with reason, can be found in Kant (2009).

10. See, for example, Escobar (1994), Mehta (1999), Said (1979), Wynter (2014), Asad (1993), Kabeer (1991), and Kothari (1988).

11. For a discussion of how sati is better understood as a product of colonial intervention and fascination than of Indian tradition, see Narayan (1997).

12. Abu-Lughod also criticizes the view that Afghan women were living in a state similar to that of Western women before the ascent of the Taliban. Her view is that this may have been the situation for women in Kabul but not for women in the provinces.

13. Universalism, as I am describing it here, does not imply a particular meta-ethical position. A range of plausible meta-ethical positions, including some described by their authors as relativist, can yield the conclusion that sexist oppression is wrong in the sense necessary for feminist politics.

14. Zerilli is arguing against the idea that the values Western feminists seek to export are already valued in all cultures.

15. Sen's critique of transcendental institutionalism sometimes seems to be an argument against theorizing about institutional design and social structure in general. I do not endorse this part of Sen's view. My argument rests only the idea that we

do not need a single view of the endpoint of justice to be able to engage in transnational normative political practices.

16. See, for example, Baier (1995), Collins (2000), Kittay (1999), Pateman (1988), and Walker (2007).

17. Narayan (1997) also shows the responsibility-deflecting character of the focus on culture.

18. Methodological individualism as a descriptive notion is the idea that social phenomena can be understood to exclusively or primarily result from the behavior of individual agents. As an approach to politics, methodological individualism suggests that acting on individual actors, rather than on structures, is the appropriate solution to political problems.

19. Mohanty's (1988) observation that the scholarship on third-world women groups them all together as possessed of the "third-world difference"—a property that is only relevant in contrasts between third-world and Western women—can be understood to be pointing out a similar phenomenon. The focus on contrast with an "Enlightened" West eclipses the contextual and historical information that is important for making actual political judgments.

20. Mahmood uses the terms "secular humanism" and "liberalism" interchangeably in other work. I take her broad point to be that the harm wreaked by Westerners is either ignored or thought to be unrelated to Western culture or Western values.

21. Philosophers typically defend criticisms of Western values by defending universalism against relativism (and thereby bypassing the possibility of universalisms not constituted or exhausted by Western values). See Buchanan (2004), Okin (1989, 1999, 1995), and to a lesser extent, Nussbaum (1999). See also Zerilli (2005) for an argument that Seyla Benhabib and Martha Nussbaum have fallen into this trap while pretending not to.

22. Though Sen shares with Charles Mills and Anderson an interest in developing a political philosophy that would improve the world we actually inhabit, I am sympathetic to Mills's (2011) argument that Sen neglects to discuss the need to repair past injustice.

23. In much liberal political philosophy, for example, the central political question is taken to concern moral coordination among individuals with diverse conceptions of the good rather than overcoming oppression and domination. See Mills and Pateman (2007) and Young (1990).

24. Some postcolonial feminist scholars, such as Oyewumi (1997), argue that the idea of gender does not exist in some contexts. The idea that feminism is opposition to sexist oppression is fully compatible with the idea that different gender categories obtain in different contexts and that gender may be less of a *determining* factor of social status in some societies than others. It is also compatible with the idea that sexist oppression does not exist in some societies because gender does not exist in them. However, most claims about the nonexistence of gender in certain societies are controversial. See Bakare-Yusuf (2003) on Oyewumi, for example.

25. Maxine Molyneux (1985) draws a similar distinction between movements that aim to change women's gender interests and their welfare interests.

26. I speak of oppression as being about the distribution of indicators of advantage and disadvantage, but the idea that oppression is the systematic subordination of a group does not require a specifically distributive conception of justice. As Young (1990) argues, oppression can be perpetuated through systems of value and control over social meanings; my definition does not preclude this—though there is some tension between my idea that it is acceptable for indicators of advantage to be context-relative and the idea that the selection of indicators itself requires normative judgments.

27. See Khader (2011) for a discussion of why people's first-person perspectives on why they seem to continue their own oppression are invaluable, even if the presence or absence of oppression is an objective phenomenon.

28. I discuss this idea at greater length in Khader (2011). For more on the debate about lists, see Nussbaum (2001), Ackerly (2000), Jaggar (2006), and Nnaemeka (2004).

29. Matua does criticize the content of human rights in one part of the paper, his discussion of the focus on rights to the exclusion of duties.

30. Sen's discussion of justice enhancement sometimes suggests that we do not need to make judgments about just social relations at all and that we should instead focus on improving individual well-being. I reject this idea since it is incompatible with the conception of feminism as opposition to sexist oppression.

CHAPTER 2

1. Okin does not advocate the elimination of "other" cultures, and I agree with her argument that "cultures" (to the extent this term is coherent) that include practices that are deeply oppressive or harmful to women should be changed. However, I take this quotation to reveal unstated background assumptions about the essential features of non-Western cultures that influence her judgments about particular cases, as well as equivocations between ideal and nonideal theoretical questions—equivocations I think her critics were justified in worrying about. Okin is plausibly interpreted as thinking there are real-world cases in which cultures should be extinguished, since the subject of the ultimatum is actual women, and the article is intended to influence policy.

2. See the introduction for discussion of the distinction between justificatory imperialism and constitutive imperialism. The allegation that individualism is justificatory imperialist amounts to the claim that it helps imperialist activity appear morally justified; the allegation that it is constitutively so amounts to the idea that the value is part of a regime of cultural domination.

3. For an example of the feminist problems with the simplistic rejection of individualism, see Saba Mahmood's (2005, 14–15) argument that societies have flourished without placing a high value on the individual or on freedom. Note that

Mahmood shifts the question to being about the flourishing of *societies* rather than of individuals and so cannot respond to the common feminist point that societies have often flourished at the expense of women.

4. One reason I create a taxonomy of the harms as thoroughly as I do in this section is to avoid framing the chapter in ways that some liberal (but not only liberal) feminists will see as begging the question. I describe the harms in ways that are straightforward and relatively intuitive and in ways that are endorsable regardless of whether one believes that collectives have independent normative status (or superior normative status to individuals) or whether one believes that harms to associations are *necessarily* harmful to women. To emphasize this, I say that the harms are perpetuated *through* damage to, or through ignorance of, associations rather than that the harm *is* the damage to associations.

5. Neoliberalism, the ideology that currently drives much of what is often positively referred to as "globalization," has become the dominant ideology largely through the actions of Northern institutions. According to it, states should strive to deregulate markets and to minimize expenditures on social services, and they should give the poor "access to markets" to end their poverty. The evidence that increased market involvement will end women's poverty is highly dubitable. See Chant (2008), Narayan (2005), Wilson (2012), Poster and Salime (2002), and Leach and Sitakaran (2002). Neoliberal reforms also often require increases in women's unpaid labor. See Desai (2002).

6. Lest it seem that the individualizing effect is benign, since women will escape poverty and no longer need associations (bracketing questions about the moral acceptability of their having to change a deeply embedded form of life to escape poverty), it is worth remembering that the informal sector work into which microcredit funnels women is itself short term and precarious (Narayan 2005, 2010).

7. See Chant (2005) for a discussion of the role the notion of the feminization of poverty plays in the feminization of responsibility; see Wilson (2012) on the role instrumentalist views of women play; and Khader (2017) for a discussion of the phenomenon in relation to global justice.

8. Another association that seems to go unacknowledged in intervention design is women's relationships with children. Given that women are likely to retain responsibility for dependents if they exit and are usually able to earn less money than men, women who exit are likely to remain in poverty (Chant 2009). Ignoring the impact of children is one part of the story, but in some cases, population control as a method of freeing women remains a part of the same development discourses that valorize income generation (Wilson 2015).

9. I intend the term "kin" to include more than relatives; see Stack (1983) for such a definition.

10. For a discussion of how parental involvement in marriage continues to be a mechanism for transmitting wealth in the contemporary West, see Khandelwal (2009).

11. See Agot (2007) for a similar argument about the persistence of severe female genital cutting and early marriage in contexts where returns for education are low.

12. See Narayan (1997) for a discussion of how language about "cultural" practices ignores the roles imperialism and economic interests play in patriarchal practices, as well as how such practices have changed over time. Archambault (2011) argues that early marriage among the Maasai is an adaptation to manage contemporary livelihood insecurity.

13. Other cases in Abu-Lughod's book besides Gateefa, those of Zaynab and Khadija, also involve women who accept sexist marriage practices and family forms because of considerations about love and care—as well as the distribution of dependency work.

14. For a discussion of the cyclical nature of women's investments in patriarchal family structures when they are young and their expectations of a return on those investments when they are older, see Kandiyoti (1988, 279–280).

15. Abu-Lughod sometimes seems to argue that the depth and importance of women's existing kinship associations tell against the value of a legal right to consent to marriage altogether; I do not think her evidence supports this conclusion.

16. See Eisenberg (2003) and Deveaux (2000) for discussions of rules of gender and cultural membership.

17. Aboriginal feminist Jackie Huggins (1994) describes feminist proposals that fail to recognize women's community attachments as follows: "In asking Aboriginal women to stand apart from Aboriginal men, the white women's movement was, perhaps unconsciously, repeating the attempts made over decades by welfare administrations to separate Aboriginal women and use them against their families" (70).

18. See Jeff Spinner-Halev (2001) for a criticism of Okin for failing to recognize this fact. I reject his argument that concerns about inequality among groups are usually more important than individual women's interests, however.

19. This policy has since been deemed discriminatory and changed.

20. Enright recommends that both culturally specific and mainstream domestic violence services be available, because women fleeing forced marriage sometimes prefer secrecy from their communities.

21. I am grateful to Elizabeth Brake, Tracy Llanera, and Catriona Mackenzie for individual conversations that helped me settle on this term.

22. Personhood individualism does not exclude the possibility that people's interests are intertwined with those of others. What it does exclude is the possibility that the importance of a person's basic interests could be lesser than, or never conceptually distinguishable from, those of others.

23. I use the term "personhood individualism" rather than "normative individualism" for two reasons. First, the term "normative individualism" suggests to many the Kant-inspired idea that fundamental source of value is the individual human person. Personhood requires much less than this and is compatible with normative perspectives besides Kantian (or other liberal) metaphysical views. Second,

independence individualism, as we shall see, is also an individualist view with strong normative elements. For feminist defenses of normative individualism without other forms of individualism, see Nussbaum (2001) and Anderson (2009).

24. For feminist views, see Fineman (1991), Kittay (1999), Walker (2007), and Code (2001). For non-Western views, see Dhand (2002), Goodman (2009), and Harris (2011).

25. See Schwartzman (2006, 26–27) for a discussion of the feminist explanatory deficiencies of methodological individualism, and Anderson (2009) for an argument that a form of personhood individualism without methodological individualism can explain what is ultimately wrong with oppression.

26. For an overview of anthropological evidence for the presence of personhood even in societies that have often been thought not to include distinct persons, see Zenker (2018).

27. However, I disagree with Nussbaum's (1999) larger claim that seeing personhood as a value at all means "speaking the language of the Enlightenment" (56), Nussbaum (2001) also revises her commitment to the idea that the value of the individual person must be understood as a liberal value in later work.

28. Of course, part of the reason children are imagined away is that the individual agent in capitalism is envisioned as a male breadwinner. I agree with this feminist criticism of neoliberalism, but am attempting to show that the association of feminism with income generation comes from colonial, and not merely androcentric, biases.

29. For an example of how, in practice, relationships become thought of as relationships of custom because of the race or ethnicity of the participants—rather than because of an internal feature of the relationships, see Akhtar (2018). Akhtar notes that unrecognized Islamic marriages are similar in structure to more general practices of cohabitation without marriage but that the former are thought of as a public policy problem.

30. The idea that relationships of custom are harmful is distinct from the idea that women should be able to choose whether to enter or exit relationships, since it is possible to follow a custom and to see one's affiliations as related to the well-being of others without being coerced or dominated.

31. An important point of contrast with the androcentric individualist ideal criticized by much of Western feminist philosophy is that the latter does not exclusively treat dependency relationships as harmful; it treats cultural embeddedness, which is assumed be valued mostly by non-Western people, as harmful.

32. Enlightenment liberalism, as I state in the introduction, is a view according to which human moral progress occurs through the abandonment of traditional values and unchosen relationships, as well as through the universalization of economic independence. It is usually made plausible by narratives that the West is the endpoint of human progress and that its putative moral superiority is caused by endogenous factors. I do not take this view to represent an explicit position in political philosophy; I instead take it to be a set of background assumptions to which public

discourse often appeals—to which philosophers and other theorists may inadvertently help themselves when making judgments about cases.

33. The UK forced-marriage case is an exception, because South Asian and Muslim women are in a late-capitalist Western context. However, it does not follow from this fact—especially in the context of a multicultural and formerly colonial state—that they are morally required shape their forms of marriage to meet the prevalent culture in the context.

34. Though Friedman allows that the value of economic independence is prudential, she argues that women in the global South, in particular, are need of economic self-sufficiency. I take the needs of women in the global South to be much more context-variant than Friedman suggests. Friedman (who is not an independence individualist) claims that economic independence is valuable because it allows women to wrest some level of control of their lives from men who dominate them; I suggest that economic self-sufficiency often fails to have this effect and that, in some cases, other changes would be more likely to reduce sexist oppression.

35. The Enlightenment teleological narrative, as I state in chapter 1, holds that the West is the high point of moral progress that all societies will ultimately arrive at, and that the differences in the current states of Western and "other" societies are caused by endogenous factors.

36. See Palmer (2016) for a discussion of the boom in the involvement of private banks in microcredit, and Narayan (2005) for a discussion of how this might constitute grooming women to consume credit.

37. See, for example, Narayan (1997), Badran (2009), Abu-Lughod (2002), Choudhury (2015), and Nzegwu (1995).

38. I borrow the term "justice-enhancing" from Amartya Sen (2009) and discuss it in greater detail in chapter 1.

39. See Sen's (1990) discussion of cooperative conflicts for an explanation of why it can be self-interested under unjust conditions for women to remain in marriages in which their interests and contributions are treated as inferior.

40. See Nussbaum (1999, 46–49) for an example of a philosophical discussion that minimizes the losses incurred through the abandonment of inherited attachments. Nussbaum attributes to her opponents the view that inherited attachments are intrinsically valuable because cultures or embedded forms of life are inherently worth preserving. Nussbaum then claims that such losses are not as worrisome as they may seem, because women can come to inhabit "new communities" through their participation in feminist organizations. I do not dispute Nussbaum's point that we should not presume to know in advance what value existing attachments have for women. However, it is striking that she treats worries about the losses women incur through changes to their inherited attachments as worries about the value of attachments *as such* rather than as worries about the value of particular existing attachments for particular women. The idea that relationships of choice can simply replace relationships of custom seems based on an understanding of relationships as

interchangeable, or a sense that all an adequate theory needs to do is render some forms of relationship acceptable.

41. See Jaggar (2006), Kandiyoti (1988), and Khader (2011, 2012, and 2013) for discussions of Western feminists' tendencies to overestimate the extent to which "other" women are motivated by false consciousness.

42. This idea is not incompatible with the idea that radical change can be a feminist strategy. Collective action can reduce, eliminate, or offset transition costs, and women's wanting to bear the costs increases their moral acceptability.

CHAPTER 3

1. Abu-Lughod (2013) coins this term to poke fun at the way North Americans homogenize Muslims.

2. Transnational feminists argue that putative feminist sentiment was one reason for Western popular support of the invasions of Iraq and Afghanistan. They do not claim that "saving" Muslim women was ever the US government's primary objective. For a discussion of the subtle ways feminists and the George W. Bush administration became strange bedfellows after September 11, see Mahmood and Hirschkind (2002).

3. See the introduction for a discussion of this dilemma. Briefly, the dilemma asks us to choose between abandoning feminism's status as a normative doctrine to respond to concerns about imperialism and embracing feminism's status a normative doctrine and accepting that normativity entails imperialist consequences.

4. See Bangstad (2011) for an argument that Mahmood's position slides into moral relativism. Abu-Lughod and Mahmood express normative commitments to anti-imperialism and feminism, so it is unclear whether their critiques of normativity are consistent with the rest of their arguments. Razakh is a notable exception among the anti-imperialist scholars of Muslim women in the care she takes to demonstrate that her position remains normative.

5. My criticism of Badinter does not require a stance about the oppressiveness of veiling in any particular context. My point is ultimately that whether veiling (or any other practice) is oppressive does not depend on whether it is traditional—and this is what Badinter misunderstands.

6. The girls around whom the hijab controversy began came from families that discouraged veiling, but the girls saw veiling as externally dictated (Scott 2010).

7. Some positive concepts of freedom posit a collective self and thus allow that the self-regarding desires of individuals undermine the freedom of the collective self (Berlin 1969, 118–172).

8. Contemporary feminist philosophers offer liberal conceptions of autonomy that are designed to take the reality and ubiquity of socialization seriously. Procedural conceptions of autonomy allow that the desire to adhere to traditional dictates can be autonomous, because values are an agent's own to the extent that they have

been subjected to processes of reflection and incorporation into the self. However, the question of whether preferences are an agent's own is, in my view, orthogonal to the question of whether they serve feminist ends. For feminist procedural understandings of autonomy, see Meyers (1989), Christman (2004), and Friedman (2006). For feminist substantive theories of autonomy suggesting that beliefs with certain content cannot be autonomous, see Stoljar (2000) and Mackenzie (2008). For an argument that substantive accounts of autonomy get in the way of feminist politics, see Khader (2011, 41–74; 2012; 2016).

9. Though Kant shares with Hirsi Ali and Badinter a sense that being thought for by others is incompatible with freedom, he does not pit traditional adherence against freedom quite so starkly. Kant leaves open the possibility of following a tradition for one's own reasons, whereas Ali and Badinter suggest that following a tradition just is the failure to possess reasons of one's own.

10. Allison Weir (2013) criticizes Mahmood for assuming liberal individualist understandings of freedom are the only possible ones.

11. See the introduction for more on my distinction between justificatory and constitutive imperialism. Values play justificatory roles in imperialism when they make projects of Northern and Western domination, such as war and economic exploitation, seem like good things. They play constitutive roles in imperialism when they prescribe parochial values as part of a regime of cultural domination.

12. Although I do not believe this is her intent, M. Jacqui Alexander's (2006) discussion of Afghan women also contains language that is easily read as repudiating normative argument. She aligns universalism with imperialism and indicts the Feminist Majority for "latent universalism within relativism."

13. Many of Okin's critics understand Okin to hold that Western cultures are not patriarchal. However, I believe Okin's stance is better understood as ranking Western and non-Western cultures in terms of degree of patriarchy. She is not even entirely consistent on this point, as she mentions parenthetically that some non-Western cultures have worked to eradicate patriarchy. Moreover, most of Okin's work is about the sexist practices of Western cultures, and her book *Women in Western Political Thought* (2013) traces sexist oppression to certain Western values.

14. The inability to respect women who do not value freedom from sexist oppression stems, according to Mahmood (2005), "from the dual character of feminism as analytical and politically prescriptive project.... [F]reedom is normative to feminism as it is to liberalism" (10).

15. According to Mahmood, feminism requires a questionable liberal value that goes by various names in the book—ranging from "the concept of individual autonomy" to "agency as the ability to realize one's interests against the weight of custom, tradition, transcendental will, or other obstacles" (Mahmood 2005, 11; see also the quotation in note 14).

16. Mahmood (2005, 191) ends the book by saying that if feminist solidarity continues to exist at all, it must involve relinquishing certainty about what feminism opposes.

17. Late twentieth-century liberalism includes a variety of conceptions of freedom and autonomy that make autonomy compatible with adherence to tradition. Rawls's *Political Liberalism* is the most famous example. See also feminist rehabilitations of the value of autonomy by Christman (1991, 2004, 2018), Friedman (2002), Khader (2011), and Meyers (1991),

18. See Barclay (2001) for a discussion of the tension between the feminist desire to acknowledge social construction and the feminist desire to oppose patriarchy.

19. Kant and contemporary liberals generally disagree on criteria for what would make a view genuinely one's own, however. Kant requires autonomous action to be morally right and consistent with the dictates of reason.

20. For a more extended discussion of the implications of Kymlicka's insistence that autonomy requires each of an agent's commitments to be subject to scrutiny and an argument that this places excessively stringent requirements on autonomy, see Christman (1991).

21. The term "relational" is used to refer to many types of conceptions of autonomy, including those according to which one can simultaneously be autonomous and socially influenced, those according to which there are normative constraints on the content of attitudes and behaviors that can be autonomously endorsed, and those according to which certain social conditions must be present for attitudes and behaviors to be autonomous. My criticism of relational autonomy in the body of the text was targeted at the third type of conception. Conceptions of the first sort are subject to my criticism of Kymlicka, and, as I have argued elsewhere (Khader 2011, 2012), I see conceptions of the second sort as conflating autonomy and the ability to flourish in problematic ways. See Madhok (2013) and Mahmood (2005) for discussions of other problems with conceptions of autonomy or agency that import substantive content into autonomy. See chapter 4 of this book and Khader (2014) for arguments that oppression-perpetuating behaviors can be genuinely autonomous and well-being enhancing under oppressive conditions.

22. More recently, hooks has also offered a definition of feminism as the struggle against all oppressions. I employ her old definition, not to deny the fact of intersectionality, but because of the need to acknowledge the presence of certain conflicts within transnational feminist praxis. Many problems discussed in this book result from the fact that the aims of opposing multiple oppressions—the end of imperialist domination and the end of sexism—can compete in practice. Keeping the forms of oppression analytically distinct helps us recognize the reality that multiply oppressed women may face tragic choices between strategies for opposing the different oppressions they face. See chapter 1 for further discussion of this point.

23. I say in chapter 1 that feminists need to agree on some list of universal indices of advantage and disadvantage. However, knowing the content of the list is not enough to know what the indices of advantage and disadvantage are in a given context. Some indices of advantage are context-specific, and even universal ones typically

have context-specific instantiations that cannot be understood without close empirical attention.

24. However, it is worth stating explicitly that denying the universal value of Enlightenment freedom does not mean denying the universal value of other goods we refer to as "freedoms," such as freedom of speech or expression. There is good reason to believe that the latter two freedoms are universally valuable and that societies that disproportionately deny them to women are oppressive. I suggested in the first chapter of this book that the goods referred to in human rights declarations were good candidates for universal goods, and that freedoms of speech and expression are among these—and can be had without Enlightenment freedom.

25. Critics of the term "Islamic feminism" argue that it entrenches the power of sexist Islamist governments by refusing to contest their fundamentally patriarchal terms (Moghadam 2002; Mojab 2001). These arguments, true as they may be, speak more to the strategic problems facing feminists organizing in certain Islamist contexts than the logical possibility of opposition to sexist oppression on Islamic grounds.

26. Feminisms in other religions also demonstrate this possibility. Consider the fact that the Seneca Falls Convention in the United States accused men of having "usurped the prerogative of Jehovah."

27. Wadud rejects the term "Islamic feminist" but meets the criteria for Islamic feminism laid out by Badran and other scholars

28. There may be feminist reasons to spread freedoms besides Enlightenment freedom. For instance, it is likely that upending sexism requires freedom of expression and the right to vote—but these are conceptually distinct from Enlightenment freedom.

CHAPTER 4

1. One section of this article initially appeared in 2015 as "Development Ethics, Gender Complementarianism, and Intrahousehold Inequality" in *Hypatia* 30 (2): 352–339.

2. Chachawarmi is an ideal of gender complementarity grounded in an indigenous Andean cosmovisions. It has become central to some decolonial feminist arguments that gender is a colonial imposition in the Americas but is also rejected by some Andean indigenous feminists for failing to support criticism of sexist gender relations within indigenous communities.

3. For another argument that Lugones romanticizes chachawarmi, one that includes references to criticisms from social scientists working in Latin America, see Giraldo (2016). Some Andean feminist groups, such as Mujeres Creando, are vocally critical of both Western eliminativism and the chachawarmi ideal (Paulson 2016, 35).

4. I use the term "gender eliminativism" in this book to refer to the idea that a person's perceived sex should not affect the social opportunities available to her. Okin's (1989) vision of a gender-free society is one example of what I would call a "gender-eliminativist" vision, whose broad contours would be widely accepted by Western feminists. Though I claim that headship complementarianism is not a feminist

ideal, I remain open to the possibility that other complementarianisms might be, so long as they allowed role differentiation to not translate into structurally engineered *disadvantage*.

5. See Baehr (2004) for a discussion of variation of gender metaphysics within Western feminism. Baehr traces view that men and women have the same nature at least as far back as the nineteenth century but also notes the existence of difference feminist and postmodern feminist views within Western traditions.

6. For criticisms of such views, see Segato (2011) and Bakare-Yusuf (2003).

7. See the introduction for a discussion of the distinction between the justificatory and constitutive roles in imperialism.

8. Some feminisms developed in the West suggest that feminized gender roles can be empowering in contexts of racial and imperialist oppression (see Collins 2000). Others suggest that revaluing and reconstructing the feminine role is the path to feminism (see Irigaray 1993).

9. Part of my point is that opposing sexism is not the only important moral concern and that we should seek feminist strategies that are consistent with other moral concerns, such as reducing imperialism. For a discussion of why I have not chosen to make anti-imperialism definitional for feminism see chapter 1 and the introduction.

10. For an example of the charge of romanticism and a response to it, see Saidi's (2010, 12) discussion of Hoppe.

11. For example, see Gallagher (2004), Mir-Hosseini (2010), and Paulson (2016).

12. For an argument for why complementarianisms that do not see women as persons should not count as reasonable in the contemporary world, see Khader (2015).

13. For discussions of the notion of asymmetrical vulnerability, see Goodin (1985) and Okin (1991).

14. It is not uncommon for headship complementarians to proclaim men's dependency on women for care, but dependency in a certain domain of life is not the same thing as vulnerability that prevents a person from accessing the spheres of life associated with power, that makes a person incapable of exiting a relationship, or that results in low bargaining power within it.

15. My analysis is thus compatible with the empirical claim that some societies do not have public/private divides; the forms of complementarianism underlying those social arrangements, when they exist, require a different normative analysis from the one I offer here.

16. The society Menon describes seems to involve a form of slightly moderated headship complementarianism, and she might argue that it is not a form of headship complementarianism at all. She argues that older women have significant household decision-making power. However, older women still live in seclusion and lack the capacity to earn income in a context where income is increasingly important (their caste is no longer able to earn a living only through the performance of religious rituals). However, having some power within the household does not mean elder women are not vulnerable to men's decisions;

nor does the fact that age increases women's power change the reality that gender is *one* significant determinant of household power and access to well-being and social advantage. Menon (2012) also mentions that men are officially the unquestioned heads of households, that women go out of their way to exercise public deference to them, and that the word for husband in their language is "lord" (91). The asymmetrical gendered vulnerability with regard to access to income and the ability to circulate in public in a world where these are important makes the arrangement characteristic of headship complementarianism. That elder women have some power just means that the asymmetry does not equally afflict all the women in a household or permeate all domains; older women make some household decisions (Menon 2000, 96).

17. For more on the idea that self-subordinating gender roles can be cultivated in the same ways as virtuous and socially desirable practices, see Tinker (1999) and Khader (2014).

18. Poor and middle-class women's resistance to feminism is often resistance to the capture of feminist movements by local elite women. I will not say much about this here, but it is of course true that the feminist reforms favored by elite women sometimes do less to improve women's lives than the reforms that would be favored by pro-poor movements.

19. See Moser (2003) and World Bank (2012).

20. She adds that this is true regardless of whether the parties involved think about the situation as bargaining—or whether they have explicitly bargained at all. According to Agarwal (1997a), the fact that explicit bargaining so rarely happens is often a testament to how advantaged men really are and how entrenched in social practices the power differentials are (7). The cost of exit may just be so high and so well-known that women do not need to threaten to exit to know what the consequences would be.

21. Criticism of practices that invisibilize or downgrade women's labor does not require the view that household labor is essentially bad or degrading. See Davis (1983) for an argument that housework is degrading. It would be unpromising for feminists to see at least once component, dependency work, as such since it is necessary in human societies. See Kittay (1999).

22. For a discussion of how Sen's related conception of "reason to value" is not value neutral, see Khader and Kosko forthcoming.

23. Similarly, Kabeer (1999), in her theoretical essay on empowerment, defines empowerment as agency expansion but mainly counts the cases in which women challenge men's authority. For an observation that the dominant feminist notion of agency is value-laden, see Mahmood (2005, 1–39).

24. There is disagreement about whether preferences to participate in oppressive practices motivated by prudential or strategic reasons can count as adaptive preferences. In my (Khader 2011, 2012) definition, such preferences can count as adaptive.

25. Papanek does not mention this, but norms around dieting and self-control in the West also suggest similar gendered compensatory beliefs.

26. It may be objected that the argument of this paragraph supposes that feminists must support eliminating, not merely reducing patriarchal risk. Though I am sympathetic to the idea that patriarchal risk must be eliminated in a gender-just society, my argument here supposes only that headship complementarians want a *degree* of patriarchal risk that feminists will find too high.

27. Similarly, Menon mentions that the women who are especially poorly off in the Oriya community are those who lack a place within a family.

28. Another conclusion one might draw from the fact that headship-complementarian views end up endorsing the persistence of IISNPs at some level is that IISNPs are not genuinely bad. I think this would involve feminists giving up too much ground, given the strength of the transnational feminist consensus on intrahousehold inequality, the amount of empirical data demonstrating the negative effects of such practices on women's opportunities, and the intuitive connection between feminism and opposition to these practices. The distinction between feminist ideals and strategies feminists can embrace in the short term that I develop here allows room for headship-complementarian strategies without requiring the strongly counterintuitive (for feminists) conclusion that IISNPs are acceptable.

29. See Kandiyoti (1988), Khader (2011, 2014), Chambers (2008), and Narayan (2002).

30. For arguments and evidence that women's empowerment programs have not had the type of cross-domain effects that were expected, or that they have increased women's well-being without reducing gender inequality, see Batliwala and Dhanraj (2007), Sen (1990), Osmani (1998), Cheston and Kuhn (2002), Agot (2007), and Khader (2014).

CHAPTER 5

1. This is not to deny that many Western feminists have questioned the desirability of women's incorporation into a gender-neutral public sphere. Within Western feminism, debates about, for example, whether women should be able to claim to special rights based on maternity and whether ostensibly gender-neutral forms of power are masculine are ongoing. I emphasize the distinct issues raised by the transnational context here, largely because I think Western feminists are more likely to dismiss feminized power by "other" women. However, there is certainly overlap in the reasons for dismissal, especially when the concerns have to do with women of color and immigrant women in the West. Many of my arguments against dismissing feminized power out of hand apply in domestic contexts as well. For discussions of how internal imperialist dynamics in the West cause the discounting of Black women's feminized power, see Collins (2000). For a discussion of disagreements among Western feminists about the metaphysics of gender, see Baehr (2004).

2. See the introduction for a discussion of these terms.

3. See Okin's (1999, 124) response to Honig; Hoppe (quoted in Saidi 2010), Bertkay (1993) on Ahmed; and Bischoff, Ening, and Acharya's (2016, 48) response which is, in part, to Nzegwu.

4. The Enlightenment teleological narrative holds that the conditions of the contemporary West are the ones toward which all human societies should aspire, because the contemporary West has morally "evolved" further than other societies have. In addition to assuming the superiority of Western societies and assuming that there is a single best form of society, this narrative obscures the role imperialism has played in sustaining the "development" of the West and the "underdevelopment" of the South. For more on the Enlightenment teleological narrative, see chapter 1.

5. Sen does not use the term "justice monist" but instead uses the term "transcendental institutionalist." However, Sen's understanding of transcendental institutionalism includes more than the view I am calling justice monism. Sen sometimes seems to use the term "transcendental institutionalist" to refer to the idea that justice concerns basic social institutions. I use the term "justice monism" so as not to have to take his anti-institutionalist critique on board.

6. In previous iterations of these arguments (see Khader 2017), I referred to the missionary feminist mistakes I describe in this chapter as abuses of ideal theory. So long as the refusal to critically consider the origins of normative concepts and the focus on what is just to the exclusion of what is justice enhancing are both taken to be characteristic of ideal theory (as they are in Mills), the characterization still holds. However, since many understand ideal theory to include only the latter, and since the relationship between the former and the latter seems to have more to do more with historical associations than with conceptual links, I have chosen to foreground the extent to which ideological associations (i.e., those constitutive of missionary feminism) are the underlying driver.

7. For a discussion of the usage, as well as of the ways in which imprecise uses of it occlude, women's power in the West, see Fraser (1990).

8. An oft-cited example of the colonial reduction of women's social influence involves women's loss of control over land and the political power that came from their roles in farming. Jane Parpart argues that women in many precolonial societies had control over farming or specific farming activities, and that formal political power sometimes came from these roles. Colonialism meant the advent of private land ownership and the idea that only men could own property, the exclusive selection of men for formal political roles, and the idea that women's appropriate role was homemaking. See Parpart (1986) and Mikell (1997).

9. For a discussion of the forms of violence against women brought about by neoliberal urbanization, see Luttrell (2013).

10. See Kabeer (2001) for a discussion of how common practices of data analysis about microcredit assume that injections of income should either cause women to take unilateral control of their households or become divorced.

11. Of course, the hijab does not cover the face, which is further evidence of the culturalist move of taking the most putatively oppressive practices to stand metonymically for the entire culture.

12. Accepting that this is an instance of the culturalist category does not require thinking infibulation is a good thing. It just requires noticing that it is one oppressive restriction among many, and that rendering a judgment about whether women in Sudan were better off than American ones would require taking into account a multiplicity of restrictions in each context and weighing them against each other.

13. Many examples of the culturalist category error occur outside philosophy because of the dearth of philosophical writing on "other" women. However, "other" examples in academic and activist forums include Monica Jardine's drawing attention to the oppressiveness of "African cultural practices" in response to a difference of strategy about how to oppose severe female genital cutting (Obiora, Hall, and Jardine 1996, 74–76); Femen's pointing to the patriarchal character of Islam (and claim that it was better to be naked than to wear a burqa) when Tunisian feminists were saying that Femen's politics were undermining of their own (Choudhury 2015); and Josie Bullock's responding to Maori women who objected to *external* criticism of a potentially sexist element of a ceremony as defenders of "silly old traditions" (quoted in Curchin 2011).

14. Honig argues that co-wives form solidarity and that this can help them divide labor and bargain with their husbands. Okin (1999, 124) replies that wives only need solidarity because of the context's patriarchality.

15. See Jaggar (2005) for a discussion of the particular responsibilities Western feminists face because of their complicity in, and power to do something about, imperialism. See Zerilli (2005) for a discussion of the ineluctability of normative judgments for feminists.

16. In some cases, the anti-imperialist claim is that women are resisting colonialism instead of sexist oppression. Resistance of the former sort would still need to be measured diachronically, but it would have distinct normative goals that might not always align with feminist ones.

17. "Empowerment" and "resistance" are both process terms that denote transitions out of nonideal conditions. I focus on resistance here because empowerment is usually used transitively—to suggest that one agent is awakening power in another.

18. I thank Monique Deveaux for helping me clarify this point.

19. See Narayan (1997) and Mohanty and Alexander (1991) on how allegations of Westernization can undermine third-world women's movements.

20. See also Margaret Walker (2007) for a related discussion of how philosophy should focus on "comparative and piecemeal justifications" (264).

21. Mills makes the same point. See Mills and Pateman (2007, 121–122).

22. Embracing a human right to shape one's community requires embracing democratic forms of government; my point is that a number of cultural viewpoints about how gender should be lived, and what kinds of social institutions (broadly construed) are compatible with both feminism and democracy.

23. See Deveaux (2016b) on how recognizing informal political participation can enhance women's social decision-making power in contexts of traditional political authority. For discussion of significant social decision-making power wielded through institutions Westerners might miss, consider the literature on the panchayats of South Asia.

24. Basu (2016) notes that a number of women's movements have arisen around such issues as restricting contraception and abortion. In some of these cases, women who have lacked social decision-making power before are using gains in that power to undermine their well-being and freedom from oppression in other domains. (In others, there is no increase in social decisionmaking power, and the movements straightforwardly undermine feminist goals; Western feminists in particular should be careful to verify that "other" women having social decision-making power is actually new, and doesn't just seem new to Western feminists.) Cases in which women are gaining social decision-making power but using it against themselves are tough ones for feminists, and decision-making power has a special kind of importance relative to other goods. At the same time, feminists should not uncritically embrace cases of women who seem to be trading one part of their oppression for another.

25. For an argument that feminist conceptions of resistance are typically normatively laden, whether their authors realize it or not, see Mahmood (2005, 6–10).

26. See Khader (2011) and (2016) for an argument that building normative content into the concept of autonomy or agency has problematic consequences for feminists, including not recognizing the self-interested character of some oppression-perpetuating behavior.

27. Ahmed (1992) explicitly criticizes Saudi Arabia for enacting a form of sex segregation that causes "every law and institution to be dominated by men and designed blatantly and unequivocally to serve and maintain uncompromising male control" (531).

28. For an example of this argument, see Berktay (1993, 118–119).

29. Fanon famously referred to the veiled woman as capable of "seeing without being seen."

30. See Ferguson (2010) for an argument that in Western contexts the incomplete transformation of the world is a reason feminist commitments can be compatible with some acceptance of patriarchy. My discussion of transition costs in chapter 2 is also relevant to this question.

31. Nzegwu uses the term "sex" rather than gender, because she conceives the refusal to imagine away biological difference between men and women to be an advantage of Igbo metaphysics.

REFERENCES

Abu-Lughod, Lila. 2002. "Do Muslim Women Really Need Saving?" *American Anthropologist* 104 (3): 783–790.

Abu-Lughod, Lila. 2013. *Do Muslim Women Need Saving?* Cambridge, MA: Harvard University Press.

Ackerly, Brooke. 2000. *Political Theory and Feminist Social Criticism.* Cambridge: Cambridge University Press.

Adato, Michelle, Benedicte de la Briere, Dubravka Mindek, and Agnes Quisumbing. 2000. *The Impact of PROGRESA on Women's Status and Intrahousehold Relations.* Washington, DC: International Food Policy Research Institute.

Agarwal, Bina. 1997. "'Bargaining' and Gender Relations: Within and beyond the Household." *Feminist Economics* 3 (1): 1–51.

Agot, Kawango. 2007. "Women, Culture, and HIV/AIDS in Sub-Saharan Africa: What Does the Empowerment Discourse Leave Out?" In *Global Empowerment of Women: Responses to Globalization and Politicized Religions*, edited by Carolyn M. Elliot, 287–303. New York: Routledge.

Ahmed, Fauzia Erfhan. 2008. "Microcredit, Men, and Masculinity." *Feminist Formations* 20 (2): 122–155.

Ahmed, Leila. 1992. "Western Ethnocentrism and Representations of the Harem." *Feminist Studies* 8 (3): 521–534.

Akyeampong, Emmanuel, and Hippolyte Fofack. 2014. "The Contribution of African Women to Growth in the Colonial and Precolonial Periods." *Economic History of Developing Regions* 29 (1): 42–73.

Alcoff, Linda Martin. 2007. "Mignolo's Epistemology of Coloniality." *CR: The New Centennial Review* 7 (3): 79–101.

Alexander, M. Jacqui. 2006. *Pedagogies of Crossing: Meditations on Feminism, Sexual Politics, Memory, and the Sacred.* Durham, NC: Duke University Press.

Al-Khatahtbeh, Amani, Darakshan Raja, Kulsoom K. Ijaaz, Tajmia Tameez, and Anonymous. November 24, 2014. "Muslim Feminists Respond, The Hypocrisy of the Male-Centric Narrative." http://www.altmuslimah.com/2014/11/muslim-feminists-respond-the-hypocrisy-of-the-male-centric-narrative/.

Alkire, Sabina. 2007. "Concepts and Measures of Agency." Oxford Poverty and Human Development Initiative Working Paper 9. Oxford University, Oxford, UK.

Amadiume, Ifi. 1998. *Reinventing Africa: Matriarchy, Religion, and Culture*. London: Zed.

Amadiume, Ifi. 2002. "Bodies, Choices, and Globalizing Neoliberal Enchantments: African Matriarcha and Mamy Water." *Meridians* 2 (2): 41–66.

Anderson, Elizabeth. 2010. *The Imperative of Integration*. Princeton, NJ: Princeton University Press.

An-Na'im, Abdullahi. 1999. "Promises We Should All Keep in Common Cause." In *Is Multiculturalism Bad for Women? Susan Moller Okin with Respondents*, edited by Joshua Cohen, Matthew Howard, and Martha C. Nussbaum, 59–65. Princeton, NJ: Princeton University Press.

Archambault, Caroline. 2011. "Ethnographic Empathy and the Social Context of Rights: Rescuing Maasai Girls from Early Marriage." *American Anthropologist* 13 (4): 632–643.

Asad, Talal. 1993. *Genealogies of Religion*. Baltimore, MD: Johns Hopkins University Press.

Asad, Talal. 2003. *Formations of the Secular*. Palo Alto, CA: Stanford University Press.

Ayotte, Kevin J., and Mary E. Husain. 2005. "Securing Afghan Women: Neocolonialism, Epistemic Violence, and the Rhetoric of the Veil." *NWSA Journal* 17 (3): 112–133.

Anzaldua, Gloria. 1987. *Borderlands/La Frontera*. San Francisco: Aunt Lute Books.

Bachetta, Paola. 2002. *Right Wing Women*. New York: Routledge.

Badinter, Elisabeth, Régis Debray, Alain Finkielkraut, Elisabeth de Fontenay, and Catherine Kintzler. 1989. "Profs, ne capitulons pas!" *Le Nouvel Observateur*, November 2.

Badran, Margot. 2001. "Locating Feminisms: The Collapse of Religious and Secular Feminisms in the Mashriq." *Agenda* 50: 41–57.

Badran, Margot. 2009. *Feminism in Islam: Secular and Religious Convergences*. London: Oneworld.

Baehr, Amy. 2004. "Feminist Politics and Feminist Pluralism: Can We Do Feminist Political Theory without Theories of Gender?" *Journal of Political Philosophy* 12 (4): 411–436.

Baier, Annette. 1995. "The Need for More Than Justice." In *Justice and Care*, edited by Virginia Held, 47–60. Boulder, CO: Westview.

Bakare-Yusuf, Bibi. 2003. "Yorubas Don't Do Gender." *African Identities* 1: 121–142.

Banerji, Himani. 2001. "Pygmalion Nation." In *Of Property and Propriety*, edited by Himani Bannerji, Shahrzhad Mojab, and Judith Whitehead, 34–80. Toronto: University of Toronto Press.

Bangstad, Sindre. 2011. "Saba Mahmood and Anthropological Feminism after Virtue." *Theory, Culture and Society* 28 (3): 28–54.

Barakat, Sultan, and Jareth Wardell. 2002. "Exploited by Whom?" *Third World Quarterly* 23 (5): 909–930.

Barclay, Linda. 2001. "Autonomy and the Social Self." In *Relational Autonomy*, edited by Catriona Mackenzie and Natalie Stoljar, 52–71. New York: Oxford University Press.

Barlas, Asma. 2002. *"Believing Women" in Islam: Unreading Patriarchal Interpretations of the Qur'an*. Austin: University of Texas Press.

Bartky, Sandra. 1990. *Femininity and Domination*. New York: Routledge.

Basu, Amrita. 2004. "Women's Movements and the Challenge of Transnationalism." http://www3.amherst.edu/~mrhunt/womencrossing/basu.html. Accessed February 3, 2015.

Basu, Amrita. 2016. *Women's Movements in the Global Era: The Challenge of Local Feminisms*. New York: Avalon Publishing.

Batliwala, Srilantha, and Deepa Dhanraj. 2007. "Gender Myths That Instrumentalize Women: A View from the Indian Front Line." In *Feminisms in Development: Contradictions, Contestations, and Challenges*, edited by Andrea Cornwall, Elizabeth Harrison, and Ann Whitehead, 21–35. London: Zed.

Beneria, Lourdes, and Gita Sen. 1981. "Accumulation, Reproduction, and Women's Role in Economic Development." *Signs* 7 (2): 297–298.

Benhabib, Seyla. 1992. *Situating the Self: Gender, Community, and Postmodernism in Contemporary Ethics*. New York, Routledge.

Berktay, Faramagul. 1993. "Looking from the Other Side: Is Cultural Relativism the Way Out." In *Doing Things Differently: Women's Studies in the 1990s*, edited by Joanna de Groot and Mary Maynard, 110–131. New York: MacMillan.

Berlin, Isaiah. 1969. *Four Essays on Liberty*. London: Oxford University Press.

Bhabha, Homi. 1999. "Liberalism's Sacred Cow." In *Is Multiculturalism Bad for Women*, edited by Martha Nussbaum, Josh Cohen, and Matthew Howard, 79–85. Princeton: Princeton University Press.

Bilimoria, Purushottama. 1993. "Rights and Duties." In *Ethical and Political Dilemmas of Modern India*, edited by Ninian Smart and Shivesh Thakur, 30–59. London: St. Martin's Press.

Bischoff, Paul-Henri, Kwasi Ening, and Amitav Acharya. 2016. *Africa in Global Relations*. New York: Routledge.

Blagg, Harry. 2008. *Crime, Aboriginality, and the Decolonization of Justice*. Annandale, AUS: Hawkins Press.

Boddy, Janice. 1989. *Wombs and Alien Spirits*. Madison: University of Wisconsin Press.

Bordieu, Pierre. 2002. *Masculine Domination*. Stanford, CA: Stanford University Press.

Buchanan, Alan. 2004. *Justice, Legitimacy, and Self-Determination*. Oxford: Oxford University Press.

Cain, Mead, Syeda Roseka Khanam, and Shamsun Nahar. 1979. "Class, Patriarchy, and Women's Work in Bangladesh." *Population and Development Review* 5 (3): 405–438.

Calhoun, Cheshire. 1988. "Justice, Care, Gender Bias." *Journal of Philosophy* 85 (9): 451–463.

Carty, Linda A., and Chandra T. Mohanty. 2015. "Mapping Transnational Feminist Engagements." In *Oxford Handbook of Transnational Feminist Movements*, edited by Rawida Bakkash and Wendy Harcourt, 82–116. New York: Oxford University Press.

Castillo, R. Aida. 2010. "The Emergence of Indigenous Feminism in Latin America." *Signs* 35 (3): 539–545.

Chambers, Clare. 2008. *Sex, Culture, and Justice: The Limits of Choice*. University Park: Pennsylvania State University Press.

Chant, Sylvia. 2006. "Re-thinking the Feminization of Poverty in Relation to Aggregate Gender Indices." *Journal of Human Development* 7 (2): 201–220.

Chant, Sylvia. 2008. "The Feminization of Poverty and the Feminization of Anti-poverty Programs." *Journal of Development Studies* 44 (2): 165–197.

Chant, Sylvia. 2009. "The 'Feminisation of Poverty' in Costa Rica: To What Extent a Conundrum?" *Bulletin of Latin American Research* 28 (1): 19–43.

Charusheela, S. 2008. "Social Analysis and the Capabilities Approach." *Cambridge Journal of Economics* 33 (6): 1–18.

Chesler, Phyllis. 2010. "The Feminist Politics of Islamic Misogyny." *American Thinker*, November 13. http://www.americanthinker.com/articles/2010/11/the_feminist_politics_of_islam.html.

Cheston, Susy, and Lisa Kuhn. 2002. *Empowering Women through Microfinance*. New York: UNIFEM.

Choudhury, Cyra Akila. 2015. "Beyond Culture." *Berkeley Journal of Gender, Law and Justice* 30: 226–267.

Christman, John. 2003. "Relational Autonomy and the Social Constitution of Selves." *Philosophical Studies* 117 (1): 143–164.

Christman, John. 2004. "Relational Autonomy, Liberal Individualism, and the Social Constitution of Selves." *Philosophical Studies* 117 (1): 143–164.

Christman, John. 2018. "Autonomy and Deeply Embedded Cultural Identities." In *Personal Autonomy in Plural Societies*, edited by Marie-Claire Foblets, Michele Graziadei, and Alison Dundes Renteln, 51–64. New York: Routledge.

Code, Lorraine. 2001. "The Perversion of Autonomy and the Subjection of Women." In *Relational Autonomy*, edited by Catriona Mackenzie and Natalie Stoljar, 181–213. New York: Oxford University Press.

Collectif 95 Maghreb Egalité. 1993. *One Hundred Steps: One Hundred Provisions for an Egalitarian Codification of Family and Personal Status Laws in the Maghreb*. Rabat, Morocco: Collectif 95 Maghreb Egalité.

Collectif 95 Maghreb Egalité. 2005. *Guide to Equality in the Family in the Maghreb*. Bethesda, MD: Women's Learning Partnership for Development and Rights.

Collins, Patricia Hill. 2000. *Black Feminist Thought*. New York: Routledge.

Connell, Raewyn. 2014. "Using Southern Theory." *Planning Theory* 13 (2): 210–222.

Connell, Raewyn. 2015. "Meeting at the Edge of Fear." *Feminist Theory* 16 (1): 49–66.

Crenshaw, Kimberle. 1989. "Demarginalizing the Intersection of Race and Sex." *University of Chicago Legal Forum* 1 (8): 139–167.

Curchin, Katherine. 2011. "Pakeha Women and Maori Protocol: The Politics of Criticizing Other Cultures." *Australian Journal of Political Science* 46 (3): 375–388.

Davis, Angela. 1983. "The Approaching Obsolescence of Housework." In *Women, Race, and Class*, 222–245. New York: Vintage.

Desai, Manisha. 2002. "Transnational Solidarity: Women's Agency, Structural Adjustment, and Globalization." In *Women's Activism and Globalization*, edited by Nancy Naples and Manisha Desai, 15–34. New York: Routledge.

Deveaux, Monique. 2000. *Cultural Pluralism and Dilemmas of Justice*. Ithaca, NY: Cornell University Press.

Deveaux, Monique. 2016a. "Beyond the Redistributive Paradigm." In *Ethical Issues in Poverty Alleviation*, edited by Helmut Gaisbauer, Gottfried Schweiger, and Clemens Sedmak, 225–245. New York: Springer.

Deveaux, Monique. 2016b. "Effective Deliberative Inclusion of Women in Contexts of Traditional Political Authority." *Democratic Theory* 3 (2): 2–25.

Dhand, Arti. 2002. "The Dharma of Ethics: The Ethics of Dharma." *Journal of Religious Ethics* 30 (3): 347–372.

Eisenberg, Avigail. 2003. "Diversity and Equality: Three Approaches to Cultural and Sexual Difference." *Journal of Political Philosophy* 11 (1): 41–64.

Enright, Mairead. 2009. "Choice, Culture, and the Politics of Belonging: The Emerging Law of Forced and Arranged Marriage." *Modern Law Review* 72 (3): 331–359.

Escobar, Arturo. 1994. *Encountering Development: The Making and Unmaking of the Third World*. Princeton, NJ: Princeton University Press.

Fatima, Saba. 2014. "Indignation without Reflection." siuewmst.wordpress.com.

Fatima, Saba, Kristie Dotson, Ranjoo Herr, Serene J. Khader, and Stella Nyanzi. 2017. "Contested Terrains: Women of Color and Third-World Women." *Hypatia* 32 (3): 731–742.

Ferguson, Michaele. 2010. "Choice Feminism and the Fear of Politics." *Perspectives on Politics* 8 (1): 247–253.

Fernandes, Sujatha. 2017. "Stories and Statecraft: Afghan Women and the Construction of Western Freedoms." *Signs* 42 (3): 643–667.

Fineman, Martha. 1991. *The Illusion of Equality*. Chicago: University of Chicago Press.

Fineman, Martha. 2005. *The Autonomy Myth*. New York: New Press.

Folbre, Nancy. 2001. *The Invisible Heart*. New York: New Press.

Foucault, Michel. 1997. *Society Must Be Defended*. New York: St. Martin's Press.

Fraser, Nancy. 1990. "Rethinking the Public Sphere: A Contribution to the Critique of Actually Existing Democracy." *Social Text* 25/26: 56–80.

Fraser, Nancy, and Linda Gordon. 1994. "A Genealogy of Dependency." *Signs* 19 (2): 309–336.

Freedom without Fear Platform. 2013. "One Year On: Statement from Freedom without Fear Platform." http://freedomwithoutfearplatformuk.blogspot.com.au/2013/12/.

Freedom without Fear Platform. 2014. "Our Letter to the Indian Prime Minister to Be Handed Today at the High Commission." http://imkaan.org.uk/post/70183730620/statement-by-the-freedom-without-fear-platform-16.

Freedom without Fear Platform. 2015a. "Protesting Narendra Modi's Visit to the UK." http://freedomwithoutfearplatformuk.blogspot.com/2015/10/protesting-narendra-modis-visit-to-uk.html.

Freedom without Fear Platform. 2015b. "Scrap the Trivializing and Racist Posters on Child Sexual Exploitation." http://freedomwithoutfearplatformuk.blogspot.com/2015/05/scrap-trivialising-and-racist-posters.html.

Friedman, Marilyn. 2000. "Autonomy Social Disruption and Women." In *Relational Autonomy*, edited by Catriona Mackenzie and Natalie Stoljar, 35–52. Oxford: Oxford University Press.

Friedman, Marilyn. 2006. *Autonomy, Gender, Politics*. New York: Clarendon Press.

Friedman, Marilyn. 2013. "Independence, Dependence and the Liberal Subject." In *Reading Onora O'Neill*, edited by David Archard, Monique Deveaux, Neil Manson, and Daniel Weinstock, 111–131. Abingdon: Routledge.

Frye, Marilyn. 1983. "Oppression." In *The Politics of Reality*, 1–16. Freedom, CA: Crossing Press.

Gallagher, Sally. 2004. "The Marginalization of Evangelical Feminism." *Sociology of Religion* 65 (3): 215–237.

Giraldo, Isis. 2016. "Coloniality at Work." *Feminist Theory* 17 (2): 157–173.

Glenn, Evelyn Nakano. 1992. "From Servitude to Service Work." *Signs* 18 (1): 1–43.

Goodin, Robert. 1995. "Political Ideals and Political Practice." *British Journal of Political Science* 25 (1): 37–56.

Gopal, Priyamvada. 2013. "Speaking with Difficulty: Feminism and Antiracism in Britain after 9/11." *Feminist Studies* 39 (1): 98–118.

Grewal, Inderpal. 1996. *Home and Harem: Nation, Gender, Empires, and the Cultures of Travel*. Durham, NC: Duke University Press.

Grewal, Kiran. 2012. "Reclaiming the Voice of the 'Third World Woman.'" *Interventions* 14 (4): 569–590.

Guilmoto, Christophe Z., and Myriam de Loenzien. 2014. "Shifts in Vulnerability Landscapes: Young Women and Internal Migration in Vietnam." *Genus* 70 (1): 27–56.

Hale, Sondra. 2005. "Colonial Discourse and Ethnographic Residuals." In *Female Circumcision and the Politics of Knowledge*, edited by Obioma Nnaemeka, 209–219. Westport, CT: Praeger.

Hill, Thomas. 1995. "Servility and Self-Respect." In *Dignity, Character, and Self-Respect*, edited by Robin S. Dillon, 76–93. New York: Routledge.

Hirschmann, Nancy. 2002. *The Subject of Liberty*. Princeton: Princeton University Press.

Hirsi Ali, Ayaan. 2007. *Infidel*. New York: Simon and Schuster.

Hoffman, Elisabeth, and Kamala Marius-Gnanou. 2007. "Credit for Women: A Future for Men?" *ADA Dialogue* 37: 7–11.

hooks, bell. 2000a. *Feminism Is for Everybody*. Cambridge, MA: South End Press.

hooks, bell. 2000b. *Feminist Theory: From Margin to Center*. Cambridge, MA: South End Press.

Hondagneu-Sotelo, Pierette. 2007. *Domestica*. Berkley: University of California Press.

Honig, Bonnie. 1999. "'My Culture Made Me Do It.'" In *Is Multiculturalism Bad for Women? Susan Moller Okin with Respondents*, edited by Cohen, Howard, and Nussbaum, 31–35. Princeton, NJ: Princeton University Press.

Huggins, Jackie. 1994. "A Contemporary View of Aboriginal Women's Relationship to the White Women's Movement." In *Australian Women: Contemporary Feminist Thought*, edited by Norma Grieve and Ailsa Burns, 70–79. Melbourne, AUS: Oxford University Press.

Hunt, Janet. 2010. "Assessing Poverty, Gender, and Well-Being in 'Northern' Indigenous Communities." In *International Handbook on Gender and Poverty*, edited by Sylvia Chant, 241–248. Cheltenham, UK: Edward Elgar.

India Tomorrow. 2015. "Modi Faces Massive Protests in London as People Chant 'Not Welcome' Slogans." Indiatomorrow.net. November 13. http://www.indiatomorrow. net/eng/modi-faces-massive-protest-in-london-as-people-chant-not-welcome-slogans-

Irigaray, Luce. 1993. *An Ethics of Sexual Difference*. Translated by Carolyn Burke and Gillian C. Gil. Ithaca, NY: Cornell University Press.

Iverson, Vergard. 2003. "Intra-household Inequality: A Challenge for the Capability Approach." *Feminist Economics* 9 (2–3): 93–115.

Jaggar, Alison. 2005. "Saving Amina: Global Justice for Women and Intercultural Dialogue." *Ethics and International Affairs* 19 (Fall): 55–75.

Jaggar, Alison. 2006. "Reasoning about Well Being: Nussbaum's Methods of Justifying the Capabilities Approach." *Journal of Political Philosophy* 14 (3): 301–322.

Jaggar, Alison. 2013. "We Fight for Roses Too: Time Use and Global Gender Justice." *Journal of Global Ethics* 9 (2): 115–129.

Jamal, Amina. 2013. "Gender and Development and Its Discontents." In *Jamaat El-Islami Women in Pakistan*, 170–207. Syracuse, NY: Syracuse University Press.

Kabeer, Naila. 1994. *Reversed Realities*. New York: Verso.

Kabeer, Naila. 1999. "Resources, Agency, Achievements: Reflections on the Measurement of Women's Empowerment." *Development and Change* 30 (3): 435–464.

Kabeer, Naila. 2001. "Conflicts over Credit: Re-evaluating the Empowerment Potential of Loans to Women in Rural Bangladesh." *World Development* 29 (1): 63–84.

Kabeer, Naila. 2011. "Between Affiliation and Autonomy: Navigating Pathways of Women's Empowerment and Gender Justice in Rural Bangladesh." *Development and Change* 42 (2): 499–528.

Kabeer, Naila. 2012. "Empowerment, Citizenship, and Gender Justice." *Ethics and Social Welfare* 6 (3): 216–232.

Kandiyoti, Deniz. 1988. "Bargaining with Patriarchy." *Gender and Society* 2 (3): 275–290.

Kant, Immanuel. 2009. "Idea for a Universal History with a Cosmopolitan Aim." In *Kant's Idea for a Universal History with a Cosmopolitan Aim: A Critical Guide*, edited by Amelie Oksenberg Rorty and James Schmidt, 9–24. Cambridge: Cambridge University Press.

Kant, Immanuel. 2010. *An Answer to the Question: "What Is Enlightenment?"* New York: Penguin.

Karahasan, Barbara. 2014. "Evaluation Report of the Aboriginal Family Violence Prevention and Legal Service Victoria's Early Intervention and Prevention Program." Melbourne, AUS: Aboriginal Family Violence and Prevention Legal Service.

Karim, Lamia. 2011. *Microfinance and Its Discontents*. Minneapolis: University of Minnesota Press.

Khader, Serene J. 2011. *Adaptive Preferences and Women's Empowerment*. Oxford: Oxford University Press.

Khader, Serene. 2012. "Must Theorizing about Adaptive Preference Deny Women's Agency?" *Journal of Applied Philosophy* 29 (4): 302–317.

Khader, Serene. 2013. "Identifying Adaptive Preferences in Practice: Lessons from Postcolonial Feminisms." *Journal of Global Ethics* 9 (3): 311–327.

Khader, Serene J. 2014. "Empowerment through Self-Subordination." In *Poverty, Agency, and Human Rights*, edited by Diana Meyers, 223–249. New York: Oxford.

Khader, Serene J. 2015. "Development Ethics, Gender Complementarianism, and Intrahousehold Inequality." *Hypatia* 30 (2): 352–369.

Khader, Serene J. 2016. "Beyond Autonomy Fetishism: Affiliation with Autonomy in Women's Empowerment." *Journal of Human Development and Capabilities* 7 (1): 125–139.

Khader, Serene J. 2017. "Transnational Feminisms, Nonideal Theory, and Other Women's Power." *Feminist Philosophy Quarterly* 3 (1): 1–23.

Khader, Serene, and Stacy Kosko. Forthcoming. "Reason to Value and Perfectionism in the Capability Approach." In *Ethics, Agency, and Democracy in Global Development*, edited by Lori Keleher and Stacy Kosko. Cambridge: Cambridge University Press.

Khandelwal, Meena. 2009. "Arranging Love." *Signs* 34 (3): 583–609.

Khanum, Nazia. 2008. *Forced Marriage, Family Cohesion, and Community Engagement.* London: Equality in Diversity.

Khoja-Moolji, Shenila S. 2017. "The Making of Humans and Their Others through Transnational Human Rights Advocacy." *Signs* 42 (2): 377–401.

Kittay, Eva. 1999. *Love's Labor.* New York: Routledge.

Kothari, Rajni. 1988. *Rethinking Development.* Liberty Corner, NJ: New Horizons.

Krishnan, Kavita. October 9, 2013. "India's Anti-rape Movement: Experiences, Reflection, and Strategies for the Future." London School of Economics. http://freedomwithoutfearplatformuk.blogspot.com.au/2013/12/indias-anti-rape-movement-experiences.html.

Kumar, Camille. January 21, 2014. "Feminism: Then and Now." London School of Economics. http://freedomwithoutfearplatformuk.blogspot.com.au/2014/02/feminism-then-and-now.html.

Kymlicka, Will. 1991. *Liberalism, Community, and Culture.* Oxford: Clarendon.

Kymlicka, Will. 1995. *Multicultural Citizenship.* Oxford: Oxford University Press.

Lawrence, Bonita. 2013. "Regulating Native Identity by Gender." In *Gender and Women's Studies in Canada*, edited by Margaret Hobbs and Carla Rice, 285–294. Toronto: Women's Press.

Leach, Fiona, and Shashikala Sitaram. 2002. "Microfinance and Women's Empowerment: A Lesson from India." *Development in Practice* 12 (5): 575–588.

Lugones, Maria. 2003. "Tactical Strategies of the Streetwalker/Estrategias Tacticas de La Callajera." In *Pilgrimajes/Peregrinajes*, 207–238. Lanham, MD: Rowman and Littlefield.

Lugones, Maria. 2010. "Toward a Decolonial Feminism." *Hypatia* 25 (4): 742–759.

MacKenzie, Catriona. 2008. "Relational Autonomy, Normative Authority and Perfectionism." *Journal of Social Philosophy* 39: 512–533.

Maclean, Kate. 2014. "Chachawarmi: Rhetorics and Lived Realities." *Bulletin of Latin American Research* 33 (1): 76–90.

Madhok, Sumi. 2013. "Action, Agency, Coercion: Reformatting Agency for Oppressive Contexts." In *Gender, Agency, Coercion*, edited by Anne Phillips, Sumi Madhok, Kalpana Wilson, and Clare Hemmings, 102–122. Basingstoke, UK: Palgrave MacMillan.

Mahmood, Saba. 2005. *Politics of Piety.* Princeton, NJ: Princeton University Press.

Mahmood, Saba, and Charles Hirschkind. 2002. "Feminism, the Taliban and the Politics of Counterinsurgency." *Anthropological Quarterly* 25 (2): 339–354.

Maira, Sunaina. 2009. "'Good' and 'Bad' Muslim Citizens: Feminists, Terrorists, and U.S. Orientalisms." *Feminist Studies* 35 (3): 631–656.

Matua, Makau. 2001. "Savages, Victims, and Saviors." *Harvard Law Review* 42 (1): 201–245.

Mayoux, Linda. 1999. "Questioning Virtuous Spirals: Women's Empowerment and Microfinance in Africa." *Journal of International Development* 11: 957–984.

Mayoux, Linda, and Jean-Paul LaCoste. 2005. "Saving for Sustainability? Self-Help Foundation Zimbabwe." GenFinance. http://www.gamechangenetwork.info/documents/GenderMainstreaming/FinancialServices/Gender%20Impact/SHDF_genfinance.pdf.

Mehta, Uday Singh. 1999. *Liberalism and Empire*. Chicago: University of Chicago Press.

Menon, Usha. 2000. "Does Feminism Have Universal Relevance: The Challenges Posed by Oriya Family Practices." *Daedalus* 129 (4): 77–99.

Menon, Usha. 2012. *Women, Well-Being, and the Ethics of Domesticity in an Odia Hindu Temple Town*. Delhi: Springer India.

Menon, Usha, and Richard Schweder. 2001. "The Return of the 'White Man's Burden': The Encounter between the Moral Discourse of Anthropology and the Domestic Life of Oriya Women." In *Cultural and Critical Perspectives on Human Development*, edited by Martin Packer and Mark Tappan, 67–111. Albany: State University of New York Press.

Meyers, Diana Tietjens. 1989. *Self, Society, and Personal Choice*. New York: Columbia University Press.

Meyers, Diana Tietjens. 2000. "Feminism and Women's Autonomy: The Challenge of Female Genital Cutting." *Metaphilosophy* 31 (5): 469–491.

Mignolo, Walter. 2002. "The Geopolitics of Knowledge and the Colonial Difference." *South Atlantic Quarterly* 10 (1): 56–96.

Mignolo, Walter, and Madina Tlostanova. 2006. "Theorizing from the Borders: Shifting to Geo- and Body-Politics of Knowledge." *European Journal of Social Theory* 9 (2): 205–221.

Mikell, Gwendolyn. 1997. Introduction to *African Feminism*, edited by Gwendolyn Mikell, 1–52. Philadelphia: University of Pennsylvania Press.

Mill, John Stuart. 2002. *The Basic Writings of John Stuart Mill: On Liberty, The Subjection of Women, and Utilitarianism*. New York: Modern Library.

Mills, Charles. 2005. "Ideal Theory as Ideology." *Hypatia* 20 (3): 165–184.

Mills, Charles, and Carole Pateman. 2007. *Contract and Domination*. Boston: Polity.

Mir-Hosseini, Ziba. 1999. *Islam and Gender: The Religious Debate in Contemporary Iran*. Princeton, NJ: Princeton University Press.

Mir-Hosseini, Ziba. October 28, 2010. "We Need to Rethink Old Dogmas." https://en.qantara.de/content/interview-with-ziba-mir-hosseini-we-need-to-rethink-old-dogmas.

Moghadam, Valentine. 2000. "Transnational Feminist Networks." *International Sociology* 15 (1): 57–85.

Moghadam, Valentine M. 2002. "Islamic Feminism and Its Discontents." *Signs* 27 (4): 1135–1171.

Moghadam, Valentine M. 2010. "Review Symposium: Gender Equality and the Power of Women." *Perspectives on Politics* 6 (1): 284–286.

Mojab, Shahrzad. 2001. "Theorizing the Politics of Islamic Feminism." *Feminist Review* 69 (Winter): 124–146.

Mohanty, Chandra Talpade. 1988. "Under Western Eyes." *Feminist Review* 30: 61–88.

Mohanty, Chandra Talpade. 1992. "Feminist Encounters: Locating the Politics of Experience in Destabilizing Theory." In *Destabilizing Theory: Contemporary Feminist Debates*, edited by Anne Phillips and Michele Barrett, 74–93. Palo Alto: Stanford.

Mohanty, Chandra Talpade. 2003. *Feminism without Borders*. Durham, NC: Duke University Press.

Mohanty, Chandra Talpade. 2013. "Transnational Feminist Crossings: On Neoliberalism and Radical Critique." *Signs* 38 (4): 967–991.

Molyneux, Maxine. 1985. "Mobilization without Emancipation." *Feminist Studies* 11 (2): 227–254.

Molyneux, Maxine. 2006. "Mothers at the Service of the Antipoverty Agenda." *Social Policy and Administration* 40 (4): 425–449.

Moraga, Cherrie, Gloria Anzaldua, and Toni Cade Bambara. 1983. *This Bridge Called My Back*. Boston: Kitchen Table Women of Color Press.

Moreton-Robinson, Aileen. 2002. *Talkin' Up to the White Woman*. St. Lucia, Australia: University of Queensland Press.

Moser, Carolyn. 2003. *Gender, Planning, and Development*. New York: Routledge.

Nagar, Richa, and Saraswati Raju. 2003. "Women, NGOs and the Contradiction of Empowerment and Disempowerment." *Antipode*: 1–13.

Narayan, Deepa. 2000. *Voices of the Poor*. Vol. 1. *Can Anybody Hear Us?* New York: Oxford University Press.

Narayan, Uma. 1997. *Dislocating Cultures: Identities, Traditions, and Third-World Feminism*. New York: Routledge.

Narayan, Uma. 2002. "Minds of Their Own: Choices, Autonomy, Cultural Practices, and Other Women." In *A Mind of One's Own: Feminist Essays on Reason and Objectivity*, edited by Louise M. Antony and Charlotte E. Witt, 418–432. Boulder, CO: Westview.

Narayan, Uma. 2005. Unpublished work on file with the author.

Narayan, Uma. 2010. "Symposium: Global Gender Inequality and the Empowerment of Women." *Perspectives on Politics* 8 (1): 280–284.

Nnaemeka, Obioma. 2004. "Theorizing, Practicing, and Pruning Africa's Way." *Signs* 29 (2): 357–385.

Nussbaum, Martha C. 1992. "Human Functioning and Social Justice: In Defense of Aristotelian Essentialism." *Political Theory* 20 (2): 202–246.

Nussbaum, Martha C. 1999. *Sex and Social Justice*. Oxford: Oxford University Press.

Nussbaum, Martha C. 2001. *Women and Human Development: The Capabilities Approach*. Cambridge: Cambridge University Press.

Nzegwu, Nkiru. 1995. "Recovering Igbo Traditions." In *Women, Culture, and Development*, edited by Martha Nussbaum and Jonathan Glover, 332–360. New York: Oxford University Press.

Nzegwu, Nkiru. 2006. *Family Matters: Feminist Concepts in African Philosophy of Culture*. Albany: State University of New York Press.

Obiora, Leslye, Julia Hall, and Monica Jardine. 1996. "Situating a Critic in Her Critique: A Conversation." *Circles: The Buffalo Women's Journal of Law and Social Policy* 4: 73–77.

Okin, Susan Moller. 1989. "Feminism, Women's Human Rights, and Cultural Differences." In *Decentering the Center,* edited by Sandra Harding and Uma Narayan, 26–47. Bloomington: Indiana University Press.

Okin, Susan Moller. 1991. *Gender, Justice, and the Family*. New York: Basic Books.

Okin, Susan Moller. 1995. "Inequalities between the Sexes in Different Cultural Contexts." In *Women, Culture, and Development,* edited by Martha Nussbaum and Jonathan Glover, 274–298. Oxford: Clarendon.

Okin, Susan Moller. 1999. "Is Multiculturalism Bad for Women?" and "Reply." In *Is Multiculturalism Bad for Women? Susan Moller Okin with Respondents,* edited by Joshua Cohen, Matthew Howard, and Martha C. Nussbaum, 9–24 and 115–123. Princeton, NJ: Princeton University Press.

Okin, Susan Moller. 2000. "Feminism, Women's Human Rights and Cultural Differences." in *Decentering the Center*, edited by Harding and Narayan, 26–47. Bloomington: Indiana University Press.

Okin, Susan Moller. 2013. *Women in Western Political Thought*. Princeton: Princeton University Press.

O'Neill, Onora. 1987. "Abstraction, Idealization, and Ideology in Ethics." *Royal Institute of Philosophy Lectures* 22: 55–69.

Osmani, Lutfun. 1998. "The Impact of Microcredit on the Relative Well-Being of Women." *IDS Bulletin* 29 (4): 31–38.

Oyewumi, Oyeronke. 1997. *The Invention of Woman*. Minneapolis: University of Minnesota Press.

Pala, Achola. 2005. "Definitions of Women and Development: An African Perspective." In *African Gender Studies,* edited by Oyeronke Oyewumi, 299–313. New York: Palgrave.

Palmer, Eric. 2016. "The Miracle of Microfinance? A 2016 Ethical Assessment." In *The SAGE Encyclopedia of Business Ethics and Society.* 2nd ed., edited by Robert Kolb. Thousand Oaks, CA: Sage.

Papanek, Hannah. 1990. "To Each Less Than She Needs, from Each More Than She Can Do: Allocations, Entitlement, and Value." In *Persistent Inequalities: Women and World Development,* edited by I. Tinker, 162–184. Oxford: Oxford University Press.

Paredes-Carvaji, Julia. 2006. "Feminismo and Socialismo." Jornadas Feministas Workshop: Mujeres Creando La Paz.

Parpart, J. 1986. "Women and the State in Africa." Working Paper 117. United States Agency for International Development, Washington, DC.

Pateman, Carole. 1988. *The Sexual Contract.* Stanford, CA: Stanford University Press.

Paulson, Susan. 2016. *Masculinities and Femininities in Latin America's Uneven Development*. New York: Routledge.

Poster, Winifred, and Zakia Salime. 2002. "The Limits of Microcredit: Transnational Feminism and USAID Activities in the United States and Morocco." In *Women's*

Activism and Globalization, edited by Jennifer Naples and Manisha Desai, 189–219. New York: Routledge.

Phillips, Anne. 2009. *Multiculturalism without Culture.* Princeton, NJ: Princeton University Press.

Pieterse, Jan Nederveen. 2001. *Development Theory.* London: Sage.

Press Trust of India. 2013. "UK Groups Call on India to Act Against Rape." *Business Standard.* http://www.business-standard.com/article/pti-stories/uk-rights-groups-call-on-india-to-act-against-rape-113012400602_1.html.

Puar, Jasbir. 2007. *Terrorist Assemblages.* Durham, NC: Duke University Press.

Rawls, John. 1971. *A Theory of Justice.* Cambridge, MA: Harvard University Press.

Rawls, John. 1996. *Political Liberalism: The John Dewey Essays in Philosophy.* New York: Columbia University Press.

Raz, Joseph. 1988. *The Morality of Freedom.* Oxford: Clarendon Press.

Razack, Sherene. 2008. *Casting Out: The Eviction of Muslims from Western Law and Politics.* Toronto: University of Toronto Press.

Robinson, Kathryn. 2006. "Islamic Influences on Indonesian Feminism." *Social Analysis* 50 (1): 171–177.

Said, Edward. 1979. *Orientalism.* New York: Vintage.

Saidi, Christine. 2010. *Women's Authority and Society in Early East-Central Africa.* Rochester: University of Rochester Press.

Salazar Parrenas, Rhacel. 2000. "Migrant Filipina Domestic Workers and the International Division of Reproductive Labor." *Gender and Society* 14 (4): 560–580.

Schutte, Ofelia. 2003. "Dependency Work, Women, and the Global Economy." In *The Subject of Care,* edited by Ellen Feder and Eva Feder Kittay, 138–159. Lanham, MD: Rowman and Littlefield.

Schwartzman, Lisa. 2006. *Challenging Liberalism.* University Park: Pennsylvania State University Press.

Scott, Joan. 2010. *The Politics of the Veil.* Princeton, NJ: Princeton University Press.

Segato, Rita. 2011. "Genero y Colonialidad: En Busca de Claves de Lectura y de un Vocabulario Es-trate' gico Descolonial." In *Feminismos y Poscolonialidad: Descolonizando el Feminismo desde y en America Latina,* edited by Karina Bidaseca and Vanessa Laba, 17–47. Buenos Aires : Ediciones Godot.

Sen, Amartya. 1990. "Gender and Cooperative Conflicts" In *Persistent Inequalities: Women and World Development,* edited by I. Tinker, 123–149. Oxford: Oxford University Press.

Sen, Amartya. 1999. *Development as Freedom.* New York: A. A. Knopf.

Sen, Amartya. 2009. *The Idea of Justice.* Cambridge, MA: Harvard University Press.

Sharma, Jaya, and Soma Parthasarathy. 2007. *Examining Self-Help Groups.* Delhi: Nirantar.

Sharp, Joanne, John Briggs, Hoda Yacoub, and Nabila Hamed. 2003. "Doing Gender and Development: Understanding Empowerment and Local Gender Relations." *Transactions of the Institute of British Geographers* 28 (3): 281–295.

Singh, Kirti. 2012/3. "The Movement for Change: Implementation of Sexual Assault Laws." *India International Centre Quarterly* 39 (3/4): 259–269.

Smith, Andrea. 2010. "Queer Theory and Native Studies: The Heteronormativity of Settler Colonialism." *GLQ* 16 (1): 42–68.

Song, Sarah. 2008. *Justice, Gender, and the Politics of Multiculturalism*. Cambridge: Cambridge University Press.

Sotero, Michelle. 2006. "A Conceptual Model of Historical Trauma." *Journal of Health Disparities Research and Practice* 1 (1): 93–108.

Spinner-Halev, Jeff. 2001. "Feminism, Multiculturalism, Oppression, and the State." *Ethics* 112 (1): 84–113.

Stack, Carol B. 1983. *All Our Kin*. New York: Basic Books.

Stoljar, Natalie. 2000. "Autonomy and the Feminist Intuition." In *Relational Autonomy: Feminist Perspectives on Autonomy, Agency, and the Social Self*, edited by C. Mackenzie and N. Stoljar, 94–112. Oxford: Oxford University Press.

Superson, Anita. 2005. "Deformed Desires and Informed Desire Tests" *Hypatia* 20 (4): 109–126.

Tessman, Lisa. 2015. *Moral Failure*. New York: Oxford University Press.

Tobin, Theresa Weynand. 2007. "On Their Own Ground: Strategies of Resistance for Sunni Muslim Women." *Hypatia* 22 (3): 152–174.

Tobin, Theresa Weynand. 2009. "Using Rights to Counter 'Gender-Specific' Wrongs." *Human Rights Review* 10 (4): 521–530.

Tobin, Theresa Weynand, and Alison Jaggar. 2013. "Naturalizing Moral Justification." *Metaphilosophy* 44 (4): 409–439.

UK Home Office. October 27, 2004. Promoting Human Rights, Respecting Individual Dignity. UK Home Office Press Release.

Volpp, Leti. 2001. "Feminism versus Multiculturalism." *Columbia Law Review* 101 (5): 1181–1218.

Volpp, Leti. 2011. "Framing Cultural Difference: Immigrant Women and Discourses of Tradition." *Differences* 22 (1): 91–110.

Wadud, Amina. 2006. *Inside the Gender Jihad: Women's Reform in Islam*. London: Oneworld.

Walker, Margaret Urban. 2007. *Moral Understandings*. New York: Oxford University Press.

Waring, Marilyn. 1988. *Counting for Nothing*. Wellington, NZ: Allen Unwin.

Watene, Krushil. 2016. "Indigenous Peoples and Justice." In *Theorizing Justice*, edited by Krushil Watene and Jay Drydyk, 133–153. Lanham, MD: Rowman and Littlefield.

Weir, Allison. 2013. "Feminism and the Islamic Revival: Freedom as a Practice of Belonging." *Hypatia* 28 (2): 323–340.

Whyte, Kyle. 2013. "Indigenous Women, Climate Change Impacts, and Collective Action." *Hypatia* 29 (3): 599–616.

Wilson, Amrit. April 8, 2013. "India's Anti-rape Movement: Redefining Solidarity outside the Colonial Frame." 50.50 Gender, Sexuality, and Social Justice.

http://www.opendemocracy.net/5050/amrit-wilson/indias-anti-rape-movement-redefining-solidarity-outside-colonial-frame.

Wilson, Amrit. 2015. "Narendra Modi, Gender Violence, and the Hindu Right's Agenda." 50.50 Gender, Sexuality, and Social Justice. http://www.opendemocracy.net/5050/amrit-wilson/india-gender-violence- is-at-heart-of-hindu-rights-agenda.

Wilson, Kalpana. 2011. "Race, Gender, and Neoliberalism: Challenging Visual Representations in Development." *Third World Quarterly* 32 (2): 315–331.

Wilson, Kalpana. 2015. "Towards a Radical Reappropriation: Gender, Development, and Neoliberal Feminism." *Development and Change* 46 (4): 803–832.

World Bank. 2012. "World Development Report: Gender Equality and Development." Washington DC: World Bank.

Young, Iris Marion. 1990. *Justice and the Politics of Difference*. Princeton, NJ: Princeton University Press.

Zeleza, Paul Tiyambe. 2005. "Gender Biases in African Historiography." In *African Gender Studies*, edited by Oyeronke Oyewumi, 207–233. New York: Palgrave Macmillan.

Zerilli, Linda. 2009. "Toward a Feminist Theory of Judgment." *Signs* 34 (2): 295–317.

INDEX

Abu-Lughod, Lila 6, 23–34, 55–56, 74,
76, 77, 82–85, 90, 93, 98, 123, 146,
147, 151, 153, 154
adaptive preferences 18, 52, 73,
87, 105, 108–112, 154n8, 159,
160, 163n26
Afghanistan 23–24, 44–45, 82–85,
119, 154n2
Agarwal, Bina 107, 109, 111, 159n20
Agency 6, 18, 29, 78, 87, 92, 100,
105–106, 108, 112
value-laden conceptions
of 108–112, 159n23
Ahmed, Leila 122, 130–132, 139–142,
161n3, 163n27
Amadiume, Ifi 101, 103, 127–128
androcentrism 63–64, 137,
152n28, 152n31
anti-imperialism/normativity
dilemma 2–3, 7, 21, 30, 37, 76–77,
84, 89, 154n3
Archambault, Caroline 55–56, 58–59,
65–66, 151n12
associational damage, *see* imperialist
associational damage
Asad, Talal 78, 80, 147n10
autonomy 3, 5, 7, 8, 18, 57, 76–97,
154n8, 155n15, 156n20
Enlightenment freedom as a specific
version of 80–81

as the ability to distance oneself from
one's commitments 88
as contrasted with
anti-oppressiveness 92
relational 92, 146n10, 156n21
substantive 110, 163n26
See also agency

Badinter, Elisabeth 79–90,
154n5, 155n9
Badran, Margot 94, 95, 98,
153n37, 157n29
Baehr, Amy 145n2, 158n5, 160n1
bargaining with patriarchy 138, 146n1
Barlas, Asma 91, 94
Basu, Amrita 37, 38, 39, 163n24
Benhabib, Seyla 89–92, 145n9, 148n21
Bhabha, Homi 80
Boddy, Janice 86
Bourdieu, Pierre 137
burqa 6, 24, 27, 82–83, 131–132,
162n11

Calhoun, Cheshire 15
care 55–56, 64–72, 108, 151n13,
158n14, 163n24
See also gendered labor burdens
chachawarmi 99, 157n2, 157n3
Chant, Sylvia 2, 53–54, 150n5,
150n7, 150n8

Obstetrics for Anaesth

Obstetrics for Anaesthetists

Edited by
John Clift
City Hospital, Birmingham, UK

Alexander Heazell
St Mary's Hospital and University of Manchester, UK

CAMBRIDGE UNIVERSITY PRESS
Cambridge, New York, Melbourne, Madrid, Cape Town, Singapore, São Paulo, Delhi

Cambridge University Press
The Edinburgh Building, Cambridge CB2 8RU, UK

Published in the United States of America by Cambridge University Press, New York

www.cambridge.org
Information on this title: www.cambridge.org/9780521696708

First published 2008

Printed in the United Kingdom at the University Press, Cambridge

A catalogue record for this publication is available from the British Library

ISBN 978-0-521-69670-8 paperback